Mindfulne___

A Guide to Mastering Your Life

M000118620

PAX TANDON

Other Schiffer Books on Related Subjects:

Get Positive Live Positive: Clearing the Negativity from Your Life. Melinda D. Carver
ISBN: 978-0-7643-5291-1

Inspiring Butterflies: A 27-Day Course of Self Discovery. Marge Richards and Ginny Zaboronek
ISBN: 978-0-7643-3969-1

Living a Life in Balance: An Elemental Journey of Self-Discovery. Cael SpiritHawk
ISBN: 978-0-7643-4748-1

Copyright © 2018 by Pax Tandon

Library of Congress Control Number: 2017955195

Designed by John P. Cheek
Cover design by Brenda McCallum
Cover photo: Girl go for a cycle ride at water with umbrella in hand © Masson.
   Courtesy www.bigstockphoto.com
Type set in Zurich BdXCn BT/Garamond Premier Pro

ISBN:978-0-7643-5525-7
Printed in the United States of America

Published by Red Feather Mind, Body, Spirit
An imprint of Schiffer Publishing, Ltd.
4880 Lower Valley Road
Atglen, PA 19310
Phone: (610) 593-1777; Fax: (610) 593-2002
E-mail: Info@schifferbooks.com
Web: www.redfeatherpub.com

For our complete selection of fine books on this and related subjects, please visit our website at www.schifferbooks.com. You may also write for a free catalog.

Schiffer Publishing's titles are available at special discounts for bulk purchases for sales promotions or premiums. Special editions, including personalized covers, corporate imprints, and excerpts, can be created in large quantities for special needs. For more information, contact the publisher.

We are always looking for people to write books on new and related subjects. If you have an idea for a book, please contact us at proposals@schifferbooks.com.

Note regarding the research and use of dimethyltryptamine (DMT): DMT should only be taken in a controlled, therapeutic setting with the right professionals. (See Chapter 9.)

For my parents, who always made sure I had
the resources to find a higher self.

Contents

Preface

I came into the world in 1978 at the hospital of the University of Pennsylvania, a first generation American born to Indian immigrant parents. They were "fresh off the boat," my father having literally arrived by boat, in 1959, and my mother (by plane) almost two decades later. My father wanted to call me Nature. He had already named my older sister Uni for "one" or "universal." It was the '70s and Dad was on a journey to find peace and enlightenment, especially in the wake of a divorce from his first wife. He was channeling his overarching philosophies of "unity in diversity" and "one ultimate reality" into our names (to this day, when my sister and I are together, he will address us as his "natural unity"). "Uni" had my dad's hippie stamp all over it, and my mom was gearing up for a veto by the time I came along a year and a half later. When my dad suggested "Nature," she rebutted with, "Sonia." One is imbued with meaning; the other, well, easy to pronounce. Where would my father project his newfound *kumbaya* if I was called "Sonia"? He volleyed the veto. They eventually settled on Prakriti, the rough translation of nature in the Sanskrit language. My sister got two syllables and relative simplicity of pronunciation; I got three—and a plethora of quizzical and contorted faces whenever someone asked me my name.

I ended up creating the monosyllabic nickname "Pax," meaning peace in Latin. Aligned with "Prakriti" in meaning, easy to pronounce, hard to butcher.

At times I wished my folks had gone with Nature. I grew up in the era of River Phoenix and his siblings, who had similarly granola-fied names like Sky and Leaf. I could have claimed to be their long-lost brown cousin, or at least gained some cool points telling kids at school my parents loved *Stand by Me* so much they too chose a crunchy name for their kid. But Nature I was not. I was Prakriti. If you Google it, these are the meanings and definitions associated with my name:

- …The primal matter with three different innate qualities whose equilibrium is the basis for all observed empirical reality.
- The feminine aspect of all life forms … a woman is seen as a symbol of Prakriti.
- Making or placing before or at first, the original or natural form or condition of anything; original or primary substance.

- Nature, body matter, phenomenal universe.
- The personified will and energy of the Supreme (Brahman).
- *And one more*: The potency that brings about evolution and change in the empirical universe.

Ah haaaaaaaaaa! Those extra "a's" beyond the usual "A-ha!" moment indicate a compilation of thousands of moments—an entire existence—coming into crisper view. The trajectory of my life makes total sense in the context of my name. My journey has led me on a path toward effecting mass positive change on the planet as my life's goal. I was literally *born*—down to the name I was conferred at birth—to do this (help others find their way to well-being, that is). Before writing this page, I didn't have such a specific notion of the meaning of my name; I knew it as "nature" or the "life force," and that was a name to endeavor to live up to in and of itself. Now, I get it on a whole new level.

The subject matter of this book is the avatar of "Prakriti." Scan back a bit and take another look at the interpretations and definitions I listed above. As you read along, hold them close to you and feel them channel through the material and my voice.

This book has taken a great deal of passion, dedication, and effort from me to write, and it hasn't been a cakewalk: countless hours penning lines, sacrifices of time with friends and family to bring it to life, days of exhaustion and creative depletion.

It also hasn't been a chore. I haven't had to force the material or drive hard at the content; the words have poured forth fluidly and authentically, as if waiting to be written. Whether they were *well* written, now that tortured me a little. I'll just hope you receive them with an open heart and a receptive mind, and that, as such, they speak to you, leading to positive change in your life. That's my only angle.

Convergence is a word I use often to denote various elements colliding synchronistically at a single point in time. It implies a divine rightness to the moment, a magical unfolding that we are privy to if we choose to see it and are willing to embrace its messages. It's the purest convergence as I sit here now, taking stock of my life from its inception, when I was given the name Prakriti. This name has tethered me to a purpose that brought me right here, to this moment, as I type these words onto a page while I look up the definitions of "Prakriti" and realize they are the very substrate of this book.

Convergence. Take a moment to close your eyes and whisper it to yourself, letting its meaning and magic sink into your cells. Know how to recognize it when it greets you in your life, and be ready to shake its hand and follow it where it wants you to go. Where it wanted me to go was right here: through a journey of life's Byzantine pathways to a place where I could speak these truths and endeavor to provide the forces of change for you to find your own evolution (i.e., the last definition of "Prakriti" mentioned earlier). I surrendered to my purpose and became Prakriti (i.e., second-to-last definition) so I could write these words. And have them find their way to you.

Life has handed me lemons, and I've learned to turn them into lemonade. Lemonade I now serve to you. I hope you're thirsty, because we're going to figure out how to help you find your flourishing, especially through your moments of greatest pain.

Here's where mindfulness matters. Its practice is fundamental to success in virtually every area of your life. In addition, matters of health and well-being, like those in this book, inevitably come down to mindfulness. Learn to focus your attention on these areas, and you will see positive results.

Acknowledgments

I would like to thank you, the reader of this book, for the time and energy you are dedicating to your health and well-being. It takes tremendous effort to prioritize that which will guide you toward your best self, and I encourage you on.

Thank you to my parents, Shamsher and Bajendra Tandon, for endless encouragement and support around learning the best practices for health, vitality, growth, and evolution. Your unconditional advocacy for education is the reason I found my way to all of the knowledge that became the foundation for this book.

Thank you to my sister, Uni, for being my soul twin and most heartfelt fan. You love me unconditionally and protectively, as only an older sister could, seeing my true spirit and helping me find my power and success. All of those audio files back and forth inspired so much of the content of this book and kept me digging deep to exhume new connections, create original inspired thought, and attend to anything that would be in the highest service to you, and, therefore, to my readers.

Patty, *bestie extraordinaire*, I'm so glad we found our way (back) to each other in this lifetime, because we've obviously traveled eons together. I love that you exist, that you get positive psychology, that you have a soul that's pure and seeking, and that, together, we can process and process and process and never get tired.

Ushi, your unwavering commitment to psychology and essential drive toward understanding the human psyche are passion personified. You validated my work with your assessment that negative emotions are a signpost for change.

Thank you to the whole positive psychology community, who inspire me with their research, their way of being in the world, and their tenacity for the field. I'd particularly like to thank Marty Seligman for being a founding father of this field, for setting up the MAPP program and becoming an important part of my life purpose, and most especially, for hiring me as editor-in-chief of *Authentic Happiness*. What an incredible opportunity to learn and grow.

A big shout-out to everyone who contributed to the editing process. Ari Moscowitz, for your diligence in the early stages when the manuscript was raw and inchoate. Your work helped me organize my ideas and find a better voice. To Seph Fontane Pennock for the courage to give me objective, candid, and pointed feedback. To Uni, for an unwavering dedication to the final pass. Your love helped bring this work to light.

To Caroline Grace Ashurst, for being a champion of my well-being. Your magnanimous dedication helped me find the confidence to see this through.

Thank you to Jamila Payne for encouraging me around "vigor" and making sure I stayed on task and deadline.

Garden Wellington-Logan, thank you for your contributions to the early stages of this book. Your dedication to my career remains unparalleled. To Jessie Holeva for keeping the embers glowing, and to Eric Michael Sales for taking the baton and seeing it to near-completion.

Thank you to Jenice Armstrong, for recognizing the power of my voice and giving me outlets for its expression.

Marilyn-Logan Paik, thank you for trusting me to work with Vincent, and to Vincent Paik, for trusting me to help. We've already changed many lives together.

Thank you to Stacey Grant, and the whole Koi-Fly team, for collaborating with me on media projects that let my voice, and its message, shine.

Andrea Killany Thatcher, I appreciate you for planting the seed of this book in my mind and helping to nurture it to life.

Thank you to the whole team at Schiffer Publishing for believing in this project and supporting me all the way through, from idea to execution.

And, to every person who lent their voice to this book, whether implicitly or explicitly, my gratitude. So many lives have touched mine, and they've all inspired the words on these pages. That's especially true for those with whom I've shared pain, heartbreak, and other challenges. Those experiences were my greatest forces for learning and growth.

Keeping It Real

Many receive advice, only the wise profit from it.
—Publilius Syrus

It was a Tuesday morning, and immediately upon waking, I was hit with intense feelings of angst, akin in their aggregate to a suicidal thought. It was an existential spiraling out, a wave of semiconscious questions needling me . . . *Why?? Why does any of this matter? Why does it feel so hard sometimes? What does it all mean? What are we all doing here, anyway?* It was dark in my mind's eye, the outlook ominous and foreboding as I contemplated the same heavy questions intellectuals and philosophers have been pondering for the ages.

Blanketed in a cloak of confounded gloom, I willed my body out of bed and distracted myself with the quotidian, brushing my teeth, downing two tall glasses of water, sitting atop my cushion to meditate, and preparing a green smoothie. Somewhere between my meditation and smoothie prep, there was another wave. This time, however, it was a swell of illumination and insight around why I was writing this book . . . .

Until now, the process had happened quite organically, the whole turn of events a product of a-to-b-to-c. I was interviewed as a subject matter expert in mindfulness and positive psychology and, as it turns out, the interviewer was affiliated with a publishing house. She asked if I had ever considered writing my own book, to which I replied that indeed I had, many times, but had never chased the notion with any real gumption. Well, here was the notion, chasing me, so I dove in. I began writing with passion and gusto about the subject matter, a journey through the struggles of the mind, body, and spirit to uncover what really brings us well-being. But I felt dissonance, like I was writing firmly from the seat of the intellect, but missing a certain resonance from the soul. I could teach you how to be happy, but frankly, I felt too happy of late to understand the opposite. The *irony*. All of my flourishing practices were doing their jobs well, but in order to do my job well writing this book, I needed to channel what it felt like to need more flourishing—to be parched for that lemonade I spoke about earlier. From there would come the passion in my words that would motivate you to imbibe the practices and make them your own, turning them into a *way of life*. Well, *Prakriti* dosed me, because not long after, I woke up on a Tuesday morning and wanted to stay asleep, deeply depressed and questioning the point of my life. In that darkness the light bulb clinked on, the purpose of writing these pages crystallized.

The contents of this book are not necessarily meant to pull you up when you are down (though they surely may, and probably will. Hey bonus, how you doin?!) Instead, this work is designed to bolster you and make you stronger, so that when dark days come, you'll flow through them with as much ease as the light, rainbow-and-butterfly-infused ones. You'll learn to see your pain more objectively. You'll note that you are *feeling* pain, but you are not that pain you are feeling. You'll observe it without judgment, allow it to wash through you without resistance, accept it without wallowing, and even begin to embrace it with verve. You'll learn to delight in your pain as your greatest teacher and force for change, realizing that each of those darkest of moments have led to your shiniest enlightenments. Understanding how to embrace every circumstance of your life with equal measure will allow you to navigate the journey with grace and fluidity, ever stronger and more resilient. When you know you can move through and forward, ever higher, no matter what shows up, without suffering, now *that* is real *living*. And as you keep going, and growing, you are evolving spiritually, and that is the sole reason we are here. We exist to grow beyond the human container we are in toward unbounded spiritual heights.

Through the words that follow I will bare my soul and speak truths I've never even admitted to my own family, much less a mass audience. But if I know one thing by now, through all of this searching, effort, education, training, seeking, and finding, it is that I am a human designed to effect positive change. I am a vehicle for truth, and just want you to feel my love for you, and use it to inspire you higher. I want you to know how to recognize your pain, tether it to you without attaching to it, and have at your access the skills, tools, and practices that will serve you in the highest and help you flourish.

There's a reason I wrote this book, and there's a reason you picked it up to read. "Trust the process," as one of my favorite professors in grad school used to say. Life is full of magical convergences that lead to your evolution exactly when you're ready for it. Writing this book was an evolution for me, a way to chronicle my life and its teachings into a meaningful experience for you to benefit from. Join me on this journey as I take you through an exploration of the human experience. I will appeal to your mind, your body, and your spirit, likely in ways you've never encountered before. Forever altered, you will then pay these learnings forward to help others evolve. And they, forever altered, will help others evolve. This upward spiral is love in action, and love is the momentum of the Universe. We are in constant movement toward balance and higher evolution, in an interplay of light and dark, to create a dance that looks whole and complete.

SECTION I
The Mind

The energy of the mind is the essence of life.
—Aristotle

What is the "mind"? Plenty of folks talk about it, but rarely does anyone actually define it. I've attended countless mindfulness forums, many of which I myself have led, and we jump right into how to steady "the mind," liberate it from attachment to thoughts, notice when it wanders . . . but what is the "it" that we're trying so desperately to bring under control? What is this thing, buzzing around like a fly, that we simply cannot catch?

Aye, there's the rub. It is incredibly hard to personify something you can neither see nor touch. Just look up the word "mind," and nearly twenty definitions appear—and that is just for contexts where "the mind" is defined as a noun. (There are a further twenty definitions for the verb form—with or without an object—and as an idiom. Don't worry if you didn't catch that, I had to crack open a grammar book from seventh grade to decode it. And it's totally not the point—bear with me as I attempt to make one.)

Let's take a look at some of these definitions. The primary definition from dictionary.com states:

(in a human or other conscious being) the element, part, substance, or process that reasons, thinks, feels, wills, perceives, judges, etc.;

The secondary definition:
Psychology. The totality of conscious and unconscious mental processes and activities;

And the third refers to a person's mental acuity:
Intellect or understanding, as distinguished from the faculties of feeling and willing.

The first definition gets at our ability to be aware and conscious; it's that part of us that is awake to our body and our environment, and can process information from it and act accordingly—like perceiving an injustice and protesting in anger, experiencing a loss and feeling sad, noticing a beautiful flower and stopping to smell it, reacting with joy to a surprise party full of our family and friends. It's the piece of us that is constantly in interaction with the world inside and around us.

Notice how there are four qualifiers in that first definition: "element," "part," "substance," and "process." It runs the gamut because we're just really not sure what we're dealing with. Is it matter, or something more? It doesn't really "matter"; just stay open to the various possibilities as you learn to work with your mind in novel—and ultimately far more productive—ways. For example, if the mind is matter (say of a quantum nature), you might be much more attuned to the weight your thoughts carry in changing the world around you. Many thought leaders (#mindpun) ascribe to this very belief. Think about abundance, for example, and abundance will flow back to you. Be in constant fear of getting robbed, and you will attract just such a loss.

To realize the immense power of your mind to perceive, judge, or reason is also how you'll discover the ways in which it can be detrimentally judgmental, or perceive inefficiently, as when you are "multi-tasking." I put "multi-tasking" in quotes because it is in fact a misnomer. What the brain is doing when dealing with more than one task at a time is task-switching, or flitting quickly between actions. We can only handle one task at a time with our full attention. When dealing with more than one task, our attention is divided. Think about every time you hop in the car and arrive at your destination with almost no memory of the journey. Chances are you were on the phone, thinking about your errands list, singing along to the radio, or any one of a number of other preoccupations that can take our attention away. It might not be critical that you remember your car ride, but the consequences of such straying attention can be much greater if, the next time, you're too busy thinking about a fight you had with a friend to focus on the nuclear fission you're performing. A distracted mind is not an optimally efficient one.

The mind will also reason too much and over-analyze when a gut instinct or subconscious awareness would have been more truthful. I'll give you powerful examples throughout the book to help illustrate what a potent or disruptive tool the mind can be, depending on how you use it. The abilities of the mind according to the first definition are all immensely powerful and also potentially harmful, and mindfulness is the tool we will use to parse out optimal functioning for you so you are able to make the best choices in every moment.

The second definition is more global than the first, encompassing all of the workings of the mind both at the conscious and unconscious levels. Much of the work we do in psychology deals with changing cognitions (thoughts) to alter patterns of behavior. Interventions like cognitive behavioral therapy (CBT) and dialectical behavior therapy (a form of CBT more specific to individuals with borderline personality disorder) are solutions-focused talk therapies highly effective for dealing with the issues of the conscious mind. We all have patterns of thought, and these become our default if we don't give our brains new ones. A negative worldview is a good example. A person with this view will consistently default to complaint and injustice. With some work, destructive or disruptive thought patterns can be replaced with productive ones. Negativity and complaint can be replaced by gratitude and an appreciation for the myriad things going right in life.

There also exists a great deal of power to effect change at the subconscious level. If you picture the mind as an iceberg, the conscious mind is the tip that is visible above the surface of the water. The unconscious mind is the large mass hidden below the surface. Much information and intelligence exists and operates "below the surface," and can be accessed if we do the work and learn how to tap into this information.

The third definition helps you to understand the mind as a powerful tool that can be used to imbibe knowledge and create intelligent thought depending on how you train it. In this book, you will discover myriad ways you can change your daily routine, diet, physical movement patterns, and more, to realize better clarity, sharpness, and functioning of the mind. You have the freedom to be the self you desire to be, not one trapped in a body with a mind unruly and untamed that chooses for you. Show your mind who's boss and let it work for you, not the other way around.

1
Mindfulness

He said, "There are only two days in the year that nothing can be done. One is called yesterday and the other is called tomorrow, so today is the right day to love, believe, do, and mostly, live."
—Dalai Lama

The quote above hangs in my office in direct line of sight when you walk in. It is a catchy, eloquent, and vitally important reminder of why mindfulness is the key to a life of well-being. We practice mindfulness because the struggle—to stay present, in flow, grateful, and joyful—is real. The planet is suffering and in dire straits, racked with pollution, destruction, and all manner of stresses and evils. Don't get me wrong; there is immense beauty and love, too. But our tenacity for dogma and homogeneity, our illusion that material wealth will make us happy, and our general perversion around what's really important in life has left us living on an Earth that is reaching a tipping point. If we don't intervene now and nurture it back to balance, the planet will not be able to sustain the population and the pollution it creates, and we'll be our own undoing.

We need an antidote. Not an antidote that will numb us out to pain (#pharmaceuticals), or one that will create division and derision (#religion). We need a secular medicine with no side effects.

Mindfulness is that medicine.

Time magazine featured mindfulness on one of its covers recently, with the caption "The Mindfulness Revolution." *Revolution.* That's a powerful word—and used quite deliberately in this context for the weight of its meaning. Mindfulness truly has the power to effect rapid and pervasive change in the practitioner. As an example, a recent article in *U.S. News and World Report* highlighted the growing popularity of replacing detention rooms with mindfulness spaces in many schools, citing the phenomenon as ". . . one example of how mindfulness is becoming a standard part of the school day, offering an alternative to the usual punishments and . . . arming kids with lifelong tools to cope with challenging situations, resolve conflicts, and feel compassion and empathy for both themselves and others."[1] Wow. Isn't that what every parent wants for their child at the end of the day? To give them the skills of resilience and kindness so they can navigate life's challenges with ease? Beyond that, to find happiness, abundance, and contentment? And all of this without an intermediary or fear of dependence on a particular method or school of thought.

We've seen the dangers inherent in situations where impressionable minds seeking grace, salvation, or an answer to life's immense challenges are enlisted into cults whose leaders abuse their positions for power. As when young minds are recruited into militancy, used for someone else's gain—usually a religious leader or figure. Mindfulness is a secular practice, meaning it has no religious affiliations. It is also autonomous. You can practice it anytime, anywhere, with the one thing you always have on you. No, not your phone. Your breath.

It is a tool to help you strengthen and hone your ability to stay in the present moment and remain grounded in the only reality you really have: the here and now. The secret to true joy is to be completely present to the present, absorbing each moment fully, with every shred of your awareness. To be fully tuned in and turned on is what it means to truly be alive. To be able to do this also means we begin to appreciate the ephemeral nature of all things and accept that life is constantly evolving. We free ourselves from being stuck in the past, which can lead to regret, or fixated on the future, which can lead to anxiety. Through mindfulness, we stay anchored in the present, open and curious about what we find, rather than judgmental or resistant. This openness and fluidity with the present moment is perhaps *the* differentiating factor between a life of ease and one of dis-ease.

Mindfulness allows for space to be created to make different choices—better choices—rather than acting on autopilot or rote. Easier stated than executed, I know, but that's exactly what this book is designed to help you with. I want you to be enlightened to why you feel sad, anxious, unhappy, or depressed, and then give you the tools to help you resolve these feelings and find a more empowered way forward. I want you to get strong in the practices I outline, and develop such fortitude and resilience that you never look back for so long that you get stuck in the past with regret—or lean too far forward into the future that you get anxious. You'll stay right here in the now, "spidey" senses sharpened and always on the ready, extracting maximum joy from every moment of this beautiful, magical, challenging ride called life.

 I was recently summoned for jury duty, and realized that I had a flight to Miami booked for the same day. My excuse for taking time away from an already jam-packed life was to do some exploratory work for this book. The more compelling reason was to visit with my best girlfriend. Now, if you don't already know how much weight your closest relationships carry in your overall levels of happiness, you will before the end of this book. Spoiler alert: They rank heavy. As such, visiting a bestie who I hadn't seen in months was a priority. We had invested countless hours over years solidifying our relationship, but I could feel tiny tears erupting in our tightly woven bond. The time apart was taking its toll in the form of miscommunications and flare-ups. As with any long-distance relationship (she in Miami, I in Philly), there was only so long the phone would sustain us. We needed face time. It mattered to me to do my civic duty; it mattered as much to make the trip down and devote time to the friendship.

When I arrived at City Hall to report for service, it was hard to say what the outcome would be; I might be released, I might be made to stay. In truth, I was the perfect candidate to serve: I'm not crazy, I'm not racist, I'm an upstanding citizen out to do right in the world. And in the interest of justice, I wanted to do my part. But, there was a small window of opportunity to make the trip given our hectic schedules, and my bestie was waiting for me. The flight was at 6 p.m., so if I were let go anytime before 4 p.m., I could still make it. Sitting on a bench with scores of other juror potentials, all I could do was patiently wait my turn until an opportunity arose to make my case for an early dismissal. Moment to moment, it was an unknown. I willed myself to stay open, curious, and present. Getting worked up about it would get me no closer to a solution, but would bring me unwarranted and unwanted stress, a colossal waste of time given all of the reading I could catch up on, the reconnecting I could do with family and friends while I waited, and the new connections I could make with the many neighbors seated to my right and left. In addition, stress would have precluded me from paying attention not just to important information on how to fill out the jury forms (ultimately, people's lives hang in the balance), but to the stand-up comedy being performed by the administrator helping to guide us all through the process. Because I was present and engaged, I found myself listening intently to every joke she cracked, giggling with glee, and appreciative of the care and concern with which we were all being treated. I was happy for the opportunity to be in a new situation learning new things with new people. The spirit was quite jovial, and I found time flying by. Because I was taking in every moment with acute clarity and presence, I was also very aware of opportunities to make my situation known in case it might help me proceed more quickly and catch my flight. So, when the friendly attendant asked if any of us had exciting plans for the weekend, I replied, "Hopefully." Everyone laughed. I explained that I had a flight later that day, and provided all went smoothly for us, I would be on it and on my way to Miami. I had made my presence—and my situation—known (added bonus, making people laugh in the process), and now I needed to just relax and enjoy the ride.

From then on, every chance I got to raise a question about the process, contribute to the good energy in the room, or ask how we were progressing, I took. The friendly administrator told us she often took straw polls to pass the time, to get suggestions from such a varied and colorful bunch on everything from good lunch spots (and ones to avoid), to fun activities in the city, and everything in between. Today's straw poll was an "in between." Her daughter's wedding was coming up, and they were in the midst of trying to find a venue. She asked if any of us had suggestions. I readily replied with one, a beautiful location near my childhood home where my niece had recently tied the knot. Had I been stressed or upset about my plight, my mind absorbed in selfish or myopic concerns, I most certainly wouldn't have been so congenial about her request, had I even been paying enough attention to respond in the first place. Further, I doubt I would have had the clarity to express my situation to the group with levity and humor, or ask timely questions about how I might serve and still make my flight. I truly wanted what was in the highest service for all involved—if that meant me staying back and being selected to help decide a fair verdict in this trial, I was at peace with that outcome.

Ultimately, staying present kept me happy and in flow as the time slipped by, and when we returned from lunch, not five minutes had passed before the cheerful admin waved me outside and said, "I suppose best-case scenario would be if we dismissed you." I replied, "Well yes, that would be great!" To which, with a growing smile on her face, she replied, "Well then, I guess you're dismissed!"

I was in such gratitude over the abundance I had just been gifted, I felt saturated in it. Operating on that vibrational frequency, I kept magnetizing more of the same. Being let out just after lunch, I now had ample time, allowing me to stop at the office on my way out to accomplish some much-needed work. My mother ended up driving me to the airport, saving me cab fare and upping the abundance ante. Just as we were leaving, my parents gave me a "tikka," a traditional Indian blessing conferred on loved ones at special occasions—like going on a journey. Tikka is usually accompanied by a monetary gift, though on my last several trips, it had been absent (an implicit assertion by my mom that she was unhappy with my destination). Today, the abundance rained down.

My father was palming me a crispy new Benjamin, and I happily tucked it into the "emergency" pocket of my wallet.

We made our way smoothly to the airport, hitting almost no traffic. It felt like the *Twilight Zone,* that much quiet unheard of (so to speak) on a Friday at 5 p.m., normally the peak of rush hour. When I arrived at the airport, the security line was as lean, leaving me time to grab a snack before I boarded the flight. I ended up seated across from a very kind gentleman, his smile emanating warmth and ease. The good energy was following me like a balmy breeze.

A mother and her two children boarded. It was clear they were all seated separately, the boy preparing to take his place in the middle seat next to the smiley gentleman. His sister was supposed to be in the middle seat to my right, and mom was in a middle seat a few rows behind us. Without missing a beat, Mr. Good Energy across the aisle offered to take her middle seat a few rows back, and give up his aisle so the two of them could sit together. I followed his lead and offered to move over to the middle seat, so the young girl could take my aisle and be across from her mother and brother. It stung a little because I had paid extra for the aisle seat and was now giving it up for a middle. But, in a flash, I had the awareness that I was being gifted the opportunity to "pay it forward." One civic duty shirked, a new one entertained. Helped by the hundred-dollar bill I had stashed in my wallet. The tikka money more than compensated for the extra I had paid for the seat. Thank you Universe . . . .

Making the Case for Mindfulness

In his 2009 Nobel Peace Prize acceptance speech, Barack Obama said that for an active peace to be achieved in the world, we need to "expand our moral imagination." Following the speech he was interviewed by Hollywood power couple Will Smith and Jada Pinkett Smith where he elaborated:

> . . . one of the critical ingredients of any effort for peace is my ability to stand in your shoes, to see through your eyes . . . . That kind of ability to imagine ourselves in different situations helps us then connect with those other people.

My ability to stand in your shoes, to see through your eyes. In other words, empathy, the definition of which is the "psychological identification with or vicarious experiencing of the feelings, thoughts, or attitudes of another."[2] Obama is saying that for peace to be achieved, empathy is vital. Turns out that one of the cornerstone benefits of practicing mindfulness is that it cultivates and hones empathy. When you sit in silence and attune to your spiritual self, a magical thing happens: Boundaries fall away, the ego dissolves, and you realize your connectedness to the ether around you, your oneness with all things. You see yourself not as "separate," but an integral part of a larger energy. With this realization comes the enlightenment that to aggress on another energy being is tantamount to an act of aggression on the self. Thus does mindfulness build empathy in inverse correlation to aggression and violence.

The Dalai Lama has famously stated that we can successfully eradicate violence from the planet in one generation, if we teach every eight-year-old child to meditate. I can't think of a better reason to make mindfulness a way of life. But maybe that's just me—and *Miss Congeniality* Gracie Lou Freebush, who just wants "world peace."

If your agenda is not such a global one, give it time. You'll soon realize how strong an impact the violence and lack of empathy in the world have on your day-to-day life, and how each act of aggression on one of your fellow beings is like a direct attack on yourself. It's all one energy, so whether you realize it or not, each action reverberates back on each of us equally. With time and practice, this notion will become more and more clear. Meantime, there's a strong case to be made for how the practice can revolutionize your life on a more obvious level, too.

Stress-Buster

It doesn't get more obvious than as a buffer to stress. We feel stress every day—in the form of traffic on the road, deadlines in the office, and relationship challenges at home. We answer to industries and jobs that compel us to produce more, faster. We live stress in our cities, not least because we are in such close proximity absorbing each others' energies, including all of the anger, sadness, and fear. We live it in our rural areas, where isolation breeds loneliness. We live it in our increasing inability to find healthy, pure, unadulterated food for our bodies, which ultimately manifests in various cancers and diseases. The stress is piling on faster and faster, spinning out of control because we're not able to deal with it effectively. You see, we've got this stress response in our bodies that served us very well for eons to keep us alive. When we sensed danger in our environment, a cascade of hormones and chemicals readied us to stay and fight the threat, or flee and evade the danger as quickly as possible. This "fight or flight" stress response happened only acutely, a reaction to spurts of danger or threat. Think: lions, tigers, and bears. You can imagine why a stress response would come in handy. Alarms bells in the form of hormones and chemicals that helped us run or fight meant we survived and carried on the species, which is the biggest payoff in genetic terms.

What used to be an adaptive response is now working against us. Our stress response has become chronic because we don't distinguish well between a lion marking us as prey and an angry boss threatening to fire us. Real danger in our modern lives is whatever we perceive or feel it to be, whether or not our survival is actually threatened. It's going to take some time for our genes to catch up, especially if not one thousand years ago in our millennia of evolution, stressing out could literally keep us alive. In contrast, modern life has virtually eradicated the need for such a powerful stress response. The odds of walking outside our home and needing to be on guard against an active threat to our survival are thankfully almost nil for the majority of the world. We must, therefore, empower our minds to make the distinction between real stress and perceived stress. Unfortunately, most of us are unable to make that distinction because we don't have the awareness to do so. We end up with a constant flood of stress hormones and chemicals that, over time, damage the body beyond its own capacity for repair.

There will be much more on that in the next section of the book. For now, just realize that you need a tool to keep you aware of the present moment to such a honed degree that you can instantly parse out a real threat from a perceived one, and then make the choice to stay calm and stave off a stress response when you are in no real danger. In this way, you can take control and step out of the chronic stress cycle. Mindfulness is a practice designed to help us cultivate our awareness of the present and use it to make the best choices in that moment, including knowing the difference between a real tiger and a boss who just growls like one.

Emotion Regulator

Speaking of growling, do you tend to find yourself surrounded by people who have trouble controlling their emotions? Or perhaps you yourself struggle with this, blowing up in anger or bursting into tears at the slightest trigger? The act of controlling which emotions you have, when you have them, and how you experience and express them is called emotion regulation. Emotion regulation plays a key role in how we interact with each other. When it is present, we find harmony and respect. In its absence, we find misunderstandings and escalation to aggression and violence. In fact, problems with emotion regulation are central to many forms of psychological illness, including attention deficit hyperactivity disorder, bipolar disorder, borderline personality disorder, post-traumatic stress disorder, autism, and Asperger's syndrome.

It bears noting here that emotions themselves are highly adaptive. They give us vital information about events in our internal and external worlds. For example, let's say we reach a milestone goal, like finishing a book. We feel a strong sense of accomplishment, leading to reward centers in the brain firing off feel-good chemicals like dopamine. This makes us happy and we'll be motivated in the future to keep reaching for goals and accomplishing them so we can again feel that dopamine rush and the consequent deep level of satisfaction and joy. It's a positive feedback loop around achievement.

Negative emotions also have their place. They serve as a barometer for when things need adjustment. If you consistently wake up with anxiety or depression, it's a sign from your inner world that something in your outer world is not working. The unhappiness you feel in the form of negative emotions drives you to make a change to get back to equanimity. As Danielle LaPorte aptly states in *The Desire Map*, "Positive feeling states are a sign that we're in synch with our Soul. Negative feeling states are indicators that we're out of synch with our Soul."[3] Emotions are valuable: It's the inability to regulate them that gets us into trouble.

As it turns out, mindfulness is a supremely effective tool in helping you cultivate emotion regulation. This has to do with the non-judgmental component of the practice; the focus is on achieving greater *acceptance* and *awareness* of emotions, instead of actually working to change emotional experience. In this way, mindfulness promotes changing your relationship to your thoughts and feelings rather than trying to change the thoughts themselves. As you gain more distance from your emotional urges, you are less likely to act on them in rash or irrational ways. This, of course, leads to more calm and effective interactions.

Given two of the incredible benefits of mindfulness just discussed—empathy and emotion regulation—can you imagine the consequences for some of our greatest social ills? Take bullying, for example. Classrooms where space and time to be mindful are staples of the children's day are seeing marked changes in behavior. I did a mindfulness training some time ago that was specific to kindergarten through twelfth graders. They showed us a video of a young boy, around nine years old, who said he no longer felt the urge to get angry or fight, and that he was calmer and preferred to be that way because it "felt better." He also described how at home, he urged his mother to "be mindful" when she got angry or upset, and how he rarely fought with his younger brother anymore.

In another testimonial, from an article in the *Huffington Post*, mindfulness expert Oren J. Sofer recounted the story of a young boy in one of his classes, who shared that he was very scared one night, having heard gunshots outside his house. His recourse was to employ mindful breathing to calm himself down.[4] That he even had a tool to use in that moment to quell his fears and bring him back to presence speaks volumes about how our children might use mindfulness to cope with the challenges of everyday stressors.

In another anecdote, Sofer describes one educator's powerful experience teaching the skills of mindfulness to her class—specifically, how to cultivate more kindness by sending out good wishes (this is like the Buddhist metta meditation, a practice of transmitting loving kindness to others, particularly those with whom we have agitation or conflict). One of the students, who had been having some behavioral and social issues, broke the classroom's marble jar. The jar represented a log of the classroom's kind acts—every time a child witnessed an act of kindness, they would put a marble in the jar. The class was discussing the matter, agitated and angry with their classmate, when one young girl voiced that he simply hadn't learned to control his angry feelings—*yet*—and that they should take a "mindful moment" and send him a heartfelt "may he find peace." The class sat together for a moment, did some mindful breathing and sending of good wishes, and then worked together to clean up the broken glass and marbles. When the boy returned, he was welcomed back with ease.

Coming from eight-year-olds, this is a truly remarkable reaction. Through mindfulness, children will quickly learn to adopt healthy and productive ways to handle stress, cultivate empathy, manage aggressive tendencies, and reformulate their environments from the inside out to become harmonious and solutions-driven.

In an ongoing study through the University of North Carolina, Wilmington, researchers are teaching preschoolers yoga and relaxation skills. After just two weeks, the tots learning these skills exhibit better attention, awareness, gratitude, and happiness compared to their peers.[5]

A seven-year study currently running across twenty-six schools in Kentucky, called the "Compassionate Schools Project," is boldly making mindfulness a part of the curriculum, alongside staples like math and science, and closely observing its effects on the children.[5a] Results are expected to be unprecedented.

Such anecdotes are increasingly common in schools where mindfulness is being taught to students. As such, the practice is securing its place in education as integral to creating healthy, kind, sharp, and resilient children. Unfortunately, school boards are still extremely resistant to changing curriculums, especially if it means including subject matter that is vastly different from traditional academic subjects or has even a twinge of ideology or philosophy that sounds like religion. Parents, educators, and administrators must enlighten themselves to the completely secular approach mindfulness employs and push for its adoption into all schools' curriculums. Ultimately, the invaluable effects of mindfulness come down to skills. Learn them, and you can live and do better. If you aren't taught, how will you know? You can also perhaps now see why the Dalai Lama's statement that we could eradicate violence from the world in just one generation if we taught our young people to be mindful is not a pipe dream, but an achievable reality.

Noggin Sharpener

Another powerful rationale for integrating a mindfulness practice into your life is that it simply makes you smarter. Some of my favorite studies look at working memory in mindfulness practitioners. Working memory is the part of your short-term memory that temporarily stores, processes, and manipulates information. It is essential for higher executive brain functioning like comprehension, learning, and reasoning. Think about the task of test-taking. Let's say you're given a reading comprehension passage full of juicy details about the mating rituals of clams. Working memory is what you would use to store all those details as you read, so that you could answer the multiple-choice questions that follow at the end of the passage. How well you do on that test, therefore, has a lot to do with how well your working memory is operating. The functioning of your working memory relies on your ability to stay on task and focus on the information being presented. If you can do that well and hold the information you have just learned in your mind, you can perform the higher-level tasks of reasoning or drawing conclusions from those newly acquired bits of knowledge. If the mind wanders or becomes distracted by other thoughts, like "I'm starving; when is this test going to be over?" or "If I don't ace this section, I won't score high enough to get into Harvard," your working memory's effectiveness has already plummeted. It is now filling up with extraneous thoughts, which are not useful to the task at hand and are in fact replacing the essential pieces of information you need with distractors. Eek. The mind can sabotage your attention if you don't train it to stay put and focus.

Mindfulness coaxes your brain to do exactly that. The more you practice anchoring your mind on a task (we will learn and practice some techniques shortly) and noticing when it has wandered away, the more you hone your ability to keep the mind from doing so. Your ability to attend to tasks without distraction is the key to performing well when you are required to use working memory. It should, therefore, come as no surprise that those trained in mindfulness outperform the uninitiated by miles. In one particular study of the GRE (Graduate Record Exam, the standardized test most graduate schools require for acceptance), those with mindfulness training had much higher test scores.[6] Enough said.

Self-Actualizer

Okay, well, there is a bit more to say. Or rather, ask. Starting with, "Who are you, *really*?" It's a question most of us don't *really* know how to answer, and that gets us into a lot of trouble. We go through life not necessarily choosing our actions deliberately, in alignment with our essential selves, but based on external expectations or superficial rationale. Have you ever been asked what you'd like to eat, and instead of acting from a place of real, mindful intention to figure out what you really want/need, you say, "I'll have what she's having." Or, you default to the same order you give every day simply because it's easier than making a different choice—and likely the more fitting choice—in that moment.

I'm not saying we don't sometimes want what someone else is enjoying, or prefer the same thing every day, but this example is just to highlight that we are giving over a lot of our alignment to habit simply because we aren't attuning properly to ourselves. And though the consequences when it comes to food choices aren't so dire (unless you struggle with health issues, in which case, they certainly are; more on that in Section II), they can be far more perilous in other contexts. A lack of attunement to our inner compass means we could stray way off course in life, living someone else's dream and not our own. This is the classic impostor syndrome of taking on others' projections of who we should be rather than really understanding who we are at our core, and operating from that essential level to live our true purpose. And trust me, you will never, *ever* be happy living an inauthentic life. In fact, it can make you incredibly sick.

When I was fourteen, I was told I wouldn't be placed in Honors Chemistry because I had received a "B" in Freshman Biology. To merit the honors class, I needed a "B+." Turns out, I already had it running through my veins: literally, because my blood type is B-positive, metaphorically, because it would become my life's purpose. Much of what I do is to study, practice, and teach others how to "be positive." Back then, however, the B+ (or lack thereof) was a trigger for one of the darkest periods of my life. At just fifteen years old, I sank into a deep and severe depression. It was mixed with bouts of anxiety, where I was robbed of my sleep, my appetite, and my spark for life. Not to mention the physical consequences. My legs grew first, just as my torso was slated to catch up; I stopped giving my body the nutrients it needed. I ended up a decent 5'5", but I think every now and again about what life would have been like had I been taller, as doctors predicted I would be.

Back then, height was the furthest thing from my mind. My only rumination was how I had failed. I recall sitting around a conference table with the head of school, the science teachers, and my parents, feeling my negative self-worth coming down to a "positive" sign. If you had told me that some twenty years later my life purpose—my true worth—would be all about that "+" sign, I would've laughed in delight at the cyclical and magical workings of the Universe and the ironical way in which it often operates. Even more ironically, the antidote to my immense suffering during that dark time, as I would learn years later in my positive psychology studies, was to focus on what was going right, and all of the ways in which I was kicking ass in school outside of that little lack of a "plus." My grades in English and French were soaring, and I was achieving a standard of excellence in those subjects that was actually quite exemplary. I consistently swept the awards in those categories, and aced any and all written and standard exams in them. I qualified for National Merit Scholarship based not on my math scores, but on my very high verbal. But our focus was on what was going wrong, and it was taking me down.

And that wouldn't be the first time. It was only part of a slippery slope of decisions in my life based not on my own innate desires and talents, but others' wishes. I have walked down many roads simply as a result of being asked to do so—like getting married because the perfect-on-paper guy was on a knee with a big honking rock asking really nicely. That choice wasn't right for me; I just didn't have the self-awareness to realize it. It wasn't until I got divorced, and had the courage to stand on my own two feet, on ground I had leveled for myself, that I stopped slipping and regained my footing.

Turns out, mindfulness helps you answer the question of who you really are by giving you space to attune to your essential self. The essential self is the spirit inside the body that lights up bright in certain contexts, that wants to fly its unique flag in the world. It represents a specific set of gifts and talents and is compelled to see them expressed. If we aren't dedicating time every day to tune back in, our essential self can get buried under a mountain of noise, messages, and distractions.

Take social media, for instance. Each platform has its own app, a quick-and-easy download that is then either pinging constantly or showing us little red numbers that track how much activity is streaming in. It becomes like a compulsion to check, re-check, and then check again. The consequence, however, is that we get caught in a constant state of social comparison. Social comparison is the phenomenon wherein we determine our own social and personal worth based on how we stack up against others. When we see snaps of all these folks "winning" out there in the world—our friends, family members, acquaintances, favorite celebrities, or random strangers—we feel inadequate. When we see posts of those less fortunate than us, like social action videos of refugees in war-torn nations, or abused animals in dire need of advocacy, we feel a whole host of negative emotions, including guilt. Point is, whether we're comparing ourselves to those we think are far more fortunate or those we believe are far less fortunate, the forecast is equally grim.

The "world's happiest man" agrees. Matthieu Ricard, a Buddhist monk, was recently given this moniker by scientists who studied his brain as part of a twelve-year investigation into meditation and compassion at the University of Wisconsin. They found levels of gamma wave activity (associated with consciousness, attention, learning, and memory) in his brain that had never been detected in another human, including activity in his brain's left prefrontal cortex that allowed him to have an abnormally large capacity for happiness.[7] Speaking to *GQ* magazine about the secret to his bliss, he said, "Comparison is the killer of happiness."

And this is to say nothing of the other pressures we encounter.

Our own parents' desires, attachments, fears, and beliefs can snag us in a generational cycle that is incredibly difficult to break out of. In my own experience, my immigrant parents' top priority was to establish security in their new homeland. As such, they wanted to set us children up with the best chances for success, sacrificing their own needs so we'd have a top-notch education and access to stable and lucrative careers. For my parents, the epitome of "stable and lucrative" was a career in medicine. Their biggest dream for my sister and me was to see us become doctors.

It's taken me years and many fits and starts to begin owning my own truth: I'm a creative spirit, a free bird who withers in nine-to-five contexts, a lover of words and writing, and a fundamental believer in prevention over cure. And it's taken my parents years to accept this truth, and reconcile my chosen path with their medically inclined hopes and dreams. God bless them—they do try, even within the confines of their fears for my future and security. But my life is in my hands, and my path is my ultimate responsibility. The choices I make toward it or away from it are mine to own. This is not an easy course to chart, for I am a product of a generational vortex that wants to suck me in. Pulling away is like separating two viciously attracted magnets.

The only time I really get the chance to put a layer between the magnets and tease them apart is when I meditate. In this space, I turn inward and realign with my true self. It gets very quiet, and all the noise, distractions, messages, and projections fall away. Decibel levels from the external world fall to zero. And in this realm of quietude, I can hear the whisper of my true nature, *Prakriti*, and what she is calling for through the vehicle of this beautiful, uniquely designed mind and body with its equally singular gifts and talents. I non-judgmentally observe what I find, so even when comparisons start needling their way in, I practice letting thoughts go and simply accept what is. What *is,* is a woman with a strong voice and sensitive heart, a willful communicator who loves to connect, finds bliss in singing, and is repulsed by the inauthentic or the passive aggressive. This work at attunement leads me directly to my true purpose, because it eliminates paths and interactions that don't suit my essential self.

It's a work in progress every day to be mindful, to re-attune, and re-align with the essential self. It requires making difficult choices, often in direct conflict with the ego and its desires (more on that soon). But if you want a truly fulfilling and contended existence, it's the only way to get there.

Sleep-Reaper

Another vital component of a fulfilling and contented life is sleep. The sad fact is, most of us either aren't getting enough sleep, or we aren't getting adequate sleep (which means we have trouble falling asleep and/or staying asleep). Surveys conducted by the National Sleep Foundation found that the majority of us have sleep problems a few nights a week or more,[8] and it's causing us a whole slew of other issues (which we'll get into in Section II). It's mindfulness to the rescue once again. A mind that is fitful and disturbed will be unable to rest, leading to disrupted sleep. A daily mindfulness practice primes you to work yourself back to a state of deep relaxation and calm by anchoring the mind in the present moment. Over time, and with concerted effort, you get better and better at hooking into this "relaxation response" so you create a reflex around it, and then can more easily call it forth in times of need.

This was the crux of Dr. Herbert Benson's bestseller *The Relaxation Response*, a term he coined based on his research in the '60s and '70s to suggest that each of us has the ability to encourage our bodies to release chemicals and brain signals that make the muscles and organs slow down and increase blood flow to the brain.[9] Though this is the exact phenomenon associated with meditation, it was already inextricably linked to religion and mysticism for many Westerners. Dr. Benson brilliantly relabeled meditation and its associated health benefits as "the relaxation response," allowing people to see beyond the old connotations to its vital function; it is a way for us to take control of our autopilot fight-or-flight stress response and counteract it with an antidote, essentially the opposite reaction, to bring the body back to pre-stress levels.

When you find yourself lying in bed at the end of the day, unable to sleep, you can evoke the relaxation response reflex (which you'll sharpen with your mindfulness practice) to help lull you into slumber.

I began my case for mindfulness on a global note, and now that we've dived into the benefits you will receive on an individual level, let's widen the lens again. Our planet is in dire need of an antidote to terrorism, global warming, and dis-ease. We're at a tipping point, and if we don't intervene on some of these destructive patterns, we'll be beyond saving. Mindfulness is foundational to the solution because it helps us to cultivate awareness and empathy, for ourselves as well as those around us. Part of this awareness is the fundamental truth that we vary only slightly in composition and structure. In more scientific terms, we all have the same biological basis: Every single human being is made up of roughly ninety-nine percent *identical* genetic material. We have the exact same organs and tissues, and produce analogous hormones and chemicals. As such, we adopt similar patterns of behavior, which is why we can relate to each other—and why we amplify our disparities; we're all so alike we can't find enough differences to suit a selfish agenda, so we make them up. We let our egos take the driver's seat and exaggerate the one percent differences of gender, skin color, age, and creed to a destructive end instead of the beautiful one we should actually be recognizing: that we're fundamentally the same. Where we are unique is in the singular way in which our spirit finds creative expression. This, not superficial characteristics, is what true diversity means. We've spent so long oppressing each other around our differences, and then fighting to be seen as equals, that we've gotten off track. Let's champion for real diversity—and invest more resources in supporting a wider representation of artistic expressions, like in film and cinema. I'm encouraged by the seismic shift we're seeing in Hollywood. More inclusion, not more energy in conversations around exclusion, is how we'll make rapid and powerful change.

Besides, can you imagine if we were all exactly one hundred percent alike? We would be genetic copies of one another with the same skin tone, same height, same everything. It would be like a paint palette with one color. What can you create with one color on a canvas? Far less than what you can create with two colors, which is far less than what you can create with three colors, and so on. How could we depict our world as it really is—in all of its varietal bounty and colorful array—if we had only one color with which to represent it? We don't discriminate the color of one fruit or vegetable as superior or inferior, like an orange as genetically superior to an apple because it is orange and the apple is red. I don't know a single person who doesn't like a fruit or vegetable because of its color—unless they're a toddler, in which case, I think I've made my point. We appreciate that they're both fruits, that look, smell, and taste a little different, and were made by nature from the same essential components.

We are also part of a singular energy. The only thing that separates one human being from another is a layer of skin that keeps the whole organic soup of cells, organs, tissue, and skeleton contained in one convenient package so we can navigate our world as spiritual energies having a human experience. That's it, one layer of skin. But just outside that porous layer exists the same molecules that are contained within it: oxygen, carbon dioxide, nitrogen, and a few others depending on your whereabouts.

The conclusion of this awareness is inevitably that we're all the same, that We—every single one of Earth's constituents including animals, plants, and inanimate objects—collectively make up one common energy. The key to peace is to operate from a place of recognition and reverence to this commonality, as the Dalai Lama and Barack Obama endeavor to remind us.

Why don't we see this truth as we aggress on each other, on all other beings, on the planet? Because we lack empathy. When we feel empathy, violence is impossible. An act of aggression against another becomes an act of direct aggression upon ourselves, as I pointed out earlier. I am part of the laptop on which I write, as it is part of the table upon which it rests, as the table is a part of the ground on which it sits, and so on.

Neuroanatomist Jill Bolte Taylor discovered this truth firsthand in the most radical way. Getting ready for work one day (she was a brain researcher at Harvard at the time), a tangle of blood vessels in her brain burst suddenly. At age thirty-seven, she was having a stroke. A divine consequence of her in-depth knowledge of the brain and its functions, she was acutely aware of what was happening, and the functionality she was losing. She stayed just ahead of it, managing to make a life-saving phone call to a colleague. By the time she made the call, she was unable to comprehend language or formulate words, but her panicked noises were enough for him to understand that she was in peril and have an ambulance sent to her home straight away.

The stroke was the result of a massive bleed in the left hemisphere of her brain, effectively shutting it down, so she was dependent on her right brain while on the long road to recovery. Taylor describes lying in her hospital bed, unable to move, speak, or comprehend dialogue. She details her awareness of her surroundings as devoid of barriers and separations. She literally could not discern where she ended and her hospital bed began. The people and furniture around her became part of one amorphous soup—all one energy, all one thing. Why? The left and right hemispheres exist to serve very different functions. The left brain helps us with our socialization; it's about linear thinking, language, words, and computations. In real terms, it's about seeing something that looks "different," sizing it up, comparing it to what you have or haven't seen before, and labeling it accordingly. In other words, judgment. The right brain is our creative center; its intelligence stems from intuition and feeling, visualization, and a holistic picture of the world. It's expansive and limitless.

You can see from the very labels of the attributes of each hemisphere that they are often diametrically opposed: linear vs. holistic, facts vs. feelings, language vs. non-verbal, and analysis vs. imagination. Jot down some of these attributes in the space provided to the left and right of each hemisphere so you can begin to get clear on the domains of your right and left brain.

Without the left brain, we could not craft language, or read and interpret teachings and meanings. We'd be unable to discern boundaries in order to make

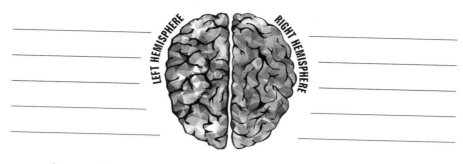

LEFT HEMISPHERE RIGHT HEMISPHERE

sense of our world and appreciate all of the objects in it. Knowing this also helps you appreciate how these very same attributes can be our downfall, engendering some our most destructive qualities. To be able to discern separateness, to analyze and judge differentials, to have different languages and computations makes us feel like we should draw borders. And then we take our variegated countries, languages, cultures, and religions and we measure them against each other. Inevitably, we come to know those systems we are born and raised into as "right." The others as "wrong." Survival has generally meant adopting the memes and values of one's environment. Learn the way of the majority and be accepted by the community. Deviate outside of it, and you risk rejection, alienation, and in the worst-case scenario, execution. If we are lucky, time and education allow us to see outside of our programming and patterns to a larger truth. Barring opportunities to see outside of these containers, however, our immediate world is the only one we know and, therefore, becomes our ultimate reality.

On the heels of a broken marriage, I was severely depressed. A romantic at heart, my faith in love had been rocked and I was at risk of becoming resentful and cynical. Maybe love didn't exist at all, or maybe I didn't deserve it. Used to achieving success at whatever I tried, I had suffered the first massive failure of my life. The bright, bubbly girl I was known to be was giving way to a self-pitying wallflower. I found myself at my sister's place one evening, suffering and in need of answers. She did a Tarot reading and had me set an intention around what it was I wanted the most. I asked for the antidote to my suffering: love.

And just like that, it arrived.

Mere weeks after leaving my marriage in India and returning home to America, I got an unexpected phone call from my cousin in Ireland. My cheery and excited "Hello!" was met with tears on the other end of the line. "What's wrong?" I implored. Through heaving sobs, my cousin managed to eek out that earlier that day, she had been part of a code team that couldn't revive the patient. He died on the table. She had just begun her training as a medical resident, and it was her first time witnessing death so up close, a healer who wasn't able to fix what was broken. I felt the strong pull to do anything in my power to alleviate her suffering, and promised I would jump on the first viable flight that I could find.

A few days later, I was sitting on a plane bound for Ireland. Mere minutes before our scheduled departure, the pilot's voice boomed over the loudspeaker: "Ladies and gentlemen, this is your captain speaking. It seems we've got some severe storms coming in from the North. All planes are grounded until further notice." A collective groan of disappointment and annoyance swept through the cabin. Then— "Since we've got about twenty planes ahead of us on the runway, don't expect we'll be going anywhere for at least a couple of hours. The flight attendants will come around now with beverages to hold you over while we wait." My stomach turned and a wave of desperation flowed through me, agitating every cell in my body. It was a foreshadowing, as if somewhere deep down I knew I would soon meet the man who would come to own my heart in a way no one ever had, the jumper cables for my quickly dimming love light.

But I didn't know it then, at least not with any mental rationality. So I simply sat there with a misplaced sense of dread at a relatively benign prognosis; I had a tight stopover in Atlanta, and if the plane was on the ground any more than thirty minutes, I would miss my connecting flight to Dublin. My arm shot up to turn on the flight attendant light. At last she materialized, having addressed more pressing concerns like pretzels, colas, and headsets; desperation was oozing out of my fidgety pores. I vomited my inquiry all over her, an anxious rush of words to inquire when the next flight out of Atlanta to Dublin would be. She replied, "Not until tomorrow, honey." My stomach churned again. "Well, can I deplane and try to find another flight out tonight?" "No, I'm sorry," came the reply. "No one is allowed off the plane unless we return to the gate. Seems like we're stuck on this runway." She flashed me a Stepford smile of plastic sympathy, and continued down the aisle. I felt something close to panic as she retreated, a caged tiger pacing. Why was I so upset, anyway? Sure, I loved my cousin dearly and wanted to be there to support her, but she would be okay. My reaction seemed unreasonable. I couldn't put my finger on it, but my body was simply reacting to a visceral sense of need.

I went into a zone. That was my word for what ensued, because back then, I had no prior reference point, and, therefore, no language for it. It was a reflex action, the only recourse to this unacceptable unfolding. Knowing what I know now about the power of intention and the quantum nature of energy, I would label it a focused meditation with the utmost purity of intention. An ask of the Universe from the deepest recesses, harnessing all of the energy one can muster within themselves. I closed my eyes and gathered all of my life-force potential into the core of my being and held it there. Then, I projected it onto the objective, willing that plane to move.

I was interrupted by the pilot's voice once again billowing from the loudspeaker: "Ladies and gentlemen, great news! Looks like we've got the go-ahead to move since the storm is coming in from the North and we're going South. Buckle your seat belts. Flight attendants get ready for takeoff, we're going NOW." If you could've seen the look on my face in that moment, you'd have borne witness to total disbelief. We were soon coasting down the runway and gliding into the air, en route to Ireland and the greatest love I've ever known.

We met that first night, and the chemistry was instant and fluid. Have you seen the movie *Brooklyn*? It helps you understand falling in love on a visceral level; the organic way it flowers into being when we least expect it and when we're not over-thinking it. The purity of it overshadows and eclipses all you knew before it, so you can take mental and spiritual leaps beyond skin color, geography, religion, culture, or kin.

Though I remember only the beauty in the way our energies intertwined, many saw us as a clash. Different races, religions, and upbringings meant that outside of our bubble, we were worlds apart. He was Muslim, born in Sudan and raised in the United Arab Emirates. I was a first-generation Indian, born and raised in the States with a Universalist approach to religion and faith. Both sets of parents were against the union and unwilling to support it. In fact, they threatened to abandon us over it. Our worlds were holding us to our differences, raising borders around them. To dissolve them meant letting go of attachment to them, and our families were not ready for this. Confronted with the reality of losing our kin, we were compelled to separate.

It was the most brutal heartbreak I've ever experienced, a pain so visceral that at times, I thought I would drown in it. There were countless pre-dawn mornings in the aftermath of the breakup when I would be shaken from slumber with a start, confronting the savage reality that it hadn't all been a bad dream. I'd gag while brushing my teeth, the anxiety was so potent. It would take years, but I'd eventually find my way through it. Meantime, that struggle was real.

*****

I heard recently that he got married to a Sudanese Muslim girl who fit the criteria his family was looking for. I hope he is happy and at peace. For me, the experience proved soul-saving, for I am now resolutely unwilling to settle for anything less than the purity and potency of what I now know real love can be. In addition, my commitment to mindfulness, beyond the myriad objective benefits, is quite personal. I want to realize a world where differences give way to commonality and love commands connection. Abiding by love means embracing our differences, and embracing our differences means deferring to our oneness. The global practice of mindfulness is a key driver of that realization of unity. I hope that is more than enough reason for you to start.

There's no time like the present to learn how to stay present, so let's jump in.

Laying the Foundation

It takes about thirty days of continuous practice to make any new endeavor a regular part of your life. Thus, the first key to getting more adept at mindfulness is to practice it with consistency. This will give it the best shot at sticking around in your life. Regularity with the practice will also make more obvious the immense positive changes that are blossoming. Once you begin to notice these, you will practice more and more, wanting to maintain all of those amazing benefits. And as you practice more, you'll get better at it. What results is the sweetest upward spiral.

In just a short while, I will outline different styles of mindfulness and practice options that you can begin to use on your own journey toward habit. But first . . .

What Is the Difference between Mindfulness and Meditation?

Mindfulness is a form of meditation, as modern "master of mindfulness" Jon Kabat-Zinn described it on *Super Soul Sunday*[10] (hands down one of my all-time favorite shows; a pioneering dive into all things spiritual and well-being on Oprah's OWN Network). I like to think of meditation as the umbrella under which mindfulness falls. And what is meditation? The primary dictionary.com definition states that meditation is "the act of meditating."[11] Thanks, Captain Obvious! The second definition states: "[meditation is] continued or extended thought; reflection; contemplation."[12] So, a protracted pondering of something qualifies it as a meditation. To be mindful is simply to be aware. Mindfulness is, therefore, the act of being aware of something for a certain period of time. That "something" you are staying aware of is the present moment.

Different Strokes for Different Folks

The practice of meditation is personal and subjective. In other words, it is not a "one-size-fits-all" model—not every style suits every person. Further, depending on the day, you may feel more connected to one style, less inclined to another. Choose what fits your schedule and state of being best in the moment you're in. So much of the joy you'll derive from this journey lies in how different methods will speak to you differently. Find your way to the right choices in your meditation selections just as you do in life with other preferences, like groceries, clothes, and home furnishings.

Also remember that mindfulness is just one form of meditation. Though it is the one I ascribe to most for its simple, secular potential and unbelievable positive impact, you can widen the sphere of your meditation practice by experimenting with other styles and philosophies.

That said, within the realm of mindfulness itself, there are many types and forms to try. Following are descriptions of some of the most popular and prominent:

Mindful Breathing

The simplest and most effective way to practice mindfulness is to use your breath. This practice involves sitting up straight, hands resting comfortably in your lap, legs hip-distance apart and feet flat on the floor. The eyes can be closed or remain open—eyes closed helps you focus on the inner workings of your body; eyes open strengthens your ability to stay serene amid external distractions.[13] Both confer important benefits, so you should experiment with each. If you choose to keep your eyes open, focus your gaze on an unmoving spot in front of you. Turn your attention to your breath, inhaling for a count of four, exhaling for a count of six. After a few cycles, stop counting and allow the breath to fall into a natural rhythm, simply being with the experience of the breath and noticing what you find there: the sensations as the air hits the tip of your nose and enters the body, as it sweeps into your lungs and the belly expands, the release of pressure on the exhale as the air is released from the body, the contraction of belly and lungs, and any temperature difference in the air as it leaves the nose once again. If thoughts arise to distract you—dinner menu, kids' science projects, or the disagreement you had with your best friend—gently release them from your present moment experience and return to your breath. In this way, you don't attach to your thoughts, or respond emotionally, but rather stay objective to them, just like clouds that do not stay fixed in the sky, but continuously glide their way through the atmosphere.

Take a moment to go back through the description of mindful breathing, familiarize yourself with the technique (posture, breath counting, anchoring cues), and then try it on your own.

The Body Scan

The body scan is a sweet two-fer in that you get the benefits of mindfulness and focused awareness along with a deep, progressive relaxation exercise. It involves scanning the body top to toe, using the power of attention to actively relax and release tension from each part of the body. Every time I guide people through this style, they fall in love with it; the dissipation of tension and stress are palpable.

I led a guided meditation at a holiday event a few years back, where stylists were offering complimentary eyelash extensions and eyebrow shaping. A seemingly unorthodox combination, I know, and exactly why it was so impactful. It's important for us to infuse meditation into all arenas of life, making it a regular part of our daily routines and an anchor-point around everything we do. This helps us stay aligned and grounded, so we don't lose ourselves in the material at the expense of the spiritual. Or vice-versa. You can find time for both, especially when you combine forces and do them in tandem.

The brow stylist later shared with me her marvel at the visible shift from tension to relaxation when I led the room through the exercise. She had a young woman in her chair when I began the practice, and as I cued everyone in the room to place their attention fully on the crown of their heads, and then use their awareness to actively release any tension they found, she said she actually saw the woman's scalp relax.

This is a great example of how effective a mindful practice can be as an immediate and potent relaxation tool using just the power of focused attention.

Mindful Eating

Another crowd favorite is the mindful eating exercise. No big surprise, since most humans love food. This method is also a two-fer in that we're simultaneously exercising our mindfulness muscles and our palettes. It's a practice in paying attention to our meals—something we rarely ever do. Most meals are inhaled on the go, in front of a screen, or scarfed down in the company of friends and family. We'd prefer to converse, rather than focus in concentrated silence on each morsel. We don't stare down our food because that could get quite awkward for our tablemates. But what if we did exactly that? It is a novel and highly potent exercise in getting you to notice what you're probably not used to noticing.

When I guide folks through this exercise in groups, I always have a few participants who fall right into the aforementioned mindless imbibing trap. I place a piece of chocolate (usually a Hershey's Kiss) at each seat before folks come in. My model examples scoop it up, unwrap the foil, and pop it into their mouths; one-to-two chews and they're done, already moving past the delectable little treat and on to the beverage sitting under their chair. I love to call them out with an expression of gratitude for their help in making my point. (Hello three-fer! A gratitude practice is one of the surest ways to increased happiness—more on that later.)

Slowing way down with our food, taking the time to savor each aspect of the experience, and perhaps even swallowing each bite with a sprinkling of gratitude is a powerful mindfulness practice. Let's take the Hershey's Kiss as an example. You might hold it in your hand for a while, turning it around, over, and upside down, carefully observing its characteristics: the shiny tin foil; the conical droplet shape; and the texture, hard and firm, or perhaps soft and melty from the warmth of your hand. Then, you might unwrap it slowly from its covering. This aspect I used to love as a child, the way the foil could untwist from the top and uncoil in one clean step if I had the patience for it. I'd pull out the long white strip of thin paper peeking through the top, and then bite off the tip of the Kiss, like a little mindful ritual. And then I'd pop the rest into my mouth and bite down.

Chances are I didn't take much time to savor it (to *savor* means "to perceive by taste or smell, especially with relish," and "to give oneself to the enjoyment of "),[14] but it's an important element of the mindful eating exercise. Really unpacking the experience of eating allows you to *taste* your food, to revel in the magic of its flavor, and hook into a bliss point we so often skirt right over. Ironic considering that an entire industry exists to determine the bliss point of various foods—that is, their optimal palatability. With a little mindfulness, we can tap into that for ourselves.

Before putting the candy in your mouth, you might first wave it under your nose and take in the aroma of the chocolate. So much of food is aroma, and the more sensory layers we add to our gastronomic experiences, the richer they become. As you put the chocolate in your mouth, letting it sit for a moment before you chew, you might notice how challenging it can be to simply taste your food and not succumb to the reflex to swallow. But if you wait, you can feel the salivary glands activate as they release enzymes that will help you break down and digest the food molecules. Chewing slowly allows you to notice how satisfying it feels to bite into different textures, the action of the jaw in helping to break down food, the miracle workings of each and every part of the body and mind to bring this simple experience of enjoying a morsel of chocolate to life.

And that's the perfect segue into gratitude; becoming uber mindful about every element that comes into play simply to take food and fuel into our bodies accords us an enhanced appreciation for how our constitutions serve us every moment to keep us alive and thriving. No doubt this will also have the added benefit of making you more mindful about what you're actually putting into your body and allow you to make better choices for your health. Anything can be substituted for the Hershey's Kiss, e.g., raisins. It's all about simply slowing down to notice each detail of your eating experience.

The exercise also works well with beverages. The Buddhist monk, peace activist, and great spiritual teacher Thich Nhat Hanh made an appearance on *Super Soul Sunday*, and taught Oprah how to live mindfully through a "tea meditation." Oprah loves her chai (Indian blend of tea with milk and spices), and I was so charmed by the delight and wonder she expressed over this newfound way to get mindful using a long-established and adored habit.

They slowed way down with the act of drinking tea, holding the cup with both hands and noticing its warmth infuse their skin, breathing in the aroma, first luxuriating in the olfactory experience, then taking that first sip and letting the warm liquid pass over their lips and sit on their tongues for a moment, relishing in the delightful taste of the leaves. . .

As you can see, almost any activity can be a mindfulness practice, and is in fact the point of the work; most of the bliss in our lives comes from being fully present to the simplest elements of our journey as it is unfolding.

How Do I Make the Practice Stick?

I hope that by now you're adequately convinced of why mindfulness is vital to your life and have some sense of how to practice it. Alas, how to make the practice a daily part of your routine given all of your other responsibilities and distractions?

What follows are some expert tips and tools to help you out. These were heavily inspired by Erin Easterly's "8 Steps to Establish a Daily Meditation Practice" as featured on chopra.com (a great site for all things holistic wellness). Remember that these are general suggestions and malleable guidelines; you can experiment with different methods and make them your own. Ultimately, I want to help ensure that this game-changing practice hangs around in your life for good, so find what works best for *you*.

Link your mindfulness practice to an instrumental task. Instrumental tasks are those deeply ingrained habits that don't require effort or forethought, like brushing your teeth or driving home from work. By linking your meditation practice to an instrumental task, you reduce the effort needed to initiate the yet-to-be-ingrained habit. This cultivates "stick-to-it-iveness."

Let's say you pair your meditation practice with brushing your teeth. Every morning, just after brushing, you sit down to meditate. Eventually, the former, already an instrumental task, will trigger the latter, until it too becomes instrumental.

I can't remember exactly when (but certainly more than a decade ago) I began to drink two tall glasses of water immediately after brushing my teeth in the morning, and one after brushing my teeth before bed (two, and I'd probably have an accident in the middle of the night). I liked the way this practice gave my body immediate hydration first thing upon waking, and replenished any depleted reserves of H_2O right before bed. Seems my body liked it, too; eventually, my mouth would go super dry right after my daily tooth-brushings, my body signaling thirst in anticipation of the impending hydration satiation. Inadvertently, I had created a link between my healthy dental hygiene habit and my healthy hydration one. You can do the same with any instrumental task and your meditations.

Don't try to be a hero and sit for an hour before you've tried sitting for five minutes. And forgive yourself the need to be a "Zen Master"—or even of the expectation that you need to "master" anything. This practice is not designed to be an outcome in and of itself (although it can feel pretty damn great to sit in silence and just be; after all, we are human *be*ings, not human *do*ings). Meditation is a means to an end. That end is about helping you navigate the life you're living with more fluidity, grace, ease, and, most importantly, joy. By *be*ing fully present to your life, you're extracting the real nectar from it. You're not doing this when you're stuck in the past or obsessed with the future because you're missing all the good stuff just as it's unfolding.

As you work the practice, also remember that it's not called a "practice" because it comes to you with no effort at all. It's a skill you cultivate over time, and as with anything, you will improve with dedicated effort. Start small and gradually increase the duration of your sessions, giving your mind, body, and spirit a chance to acclimate to this new endeavor. Whatever resistance or discomfort you may encounter as you venture into mindfulness meditation, allow it with acceptance, and give yourself time to find your flow with it.

Blood flow, in my case. When I first began to sit in meditation, my feet would invariably go numb and begin to tingle. My legs were not used to being in a cross-legged position, the blood vessels and veins unaccustomed to such constriction. As it is, I've got low BP, which means teeny tiny veins and hands and feet that are perpetually cold. It took time for my extremities to develop an intelligence around this new position, and eventually, my body adapted and learned how to channel blood flow through the posture more effectively. The breathing aspect of meditation surely also helped regulate a more even blood flow through my body.

I recommend beginning with as little as one minute of meditation. Simply focus your mind on the breath, releasing it of attachment to thoughts. You'll find that within seconds, the mind wants to wander away and take over the driver's seat. Notice this compulsion it has, and bring it back to your breath. Eventually, you will find you can quickly access states of calm and contentment because you're creating space from ruminating about things that bother or excite you. In addition, taking in fresh oxygen literally feeds your body with renewed vitality and calm; deep, slow, deliberate breaths activate the hypothalamus in the brain to release chemicals that inhibit stress-producing hormones and trigger a relaxation response in the body.[15]

Experiment with guided meditations. Sitting in silence for any duration of time and trying to focus the mind is a daunting task for beginners. Relying on yourself to remember to bring the mind back to the breath when it wanders is like reminding yourself to wake up from a dream while you're still in it. *Inception*-style, a trigger to bring you back to awareness is a very helpful tool. Guided meditations function nicely in this capacity. The instructor will periodically remind you to bring your awareness back to the breath if the mind has wandered away. They may also give you helpful analogies for the mind to concretize principles, like "observe your thoughts as clouds in the sky; acknowledge them, and watch them float on by without any need to fixate on them."

There is a wonderful video by Mingyur Rinpoche, a meditation teacher of the Tibetan Buddhist lineage who presents the oft esoteric concepts of mindfulness in very approachable, fun terms. He describes our tendency to get lost in our thoughts as the "monkey mind." Like the animal that jumps from branch to branch, excitable, restless, and hard to tame, so too our mind can behave the same way. Training the mind to be present and aware so it is your "employee" and not your "boss" is like training the monkey to be still and focused by giving it a "job." That job is the action of focusing on your breath, mindfully savoring your tea, or any one of a number of other actions to keep the mind anchored and focused on the present moment.

There are many resources out there to support you in your mindfulness efforts and help you establish a flow with your practice. Among them, apps that you can download and practice with anytime, anywhere. Given a variety of lengths and styles to choose from, you can select what speaks to you best in any given moment. Short mindfulness practice, longer mindfulness practice, visualization meditation, loving-kindness meditation, body scan, breath work, etc. By giving you freedom and choice, guided meditation apps are a lovely way to have your meditation practice work for you rather than the other way around. Many of them also offer a timer option so you can simply be in silence with your thoughts for whatever duration you choose. I have personally loved working with the Insight Timer app, though that has a slightly more advanced tonality. You might also like to explore Buddhify, Headspace, and Calm.

Enroll in a meditation course. I first learned to practice mindfulness during an eight-week "mindfulness-based stress reduction" training held through the University of Pennsylvania's School of Medicine. Led by Dr. Michael Baime, a preeminent scholar and teacher of mindfulness, the class was a comprehensive exploration, from the myriad benefits to the many challenges one experiences on the journey. Each week, our group of about twenty gathered for two-and-a-half hours on a Tuesday evening, to meditate, canvass, and walk away with homework to deepen our practice outside of the classroom.

I remember one of my classmate's experiences as being particularly striking; she suffered from Lupus, a disease where your body's immune system attacks its own tissues and organs, and the body ends up in a chronic state of inflammation. She found her way to the course in a desperate attempt to manage the persistent and often severe pain caused by her disease. At the beginning of the course, her discomfort was apparent on her generally unsmiling and withdrawn face. As we got farther into our journey, a marked change came over her. She seemed more relaxed, content, and at ease. By the time we wrapped up, she had shed layers of pain—or rather, learned an effective technique for alleviating her attachment to it—and her inner light emanated radiantly. She was more engaging in class, visibly buoyant, and interested in making conversation. Of the erstwhile most reticent member of the group, this transformation was impossible not to notice (taking that with a grain of salt, given the context of being in a room full of people learning precisely how to notice more). It was directly related to mindfulness, as she herself pointed out to the class. The practice had allowed her to free her mind from the pain signals her body was sending nonstop to her brain. By focusing on her breath and bringing her mind to a place of quiet suspension, she was able to notice her pain without attaching to it . . . without *becoming* it.

I highlight this story to underscore not only how effective a tool mindfulness can be in managing pain, but also the level of impact it can have across a variety of contexts and situations. In addition, working in a group has a funny way of making mindfulness more accessible. I chalk it up to energy—a group of folks practicing in tandem creates a force field of high vibrational frequency, that a mind, like a homing device, can find and hook into. This would explain why communities with concentrated groups of meditators are more peaceful, writ-large. In fact, studies done in crime-ridden communities where meditators were introduced saw violence decrease in direct proportion.[15a] Deepak Chopra showed a video of such a phenomenon during a course I attended at the Chopra Center, and it demonstrated powerfully the impact of collective energy in meditation.

On my last visit to India, I had an epiphany moment around this sort of phenomenon. Under the hazy, milky-sun sky characteristic of winter mornings in Delhi, I rolled out my mat on the third-floor terrace of my sister's house, and sat down to meditate. Despite the various distractions pervading my senses, including the chilly haze raising small bumps on my skin, my niece and nephew playing around me, and various animal noises oscillating in my ears, I hooked right into my meditation. The ease with which I was able to drop in was surprising and refreshing, noticeably different than when I try to practice in my home city of Philadelphia; my desultory monkey mind struggles to remain still amidst the frenetic pace of the East Coast.

Oprah Winfrey has observed that India is simply infused with baseline spirituality that is palpable—it's in the air and in the airs of its people. The

Beatles, Madonna, and Alanis Morissette would undoubtedly agree; they were "vocal" about this phenomenon through their music.

I'm not saying you have to get yourself to India to meditate, but do go and find a group where you can be among meditators regularly, and you will notice how much more easeful your own practice becomes.

Erin Easterly rounds out her list of "8 Steps to Establish a Daily Meditation Practice" with this suggestion: Create a space in one corner of your room exclusively for meditation. Easterly observes that over time, the space will absorb the vibrations of presence and clarity that you cultivate there, and begin to carry that energy within it. When you enter it, much like any spiritual vortex, you will immediately attune to the higher vibrational energy and hook into a state of calm and peace. I alluded to this in reference to groups of meditators, and India, and the same energetic logic applies here.

Resting stately in the right-side corner of my own bedroom is an altar, a tree trunk atop which sits a Buddha statue, a Tibetan singing bowl, a little green plant, and a candle. I must admit, I hadn't enjoyed a meditation at my altar in many months, choosing instead to sit on a couch or in an armchair to practice. And here's what's fascinating and heartbreaking: The plant withered and died. When I meditated there regularly, it flourished. Most of my meditations include a practice of gratitude or loving-kindness, both of which are replete with good feelings and positive affect. My plant would feel it and feed off of it. When the positive energy cloud I was generating was absent, it was deprived of the one nutrient it really needed: love.

Dr. Emoto is a Japanese research scientist made famous by the film *What the Bleep Do We Know*, which features his experiments with water to demonstrate the materiality of the energetic phenomenon I observed with my poor plant.[16] Emoto introduced different focused intentions through written and spoken words to molecularly identical water samples, and purported to show that the molecular structure of the water changed depending on the intention. Those water samples that were labeled "Hitler," or hurled insults or slurs at through thought or literal verbiage, ended up with misshapen and malformed structures. Those molecules that were thrown good vibes and kind thoughts, well, they were pretty and pristine. Though many have claimed Emoto's experiments didn't exactly "hold water," I think he's ultimately making the point that our energy is affected by everything else around us, and vice versa. And considering all we are is energy, that makes absolute sense. It also makes a solid case for living in accordance with the principle that energy is potent and malleable, and we have a duty to use it responsibly and with good intention.

I remember having my Uzbekistani neighbor over not too long ago. He was studying for his MBA at Wharton, the epitome of an analytical mind. When he noticed the altar in the corner of the living room, he moved closer to observe its contents. Just as he did, he swooned. He immediately sat down and commented, "That little guy is powerful," referencing the small wooden Buddha statue sitting cross-legged with a peaceful expression on his face, eyes dozing closed, fingers tented across his chest. I giggled, amused and charmed, and then grew solemn, deeply affected by the purity of the moment. Here was this man who grew up Muslim, studying at an institution predicated on the rational and objective, legitimately acknowledging not just the Buddha statue so endearingly, but also the energy that the space around it carried.

*****

This has nothing to do with religion; and if you are religious or affiliated with a particular style of prayer, you need not fear that you are somehow diminishing your faith by acknowledging the power of another. It just means you're an open, aware energy recognizing your molecular tag-team with the Universe. And this is exactly what the world needs more of: a decisive awareness of the oneness of all beings rather than the separateness of them. When we focus on differences, claiming the superiority of one being over another, like Hitler and other dictators who made that their primary agenda, we find racism, holocausts, and genocides. When we embrace unity, and a common agenda, we find balance, peace, and harmony. Seek out places with inherently high vibrational frequencies (or create one of your own), and then use that energy to hook quickly and fluidly into your bliss. Accessing that bliss point will in turn contribute to the entirety of bliss in the Universe. Everybody wins.

2
Positive Psychology

You can't stop the waves, but you can learn to surf.
—Jon Kabat-Zinn

Positive psychology will flip the script of your life. If you let it. You can shape your existence into something so much more purposeful, powerful, meaningful, and downright happy just by putting the interventions and exercises into practice. I hope you're thinking, "YES, sign me up!" because I'm about to give you a crash course in the essentials so you can literally be on your merry way.

Let's start at the very beginning (any *Sound of Music* fans out there?) with a definition: Positive psychology is the science of what enables individuals and communities to thrive. To thrive means you're growing more prosperous, and in the context of what *really* matters, this extends far beyond financial abundance. Yes, a certain level of income and wealth to meet basic needs like food, clothing, and shelter, is necessary. But there is a certain point at which the correlation between wealth and happiness plateaus, and those extra dollars don't actually equate to more flourishing.[17] Positive psychology is the science of what actually does influence prosperity.

It's helpful to think of mental health on a continuum, with a "minus" side, a "0" or "neutral" point, and a "plus" side.

It's helpful to think of mental health on a continuum, with a "minus" side, a "0" or "neutral" point, and a "plus" side. To be on the left side of "0" is to be in an acute state of deficit, wherein you require some remediation to get back to neutral.

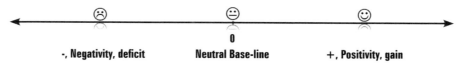

-, Negativity, deficit   **0**
Neutral Base-line   **+, Positivity, gain**

To be on the left side of "0" is to be in an acute state of deficit, wherein you require some remediation to get back to neutral (if that sounded overly technical, don't worry, plain English salvation lies ahead). Examples of such states of deficit include severe depression, chronic anxiety, and bipolar disorder. "Traditional" psychology, that is, the pathology or illness-focused approach we tend to associate with the field in general, plays an integral role in this remediation. When something is wrong, we try to make it right. If it ain't broke, don't fix it. This style of psychology, therefore, comes into play only when we feel that our mental health is suffering. It's an imperative part of the equation when it comes to flourishing; it is very hard to fill up a cup that's got a hole in it. We have to patch up the hole before we can think about a glass that's half-full, or better yet, full-full.

It's funny (though, of late it ceases to be in the "haha" way), when I tell people I am an expert in positive psychology, the inevitable quip is, "What, as opposed to negative psychology?" We share a giggle, mine usually more in the spirit of camaraderie than genuine amusement, the query by now prosaic. But I do appreciate the quick-witted nature of the distinction, and it underscores the fundamental difference I am trying to highlight: Psychology as we know it is not a "negative" science, but it is a science traditionally focused on negative states of being. Positive psychology, on the other hand (or rather, on the other side of the spectrum) is a science of what's going right so we may focus our efforts there, and capitalize on the findings. It "takes seriously as a subject matter those things that make life worth living."[18] It is the space to the right of zero, the "plus" side where there exists immense potential to make life better and better.

Positive psychology deals with how to enhance our states of mental health; we learn to cultivate more resilience and bounce back quickly when adversities occur, we extract more joy and happiness from each day, and we end up in a place where we're not just surviving but thriving.

Positive psychology is a science that acknowledges there is always work we can do, energy that we can expend, on living happier and more fulfilling lives. Always. Because every day that we are alive, we are changing, growing, and evolving. Whilst all of this growth and change is occurring, we can receive our lives in pure joy and gratitude, to the very last moment, or we can shrink and wither. Happiness is fundamentally a choice (with limited exceptions), and if we choose to do the work, we have access to the psychological "plus" side.

Not only that, a bevy of research shows that there are some very real physical benefits to being happy, too. One of my favorite studies showed that happy people get sick less often and when they do get sick, they exhibit less severe symptoms.[19] This was tested by shooting rhinovirus and influenza (common cold and flu, respectively) into the noses of two groups; one group had a PES, or "positive emotional style," meaning they were characterized by a happy, lively, and calm demeanor. The other group had an NES, or "negative emotional style," characterized by anxiety, hostility, and depression. So, what happened when both of these groups were exposed to the germs? The positive group had lower risk of developing any illness, and also reported fewer symptoms than their negative peers.

This edgy study showed what an important role emotional style seems to play in health, making a strong case for learning the science of happiness and putting it into practice. Essentially, choosing positive states of being over negative or toxic ones seems to make or break immunity.

Happy people are less stressed, and stress is responsible for a whole host— if not the majority—of illness and disease in humans, including the lowered immunity referenced above (we'll get into more of the toxic effects of stress in the next section). Happy people also enjoy better quality relationships, and you may remember that our connections are among the primary drivers of our well-being.

The A-List

In the Universe of mental health, positive psychology is a vast constellation with many bright stars. I've listed some of the most well known here, so you have a reference point for the major players in the field and the research they have done to contribute to it. As you dive into the world of positive psychology further, you'll get acquainted with many other brilliant stakeholders and their works. It's also an ever-expanding galaxy, with new stars born every day, so by the time this book goes to print, we might have a whole other galaxy. I hope so. My intention is to give you a working knowledge of the subject matter and enough exposure to the jargon that you are primed to expand your positive psychology lexicon further. I hope this will in turn open doors to continued exploration, instruction, and application. Thus, the list that follows is by no means comprehensive or exhaustive. Think of it as a highlight reel:

Martin Seligman is often called the "godfather of positive psychology" for the iconic role he plays in the field. Like Marlon Brando's character in the film *The Godfather*, he's truly the patriarch of a dynasty. Seligman coined the term "positive psychology" some two decades ago, when, after years of studying depression, he realized the need to change course. In 1998, as president of the American Psychological Association, he proposed the following call to action:

> We can articulate a vision of the good life that is empirically sound and, at the same time, understandable and attractive. We can show the world what actions lead to well-being, to positive individuals, to flourishing communities, and to a just society. Ideally, psychology should be able to help document what kind of families result in the healthiest children, what work environments support the greatest satisfaction among workers, and what policies result in the strongest civic commitment . . . . We have misplaced our original and greater mandate to make life better for all people not just the mentally ill. I, therefore, call on our profession and our science to take up this mandate once again as we enter the next millennium (APA President Address 1998, *American Psychologist*, 1999).

For the last two decades since his address, Seligman has been leading the charge toward a thriving new field. The research and interest in positive psychology is gaining exponential momentum, and if it continues on this path, Marty's goal of fifty-one percent of the world flourishing by 2051 can and will be achieved. Marty Seligman works tirelessly toward this humanitarian goal, and I am proud to be one of the "architects" of the movement (as he refers to us Masters of Applied Positive Psychology grads). I implore you to take a seat at the drafting table, too. Study the science, imbibe it, integrate it into your DNA, become the change we all wish to see, and carry the torch of it forward to others you encounter.

One of Seligman's more recent offerings to positive psychology is PERMA, an acronym for the five elements that together make up well-being. PERMA provides a theoretical framework for achieving holistic flourishing, and has already had significant impact on the field for its concise formula and uncomplicated approach. The five elements of PERMA are:

P: Positive Emotions . . . Feeling good.
E: Engagement . . . Finding flow.
R: Relationships . . . Authentic connections.
M: Meaning . . . Purpose in life.
A: Achievement . . . A sense of accomplishment.

P

The "P" in PERMA has to do with your ability to be optimistic, and view the past, present, and future from a positive perspective. Cultivating positive emotions is about more than just smiling. You've probably heard the word "hedonism," likely in association with some "wild on" reality show or spring break vacation spot. It's a word that means "pleasure-seeking," and equates happiness with enjoyment, and satisfying bodily needs like hunger, thirst, sleep, and sex. The "P" in PERMA doesn't stand for pleasure seeking—it's more *perma*nent than that. We want to think beyond this definition, and the simplicity of those smiley-face bumper stickers to a more substantial view of happiness called "eudaimonism." In contrast to hedonism, this philosophy equates happiness with the human ability to pursue complex goals and contribute meaningfully to society. Even when I have a full belly, a quenched thirst, and scratched the itch of my sex drive, I still feel a longing for more. That's my fulfillment bucket needing satiety. That's the deep drive for eudaimonia.

E

Are you getting enough "E" in your life? *Engagement*, that is? When we are engaged in a task or activity, we are fully absorbed in it. This complete immersion is where we find flow, the blissful present moment melding of skill and challenge where time seems to stop. Finding flow through engagement is vital for our intellectual, emotional, and spiritual growth. Think, "If I am flowing, then I am growing." When we use our brains in novel and exciting ways, as when we are in flow, we grow new connections between neurons and build more functional and adept brains. That's evolution in action, and to evolve is what we are fundamentally designed to do. Whether or not you believe in Darwin's theories, you can't deny that we human beings find it deeply satisfying and gratifying to use our creative gifts to reach higher heights. That's why we're so committed to growth. When we find flow, we are fulfilling our highest potential by harnessing each of our skills to maximize creative output. We generate absolute beauty and magic from that place, and man does it feel amazing.

R

Relationships and social connections rank among the most important aspects of human life. From an evolutionary perspective, isolation was one of the worst outcomes for a human being[20] because for thousands of years, our survival depended on our ability to stick together so that we could better defend ourselves against predators, forage for food, and, of course, procreate. Think about those nature shows where a herd of animals is being chased by a predator; as long as they stick together, they greatly increase their chances of survival. When one of the animals gets separated from the herd, which is usually the objective of the predator, well, they tend to meet a dismal end. That was also our reality not too long ago. Thus, when we are at risk of being isolated, pain centers in the brain light up. When we connect, we are rewarded in the form of a flood of feel-good chemicals. As such, we crave connection in the form of love, intimacy, and bonding experiences.

M

Does your life hold meaning? In other words, do you feel like you have a compelling reason for being on this Earth? The French call this *raison d'etre*, literally "the reason for being," and it gets at the essential reason a person exists. Fulfillment comes from feeling a clear sense of purpose and having a deep attachment to that purpose. Fulfillment is one of the cornerstones of a life of well-being. When I see the word, I am reminded that "fill" is contained within it; when you are fulfilled, the cup feels full. When you are not, there is a void.

I, for one, am constantly searching for the larger meaning in my experiences. When I can find significance that aligns with my higher sense of self and purpose, I feel content and at ease. This is especially true for adverse events. If I can see how they contribute to my growth, or that of the people and world around me, they are laden with meaning and therefore worthwhile.

A

"A" is for "apple." And "achievement." Just as an apple a day contributes to your health and vitality, so does a daily dose of achievement. Having goals and working towards them gives us something to aspire to, and when we actually accomplish what we set out to do, we feel gratified. Along the way, we won't necessarily feel positive emotions around our work, or even derive any meaning from it, but achievement still contributes to our well-being.

It is worth noting here that what I just articulated in that last sentence re: achievement also applies as a rule of thumb to the other elements of

PERMA; they are each pursued for their own sake, not necessarily to get any of the other elements. As an example, an investment of time in important connections may not lead directly to positive emotions, or even make you feel a sense of accomplishment, but it still enhances your life. For this reason, each of the elements is also measured independently of the others.

Working on cultivating more of each of the PERMA elements contributes to your overall sense of well-being and flourishing. If you're checking boxes in each of these areas, you're well on your way to a happy existence. Miss out on any one of them, and you'll feel the void. For example, imagine you are a ballet dancer and have worked tirelessly for many years perfecting your craft. Your blood (literally, as evidenced by the stains in your pointe shoes), sweat, tears, and countless hours at the bar are bringing you to the forefront of triumph, as you stand on the cusp of being named a principal in one of the world's preeminent ballet companies. Your efforts over many years are translating into this huge payoff, and you feel a robust sense of mastery. #achievement. Every time you perform onstage, the high degree of skill you've cultivated matches the dexterity required to nail the complex dance routines, and you find yourself in flow. #engagement. The audience's reaction and interaction with you is a greater rush than anything you can describe. It's pure joy. #positiveemotions. You know you were born to do this, and your life is replete with purpose. Your dancing engenders emotion and deep appreciation in those who watch you. #meaning. But you are lonely. You had to give every spare hour to your dancing, and you lost track of your close friendships along the way. Connections you once derived so much satisfaction from have withered and faded. You wish you had someone (indeed several someone's) to share your joy with. You have friends in the ballet company, but they're also your competitors, so you're not sure you can ever really share your vulnerabilities with them. As a result, you keep your distance. You're missing close connections. #relationships.

The point of this little anecdote is to illustrate in real life terms how each of the PERMA elements can show up in your life, and how each serve a very vital and important function. To be lacking in any one of them means you won't truly feel you are flourishing. In the example above, cultivating relationships may have come at the expense of cultivating skill. Authentic connections are an investment, an energy exchange requiring time and trust. For our ballerina, putting in the extra hours to build relationships may have meant the difference between becoming a principal and a member of the company. Would that have been a worthwhile sacrifice?

There's a good amount of material on the observations of those working in hospice or end-of-life care, and the regrets of the dying tend to follow the same patterns. One of my recent favorites comes from a blog in the *Huffington Post* by Bronnie Ware called "Top 5 Regrets of the Dying." Number 4 on the list is: "I wish I had stayed in touch with my friends." Number 2 is: "I wish I didn't work so hard." Ware writes, "It all comes down to love and relationships in the end. That is all that remains in the final weeks, love and relationships."[21] A compelling argument for reconsidering how much time you devote to work and career at the expense of your relationships.

Make time for the people that matter to you, even when you don't think you have enough or work seems prohibitive. Chances are if you don't, you'll be sitting under a mountain of regret as you look back on your life. Devote energy to each avenue of PERMA to find flourishing, but none at the expense of another. Find balance among them, and be willing to sacrifice some of one bucket to enjoy the fruits of another.

Along with Martin Seligman, Mihaly Csikszentmihalyi (pronounced *Cheeks-sent-me-high*) is one of the founding fathers of positive psychology. Dr. Csikszentmihalyi and Dr. Seligman officially announced the birth of positive psychology in the primary issue of the *American Psychologist* at the turn of the new millennium. Talk about symbolic. Since then, Csikszentmihalyi has become most well-known for his pioneering research on *flow*, a term you may remember from the "E" in PERMA. "Flow" is a term he coined for the optimal experience one can attain when mastery of skill meets challenge of situation in the perfect congruence. The language and theory of flow find application in nearly every sector of society, from gaming (flow is cited as the main reason people play video games) to athletics (being "in the zone") to religion and spirituality (being "at one with things").

The late Dr. Christopher Peterson is another of the founding fathers of positive psychology. His work with Dr. Seligman in crafting a tome called *Character Strengths and Virtues* (a positive counterpart to the *Diagnostic and Statistical Manual of Mental Disorders,* or *DSM)*, has been a formative contribution to the field. While the DSM focuses on what is going wrong, *Character Strengths and Virtues* places emphasis on what can go right. Seligman and Peterson's in-depth research spanned cultures and millennia to cull together a list of six core virtues, made up of twenty-four measurable character strengths that, when practiced, lead to increased happiness. They are:

 Courage—Bravery, Honesty, Perseverance, Zest

 Humanity—Kindness, Love, Social Intelligence

 Justice—Fairness, Leadership, Teamwork

 Temperance—Forgiveness, Humility, Prudence, Self-Regulation

 Transcendence—Appreciation of Beauty and Excellence, Gratitude, Hope, Humor, Spirituality

 Wisdom/Knowledge—Creativity, Curiosity, Judgment, Love of Learning, Perspective

Character strengths are different from other strengths, like talents, skills, resources, and interests, because they represent the "real you." That is, who you are at your *core*. Character strengths influence how you think, behave, and act at a fundamental level, and, therefore, feed directly into who you are at your best. When you apply them skillfully, they can have a significant positive impact on your life. There are several online resources that you can use to take a free test to assess what your top strengths are, in ranked order. Simply Google "character strengths" to find them. From there, you can begin tweaking your use of various strengths to work to your highest benefit, and that of others around you.

 Social psychologist Barbara Fredrickson is among those at the forefront of positive psychology research. Perhaps her most salient contribution to the field is the "broaden-and-build" theory, which suggests that positive emotions broaden one's awareness and encourage novel, varied, and exploratory thoughts and actions. In other words, positive emotions breed creativity and innovation. In contrast, negative emotions engender narrow, immediate, survival-oriented behaviors. Not only is the broaden-and-build theory an exploration of the evolved function of positive emotions, it helps us understand the importance of cultivating more of them in our lives; when we are in a positive frame of mind, our ability to see new possibilities and find creative solutions is greatly enhanced. This leads to more flourishing and satisfaction in life. In the workplace, for example, if you can come up with innovative ideas and solutions, you're winning. You enhance the productivity of the company, you are quicker to get promoted, and you feel a deep sense of satisfaction over your contributions. In general, growing and expanding your life instead of simply reacting and surviving are signs of a flourishing existence. Don't just survive, *thrive*.

Angela Duckworth's research on *grit* has made her something of a rock star in a variety of sectors and contexts. A recipient of the MacArthur "Genius" Prize (label kind of says it all) and *New York Times* bestselling author, she has revolutionized the way we think about success. "Grit" is the combined passion for a goal with a powerful motivation to achieve it. What Duckworth has found is that grit, that special blend of passion and perseverance, is a higher predictor of success than talent or I.Q.

Alain Passard, one of the finest chefs on the planet and the recipient of multiple Michelin stars, says his success boils down to one simple thing: He decided to be a chef at age fourteen, and he never wavered in his resolve. He had *grit*. Staying the course from that young an age and never deviating, no matter what challenges or distractions he encountered (and on the way to Michelin stars, you can bet there were plenty), led him to the pinnacle of achievement. Think about that next time you feel "stupid" or unmotivated; are you putting in the effort? Are you passionate about what you're doing? The answers to these questions are likely the key to what's holding you back from success. Check out Angela's grit scale online to see how you measure up, and then get about the business of becoming more "gritty" if you fall short.

Grit can be learned and cultivated in a process involving roughly four steps:

1. Discover a burning interest.
2. Immerse yourself in it (practice it a lot).
3. Identify a sense of higher purpose around it. (How will this passion make the world better?)

4. Cultivate a growth-mindset (the belief that your intelligence is not fixed, but can be developed).

Stephen Post is best known for his research on the power of helping others en route success to more happiness, better health, more resilience, more creativity, more hope, and more success, all hallmarks of a flourishing existence.[22] That's a lot of "more's," and a lot of solid reasons to give and help wherever you can. Post encourages us to follow the "Golden Rule of Flourishing": When the happiness and security of others is as meaningful to you as your own, you are a person of love, and you will flourish.

This research had a profound impact on me in graduate school, and is foundational in my lectures, workshops, and client sessions around why service is "thy medicine."

You've probably heard of post-traumatic stress disorder (commonly referred to as "PTSD"). It is characterized by a decreased ability to function after a traumatic event, and is often accompanied by debilitating symptoms like flashbacks, insomnia, and panic disorder. Researchers Richard Tedeschi and Lawrence Calhoun coined the term "post-traumatic growth" (PTG) to signify the opposite; positive psychological change occurs following an adversity or challenge, and one rises to a higher level of functioning than before.

Individuals with PTG come out of a trauma resilient, stronger and more capable than before. This is generally the exception and not the rule, likely a result of how able we are to effectively process the trauma (often based on access to mental health professionals), and the amount of resources we have to channel our trauma productively. The bottom line is that we *can* leverage our biggest challenges toward positive change; adversities can be our allies. The underlying difference in people with PTG is that they are able to extract meaning and purpose from their traumatic event. This leads to flourishing in the aftermath.

Now that you have an understanding of what positive psychology is, and of how it can change life for the better, how can you put it to work for you? The answer is by practicing what it preaches. Luckily, the human brain is plastic, meaning it is consistently able to take in new information, process it, and formulate novel connections accordingly. Learning never stops, nor do we ever have to be stuck in any pattern of thought or behavior. Our adaptable brains give us a choice: We can re-route the directions of our lives and take a new path, or we can stay where we are. Sometimes we engage in unhealthy patterns of thought and behavior, like seeing the world through a cynical lens, and assuming everyone has a negative or selfish intention. Or choosing to focus on what we don't have, rather than being grateful for all the things that we do have. Or harping on the bleak and dismal outcomes of every scenario instead of recognizing the positive potential ("glass half-empty" vs. "glass half-full" sort of metaphor). In the "glass half-full" scenario, we are cognizant of abundance, in the "glass half-empty," of lack. Another unhealthy route may be to numb out with drugs and other addictions when the emotions we encounter feel too painful or difficult to confront; we engage in avoidance instead of embracing the pain and learning from it. The point is, we can choose. There are practices that lead to withering and suffering, others that lead to joy and flourishing. If you decide to infuse your life with the best practices of a flourishing existence, that is exactly the sort of life you will have.

The Interventions

There are several exercises that represent gold as far as best practices in "flourishing hygiene" (my phrase for behaviors that promote health and vitality). These best practices are called "interventions" in positive psychology. People tend to have pretty specific associations with the word "intervention," helped along by the eponymously titled reality TV show of the 2000s. It conjures up images of a friend or loved one drugged-out or teetering on the edge of sanity, and a huddle of family members stepping in to halt the downward spiral. This is a bit more extreme than the context in which we positive psych people use it, but I like the nature of the word *intervention* because it underscores the level of seriousness with which we take these flourishing hygiene best practices. Why should interventions be reserved for acute issues like drug addiction or eating disorders? The very premise of positive psychology is that we must attend to our mental health not just when there is a problem, but throughout the lifetime. This keeps our happiness levels on an upward trajectory, and helps stave off problems *before* they occur. Enter the old adage "an ounce of prevention is worth a pound of cure." Dealing with issues once they have taken hold is far more challenging than preventing them from happening in the first place. Would you rather put healthy measures in place now, or risk your life and well-being later? I know that immediate gratification usually trumps delayed rewards, but take cues from Angela's grit research: Patience and perseverance feed more significantly into success than standard measures of intelligence like I.Q. We can't always predict the long-term consequences of our current behaviors, but if we have some self-regulation, we greatly increase the probability of living long, healthy, successful lives.

Contemplate this: You have a heart attack, and the lack of oxygen to your brain causes you to lapse into a coma. The prognosis is that the damage done to your heart muscles is severe, your brain was deprived of oxygen too long . . . you won't wake up. The doctors run some tests and discover your arteries are completely blocked with plaque from years of unhealthy eating. You could have prevented this had you just cut out saturated fat from your diet; years of that daily burger and fries are now cutting your life short by as many years. And that's just *your* life. What about those you are leaving behind? Your family and friends are bereft and in a great deal of pain from the shock of your sudden demise. If you could go back and do it over, knowing you could save your own life and have years more left with your friends and family, wouldn't you?

Think back to a time when you've been really sick or in pain, like with a searing headache, a bad case of the flu, or severe nausea. The one thing you probably wished for more than anything was to feel well again, yes? If you could go back and nip the source of your agony in the bud, wouldn't you? Be honest—even if it meant some sacrifices like skipping the tequila shots to wake up headache-free, cutting out of the party early in favor of more sleep (more on the importance of sleep in Section II), or choosing home cooking over the fast food that gave you food poisoning? Self-regulation around maintaining best practices of flourishing hygiene is like that. It requires that you expend more energy prioritizing your health than indulging in your temptations. Inevitably, it's worth it.

Granted, sometimes life hands us challenges over which we don't have much control despite our best intentions and preventive efforts. The teachings of this book are meant to help you deal with those effectively, too. Should they find their way to you, you'll know how to recognize them as your greatest teachers, embrace them as your forces for change, and have the resilience to come back fighting for your growth, stronger than ever.

Mindfulness

Though not traditionally cited as an intervention, I place mindfulness here, at the top of the list, to underscore its importance as a "best practice." Bringing the mind into a state of steadiness, control, and focus has the myriad positive benefits we've already covered. It's also a skill that is foundational to your ability to adopt other good practices and habits; an unfocused mind is not capable of taking in large amounts of new information with any real success. Imagine trying to wipe up a spilled glass of water from the counter with a full sponge. How much will it absorb? Now, wring out the sponge and try again. Bingo. The mind is like the sponge: It runs and it gets full. We need a regular practice to empty it of thoughts and allow it to recalibrate to a place where it can do its best work again. Mindfulness is the wring-out.

Researcher and Harvard professor Moshe Bar characterizes a full mind as one that is in "exploitatory mode," that is, a less creative space where we rely on existing knowledge and predictable situations.[23] His research shows that a cluttered brain gets in the way of deep and agile thinking. When we clear our mind of its mental load, we can enter "exploratory mode," a zone where we're open to new experiences and have a desire to learn. Conclusion: In order to prime the mind for successful adoption of the best practices, a regular mindfulness practice must be a foundational part of the routine.

I introduced you to Mindful Breathing in Chapter 1, and we got our feet wet (rather, grounded) with the practice. Let's try it again now.

Begin by sitting in an upright position and planting your feet firmly on the ground. Straighten your spine and feel it grow longer and stronger, even as you relax your shoulders back and down. Allow a slight downturn of your head as you take tension out of the back of the neck. Let your eyes close, or, if you prefer to keep them open, gently focus your gaze on an unmoving spot in front of you.

This is called a "mindful body posture," and you can adopt this position whenever you are in a seated chair meditation.

Inhale for 6.
Exhale for 6.

Inhale for a count of six—hold—and exhale for a count of six. If six counts feels forced or difficult on the inhale, you may have to work up to this, and that is fine. Begin with three or four counts, as we practiced before. Repeat this cycle several times. Practicing controlled breathing like this for ten to twenty minutes a day will give you familiarity and comfort with the technique so that in moments of stress, you can hook in without too much thought. You'll naturally just "go there" to calm yourself down and bring the body quickly and fluidly back to equanimity (the "relaxation response" from Chapter 1, cultivating a relaxed state that encourages the body to release chemicals that make the muscles and organs slow down and increase blood flow to the brain).

This practice has worked wonders in my own life. Among my avatars are that of public speaker, improvisational comedian, singer-songwriter, and storyteller. I used to get very nervous being onstage and baring my soul in these contexts. My heart would start to pound, my fingers turned clammy, and my palms and armpits would go slick. This translated as a dry mouth, a frozen brain, a shaky voice or slippery fingers on guitar strings. Such symptoms of nervousness were *no bueno* with respect to performance.

It took dedicated effort and practice to train my mind to invoke the relaxation response in performance contexts, but it revolutionized my experiences. Beyond the technical benefits, I learned to receive these incredible gifts of public presence not as threats (which trigger a stress response) but rather opportunities to share my voice with people who might benefit from hearing it. Part of the training meant making the focus of my singing the work and the service, not any judgments that might ensue, or other ego-based concerns.

Gratitude

 Also called "Three Good Things," the gratitude practice is perhaps the single most popular intervention in positive psychology. This is because it is incredibly effective in changing our perspective from what's going wrong, or what we don't have, to becoming mindful of the myriad other things going right, and all that we do have. Life is full of blessings, including the very fact that we are alive. There are more than thirty-seven trillion cells in the human body all working together to create the beautiful you that you are. That's thirty-seven trillion reasons to be grateful, and indeed trillions more things going right than going wrong. *This* is where we want to place our focus, rather than the relatively infinitesimal number of things not going our way or bringing us pain. Of course, any and all of these obstacles and pain-points can become our greatest allies, but it takes work to change our perspective in this way. Until we do the work, we are hardwired to spot the negatives. This "negativity bias" fills us with emotions like hopelessness, anxiety, and depression. The practice of gratitude is simply a matter of refocusing our attention and awareness on the blessings inherent in our lives to cultivate more positive emotions and ramp up our well-being. Singer/songwriter and all-around spiritual goddess Jewel says that when you are grateful, you can't be angry or resentful because you are already full. The word itself implies being full— *grateful*—leaving no room for other, less productive, emotions. Because this intervention may be practiced many ways, I encourage you to explore different versions and styles. Tweak them and make up your own! Here are a few to get you started:

Night Write

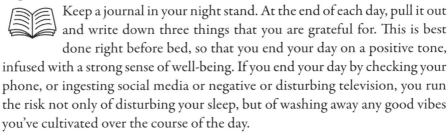 Keep a journal in your night stand. At the end of each day, pull it out and write down three things that you are grateful for. This is best done right before bed, so that you end your day on a positive tone, infused with a strong sense of well-being. If you end your day by checking your phone, or ingesting social media or negative or disturbing television, you run the risk not only of disturbing your sleep, but of washing away any good vibes you've cultivated over the course of the day.

When reflecting on my own blessings, I like to cite one from that particular day, one from life in general, and one from relationships/connections. You may recall that investing in your relationships is one of the most important facets of a happy human life. It is also one we tend to take largely for granted. Try getting specific about which connections and forces support you and how/why they add value to your life.

Here's an entry from my own gratitude journal:

1. *I am grateful for the exchange of pleasantries I shared with an elderly man in my neighborhood this morning. It made me feel wonderful to smile at him, and say hello, and then hear him wish me a good day ahead. Blessings from strangers are divine.*

2. *I am grateful for my home; it is cozy, beautiful, and quiet like a cocoon. It is my haven, and I have heat, light, and comfort. Thank you Universe for a roof over my head and walls around me to keep me safe and sheltered.*

3. *I am grateful for my mother; through her struggles, she teaches me how to be a more patient coach, and a more loving daughter. She challenges and inspires me to infuse all of my work with love.*

Gratitude Grace

Make a habit of expressing gratitude at the beginning of every meal, including when you are dining alone. If you are alone, you can speak your prayer aloud or to yourself. If you are among company, ask that each person around the table take a turn sharing one thing they are grateful for. Or, one person can take the lead at each meal, as "table representative," to vocalize gratitude. Gratitude grace is a regular event around my family table, no matter who is present. When I vocalize the blessings, it usually takes the form of appreciation for every being that contributed their energy to bringing fuel to the table, with a special shout-out to whomever actually prepared the meal on that day. It sounds something like this:

Let us be grateful to every being that played a role in bringing this bounty to our table (list all of the players for added potency; the farmers who grew or raised the food, the bacteria in the ground who nourished it, the oxygen in the air that gave it life, the transporters that ferried it from farm to table, whoever bought the groceries, whoever cooked the meal, and so on), so that we may feed our bodies and nourish our minds with the healthiest fuel, and that this fuel may in turn help us to do better work in the world, and serve our fellow beings and planet in the highest.

Phone a Friend

Designate a friend to text or call, at any time of the day you both choose, and express gratitude to each other. Making this a regular practice with a friend holds you both accountable, so it's harder to forget or blow off. You also get some bonus gratitude, because you're vocalizing not just yours, but hearing someone else's.

To the Letter "T"

It is so important to express appreciation to the people who contribute to your life in meaningful ways. Were it not for these key players, the game of your life could not be played. Writing a letter of thanks is a powerful and beautiful way to convey your gratitude to them. Even more stirring is when the object of your appreciation has perhaps no notion of the impact they've had on you—at least not from your perspective and through the lenses of your eyes. The "Thank You" letter extends the practice of giving thanks from something originating and emanating from the self, to something very inclusive and expansive. It's not just about "me" and what "I'm grateful for," but about "you," and how "you've changed my life for the better."

Begin by identifying someone who you feel has had a profound impact on your life. Write your expression of gratitude in the form of a letter, addressed directly to the recipient. Take your time with it and be comprehensive, pouring all of this person's various good-doings into your words. Perhaps even revisit it a few times to be as thorough and detailed as you can be, as you would any significant piece of writing. Really let this letter speak through your heart. Your objective should be to make them cry. Not because you are sadistic, but because things that evoke the level of emotion that bring you to tears really touch your heart, and that's what you want your gratitude letter to accomplish. If Hallmark commercials can do it, so can you. Remember, this is not just a laundry list of someone's niceties, nor a rambling enumeration of their good qualities. It is an earnest attempt to verbalize in pure, authentic prose a view only you could have about another being's efforts to give love. Deliver the letter in person, as a soliloquy (read aloud), to the recipient.

"Thank You" letters represent a highly undervalued currency that we need to begin exchanging with more frequency. Believe it or not, writing this book was the impetus for me to pen my own first ever "Thank You" letter. Now before you go thinking me an ingrate, let me qualify by saying I express gratitude often in my daily life, using all of the suggested avenues above, and others, like short form text messages, quick manifestos to my best friend, spoken words to my loved ones, audio files to my sister, and spontaneous Facebook messages. Crafting the gratitude missive as a letter, with the intention of then delivering it to a recipient in person—*that* I had never done.

As I pondered my letter, it occurred to me that I had already crafted several drafts in my mind, in the form of a eulogy for my dad. I know that sounds morbid, but my father recently turned eighty-four. I see my parents on a regular basis and am deeply attached to them. I understand and appreciate my father in a way no one else can, and our genetic thread means I share much of his humanitarian philosophy and deep reverence for life. When I force myself to acknowledge the ephemeral nature of our time here on Earth, I have to confront that I will lose him one day. It brings me to tears when I think about it, not just because of how dear he is to me, but because the world is a far better place with him in it. He is the most honest, thoughtful, jovial, and intelligent person I know.

And so I've imagined the words I'd say when friends and family gather to celebrate his life and memory, the absolute gratitude I'll feel for the fact that his is the voice in my head when I ponder what a truly *maha* (Sanskrit word for *great*) human being would do. And how that always makes me take the path of more generosity, more compassion, more mindfulness, and more laughter. How ironic that in my mind, I've spoken my gratitude letter to my father many times, but only in the context of his passing. Why *then*? Why not *now*?

Below is my "Thank You" letter to my father. I'm hoping that sharing it with you may just inspire you to write your own.

Dear Dad,

Even though I know your style, which is rather too humble to accept a "thank you" before pre-empting with something like "It's not my life I'm carrying, it's your mother's, and grandmother's, all the way back to grandmother amoeba who deserve the credit . . . ." Thank You.

Thank you for being brave enough to come all the way to America as a young man, alone, with only $5 in your pocket (I know the story well; it's what was left of the $10 you started with after buying your first beer ever on the boat. You had to chuck it, because you found it bitter and awful. I know that still really bothers you).

Thank you for not faltering when your first wife left you, but instead fighting hard against your depression to find a spiritual path, and on your way to that, for finding Mom. And then making me.

Thank you for keeping yourself alive and out of harm's way even when it tried so hard to find you. I remember every time your life was spared by a hair and hold each close to my heart as a reminder of how grateful I am that you are alive. The time you almost died in a toxic spill while working as a chemical operator that made you realize that life—and the preservation of it—is the only thing that really matters. Or the time you were held at gunpoint in our rough-and-tumble West Philadelphia neighborhood, which was the only real estate you could afford on the come-up. Or even the time you were driving on the highway and the tire of the truck in front of you blew out and smashed through the windshield, totaling the car. All of those narrow escapes meant I have had a father in my life, to teach, guide, and care for me. To tell me "I love you," which you do so often. Thank you.

Thank you for abiding by the credo "simple living, high thinking" and investing in our education. Even though we had very little money to spare, and it could've gone to so many other sources, like paying down debt on the rental properties, or buying a bigger house, or a better car, you chose to prioritize our minds. I was able to build a brain I am so proud to call my own. I am proud to espouse good values and I work on my character every day. I have also forged some of the most meaningful connections in my life, all such honest, hard-working, kind, and supportive people, through the schools you sent to me to.

Thank you for ensuring that we traveled in our youth. This was an essential part of my education and the reason I respect and appreciate other cultures and customs. You planned detailed itineraries so we could hit as many places as possible on our limited budget, making carbon copies for the family so we'd all have the schedule in our pockets. Some of my fondest and most salient memories are from these trips, like visiting remote pockets of India and standing upon the ground of our ancestors. We were imbued with India's sounds, smells, and colors, reconnected to our roots. There were the backyard trips to Europe; you were intrepid as you led us on a trek to see the Berlin wall come down. We still have pieces of it, symbols of unity unfolding. Or the time we found our way to a Philadelphia friend's relative's wedding in a remote village in Poland. She says even now that she never expected us to actually show up and was floored that we made the effort. Our three brown faces were certainly an uncommon contrast in this all-white town. Everyone there fell under the spell of your commitment to fostering communion and connection, with all of our "distant cousins," because you believe in One Family of Humanity.

And most of all, thank you for being the reason I have so much good inside of me. When it comes to honesty, integrity, and the righteous path, yours is the voice guiding me to the higher road. You are the reason I live so much of my life in service, seeking a better way for all of humanity's constituents, instead of myopically focusing on my own or that of my kin. You are the reason I never lie (with rare exceptions for the white kind), cheat (with rare exceptions for card and board games) or steal (no exceptions. Well, except for pranks).

Everybody loves you Dad, even when they think they don't. Thank you for being you.

Learn Your ABCs

The "ABC" model is a powerful intervention for how it can be used to unpack and understand behavior, so that we can change our actions. It is commonly employed in cognitive behavioral therapy (CBT), a popular therapeutic technique for analyzing thoughts, behaviors, and emotions. CBT works on the assumption that beliefs influence behavior and emotions, and that by identifying and addressing problematic thoughts or cognitions, you can change your behavior and experience of life for the better. CBT has gained in popularity since its introduction to the world of psychology, largely because it is so effective in behavior modification. In the ABC model, you take a deeper look into how your thoughts affect your actions by becoming aware of a triggering or "activating" event, analyzing your beliefs around it, and understanding how those beliefs, in turn, motivate you to behave:

A: The Activating event. Also sometimes called the "trigger" for how it sparks the other pieces into motion.
B: Beliefs. What thoughts, cognitions, or ideas are engendered within you when the activating event occurs?
C: Consequences. How do you feel and consequently behave based on your beliefs following the trigger?

The ABC model is often depicted in table format to make it easier to work with. Here is how it would be laid out:

A: Activating Event	B: Beliefs	C: Consequences

In column A, you would write down the event or situation that triggered you. In column B, you would record what you were thinking/feeling when the activating event occurred. In column C, you would record the consequences of the beliefs you wrote down in column B.

Let's look at a hypothetical example (I used Dr. David Bonham-Carter's tables[24] for inspiration), written in the personal passive voice to emphasize the relevance of thought patterns in this process:

It is nearing the end of the workday when my boss rushes into my office and asks if I have completed the new client proposal she had requested. *She literally just asked for it this morning! I've got tons on my plate and am doing the best I can! Here she is, trying to call me out. She thinks I'm not working hard enough.* Defensively, I tell her that I am almost finished, but it was a big task and I wasn't given that much time. I feel resentful, annoyed, and angry. I go home and lash out at my partner.

A: Activating Event	B: Beliefs	C: Consequences
My boss asked if I had completed the work.	She was diminishing me and assuming I haven't been working hard.	I was defensive and resentful and took out my anger on my partner when I got home.

Can you see how quick the mind can be to catastrophize? We jump to conclusions, even if there is no real evidence to support them. Worse still, we take on undue stress as a result, flooding our bodies with hormones and chemicals that put our health at risk, only to then realize the negative feelings were unjustified and unnecessary.

The example above is such a salient one because most of us can relate to feelings of anxiety or fear when it comes to our jobs and professional security. Our work is our livelihood, and to have that jeopardized equates to our very survival being threatened (in our minds anyway). That's why we tend to make panicked leaps toward a horrifying outcome—like being out on the street, penniless, and destitute, all because our boss asked, "Have you finished the presentation for the new client?"

How many times has your mind run away with you based on an activating event, perhaps leaving you with sweaty palms or a churning stomach? Or worse, a complete shutdown of the nervous system culminating in a panic attack? The ABC model is a fantastic way to become mindful of the places your thoughts can lead you; by choosing a different perspective, you can begin to stave off negative emotions and unproductive behaviors before they occur, and instead stay present and calm. Isn't that a better way to live?

Use the table below to practice using the ABC model to unpack triggering events and your beliefs around them. Think back to a recent event in your life that triggered you. Briefly describe the event in column A. In column B, jot down your beliefs at the time of the trigger. What were the consequences of these thoughts?

A: Activating Event	B: Beliefs	C: Consequences

Journal about your experience with the ABC model. How did it feel to deconstruct your thoughts in this way? Did you learn anything new or surprising? How might this exercise help you change your life for the better?

_____

_____

_____

_____

_____

_____

_____

_____

_____

_____

_____

ACR

Use It or Lose It ("It" being your closest relationships)

When it comes to communication, specifically, receiving good news, it turns out there's an optimal way to respond that leads to healthy, flourishing relationships. It's called Active-Constructive Responding (ACR). A theoretical framework first proposed by psychologist Shelly Gable, ACR exists in a matrix of four possible response styles. When you respond "actively and constructively," you are giving authentic and enthusiastic support. When you employ one of the other three—"passive-constructive," "active-destructive," and "passive-destructive" (*dunh-dunh dunhhhh*, cue ominous tones for the worst of them all)—you are headed down a dead end in the maze leading to the "optimal relationship" cheese.

I remember when I first learned ACR. I didn't take it too seriously, and thought it sounded obvious, even a little hokey. And then I began to notice communication breakdowns everywhere: avoidance based on social media and cell phones, distractions, multitasking, less-than-graceful interactions. These are all realities of our world, and here to stay at least until we become mindfulness mavens. In the interim, given all of these potential relationship-wreckers, we must learn to communicate better, or we'll erode the one thing that matters most in a flourishing life: our connections.

Married psychologist-and-relationship experts Drs. John Gottman and Julie Schwartz Gottman have been researching couples for the last several decades, and can predict with a high degree of accuracy which marriages will last, and which will end in divorce. The marriages that last share some common characteristics, which the Gottmans have distilled down into: 1) Express interest, 2) Be gentle in conflict, and 3) Repair negative interactions.[25] ACR feeds right into that first one, because it gets at how to respond optimally when receiving good news, the key of which is to be engaged and interested. As the Gottmans discovered, when we express genuine interest in our partner's day-to-day life, taking the time to check in and connect, we're nourishing the vitality of the relationship. The couple that praise together, stays together!

When we respond actively and constructively, relationships flourish. In contrast, we can deeply wound those we interact with just by following one of the other communication styles in the matrix. An active constructive response gives both the deliverer and the receiver of good news a positive outcome.

I take every opportunity to teach ACR, not least because it's so much fun when I do. I usually set it up as a role-play, where I get a volunteer to be the deliverer of good news, and I play responder. I have them share the news with me four times, and I respond using each of the styles. ACR is one of my favorite interventions for the "aha" moments it conjures up, the giggles and smiles elicited when we role play examples of the suboptimal styles, and the emails I get afterward telling me how much the learning of ACR has revolutionized lives.

Use It

Let's say your partner comes home from work and shares with you that they got a promotion. An ACR responder might say something like, "Congratulations baby! It's amazing that your hard work is being recognized in this way! Go get ready, I'm taking us out to dinner to celebrate." When people share their good news, they want you to revel in their joy with them. Conveying genuine interest, curiosity, and pride are all hallmarks of the ACR style.

This goes far beyond a lukewarm fist-bump or a distracted high-five, which would fall more in the category of a passive-constructive response. An example of a passive-constructive response might be a one-word answer like, "Awesome," while simultaneously checking social media. In a passive-constructive response, you're giving positive feedback, but you're missing the engagement piece. There's no active, elaborative component.

An active-destructive response might look something like this: "Oooooh wow. That's going to be a lot of extra work, and in an area you're not really familiar with. You were already stressed in your current role . . . are you sure you can handle it?" Eek. We have engagement here, you're listening and responding accordingly, but the response is destructive. Total storm cloud eclipsing the just-unleashed sunshine.

Now enter the worst of the lot, the passive-destructive response, which might look something like, "Huh, so what should we eat for dinner?" You're not actively engaged in the topic at hand, rather you've completely ignored it and instead decided to focus on mealtime.

Here are the responses in table format to help you see them more clearly:

Scenario:
Your Partner received a promotion at work.

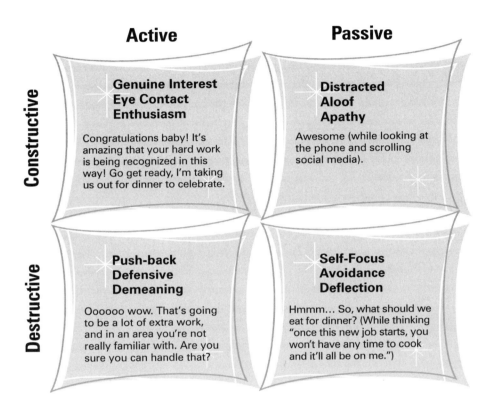

	Active	Passive
Constructive	**Genuine Interest** **Eye Contact** **Enthusiasm** Congratulations baby! It's amazing that your hard work is being recognized in this way! Go get ready, I'm taking us out for dinner to celebrate.	**Distracted** **Aloof** **Apathy** Awesome (while looking at the phone and scrolling social media).
Destructive	**Push-back** **Defensive** **Demeaning** Oooooo wow. That's going to be a lot of extra work, and in an area you're not really familiar with. Are you sure you can handle that?	**Self-Focus** **Avoidance** **Deflection** Hmmm… So, what should we eat for dinner? (While thinking "once this new job starts, you won't have any time to cook and it'll all be on me.")

Come up with a hypothetical "good news" scenario of your own (draw from real life or make it up!), and then fill in the matrix that follows with each of the response styles we've covered: active-constructive, passive-constructive, active-destructive, and passive-destructive.

Have fun with this—role-play with a partner or a friend. Focus on the "active-constructive" style, and make sure you really understand what characteristics distinguish that style of communication from the other less optimal ones.

Scenario:

_____

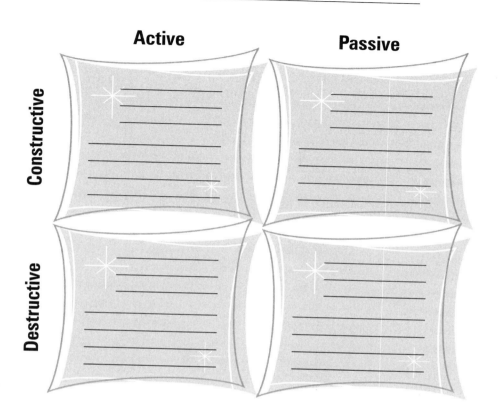

	Active	**Passive**
Constructive		
Destructive		

Now, you might be asking yourself, "What if I'm upset, or preoccupied, or really don't think I'm in a space to share authentically in the other person's joy?" Like if one of your work colleagues gets a big promotion and you are passed over. Or if you and your spouse are fighting, and you want to support them in their joyful news, but you're still livid that they forgot to buy tickets to the Adele concert and now they're sold out. Try to think of your partner's good news and your own feelings as separate issues. (This requires real maturity, but I have faith in you to bring it!) In their moment of exaltation, put your own pride or negative emotions aside. This isn't about squashing or ignoring your own feelings—there will be a more appropriate time to deconstruct any doubts, concerns, or jealousies.

Get over yourself and remember that their initial exuberance and your reaction to it is a one-shot deal, you won't get a do-over. So channel Obama and Stephen Post, put yourself in their shoes, and make their happiness as meaningful to you as your own.

Here, incidentally, is where all of your mindfulness practice—and the concurrent empathy cultivation—can really serve you. Taking some space simply to be mindful and to observe your negative states or feelings objectively will help you clarify and label them, without attaching to them or having an angry or emotional response you'll come to regret. Furthermore, once you *are* ready to communicate them, you can do so from a place of humility and honesty. Honesty doesn't have to diminish someone else's accomplishment to hold merit or be recognized, it just needs to be expressed with grace, at the right time and place.

Random Acts of Kindness

A random act of kindness is a spontaneous or unexpected gesture of good will. Á la Stephen Post's research, such gestures are intensely gratifying, and one of the surest ways to more happiness. There are many reasons why, but among the most compelling are the physiological changes that are triggered. Acts of kindness: increase levels of oxytocin (a hormone that lowers blood pressure, improves heart health, increases self-esteem and optimism), stimulate the production of serotonin (the "happy" hormone), light up pleasure centers in the brain (a phenomenon known as "helper's high"), and produce endorphins (the brain's natural painkiller).[26]

I like the "random" aspect of this intervention because it's so pure, an act of generosity without the expectation of something in return. One of my favorites is to drop a quarter into a meter that is about to expire. I feel bad for the parking authority officers; they have quotas to fill, too. But I feel worse for the vehicle owner. I empathize deeply with that sinking feeling that takes hold as you approach your car and spot it, tucked ominously under the windshield, "Violation!", an "F-U" with a fine attached. Spare someone the agony of that feeling by plunking a quarter into their meter, or any other surprise turn that will make their day just a bit brighter.

The idea is to endeavor to live in a space where you are constantly on the lookout for ways you can get someone's back. Not only will you feel *koselig* (a delightful Norwegian word for "warm and cozy"), you add large doses of kindness into the world that get paid forward. When a kindness is conferred on someone, they'll pass that *koselig* feeling on in other ways, even if it's just to smile that day. And sometimes a smile is all a person really needs to make them feel seen and cared for. Random acts of kindness also get us out of the habit of needing reciprocity to be magnanimous. Think of Martin Seligman's caveat for the PERMA elements—that each happens for its own sake, not to increase one of the other elements, or for some extrinsic reward. We've gotten too accustomed to giving only in the interest of getting something back. Or, we hold people in our debt when we help them out—"I lent you my car when yours broke down. Now you owe me." Try just being a baseline good human being, helping wherever and whenever you can. If you find yourself caught in small or petty thinking, use the ABC model to break down such thought patterns so you can begin to shift into a more abundant way of thinking: *more*, not less. *Big*, not small. The more you do for others, the better you'll feel; that's a fact. And what results is a sweet upward spiral because as you up the ante of kindness in the world, you end up swimming in a sweeter fishbowl.

In the space below, write down ten ideas for random acts of kindness you can perform in your own life. Set about the goal of executing one each day for the next week (I had you list 10 so you have options in case one doesn't work on a given day, or you feel more inclined to another). At the end of the week, spend some time savoring the experience in your gratitude journal, share it with others (could even be an initiative you start on social media!), or simply meditate on it in silent reflection.

1. _____

_____

2. _____

_____

3. _____

_____

4. _____

_____

5. _____

_____

6. _____

_____

7. _____

_____

8. _____

_____

9. _____

_____

10. _____

_____

Working Out Your Issues

Exercise is one of the most powerful interventions that exists for turning a frown upside down. Whether it's a run on the treadmill, interval training, or a hot yoga practice, the way back to light when you're hit with a wave of dark thoughts or emotions is to get up, get out, and get moving.

It's a part of my constitution to wake up feeling depressed sometimes. When I do, my medicine is a stressful sweat-session. *Wait!* You're thinking. *Did she just say* stressful? *I thought the objective was to feel the opposite?!* It is if we are talking about unhealthy stress, like the chronic kind we place our bodies under when we don't know how to relax or reign in the mind. When we say we are "under stress" in colloquial speech, we usually mean we feel unduly strained or pressured. The literal meaning of stress, however, is just a force exerted on one thing by another.

We'll take a much closer look at different types of stress, "good" and "bad," in the sections to follow. We'll also discover why exercise is such a powerful mood elevator on a brain chemistry level. For now, just note that exercise is "good" stress. The example of weight lifting illustrates the point nicely. When you lift a weight, you are placing force on your muscles that they have to resist. This resistance causes tiny tears in the muscles that your body then sets about repairing. When it does, the muscles become incrementally stronger than they were before. This is the whole essence of fitness; placing stress on the body so that it becomes stronger, performing better and better under increasingly stressful (that is to say, physically challenging) circumstances.

My father was preparing to leave for India on one of his frequent business trips. He had earned himself high status on the airline clocking all of those miles and was allowed three suitcases and a higher weight limit. He capitalized on this perk by filling his bags to the maximum weight allowance, usually with whatever he could get his hands on to ensure his benefits were not ceded to "the man." On this particular occasion, the bags were offensively heavy. As my dad wheeled the first case toward the car, I assumed the weight lifter position and scooped my arms around the bag, using the strength of my legs to hoist it into the trunk. It still makes me giggle thinking about the look on my dad's face in that moment, a mixture of total shock, delight, and admiration. He exclaimed, "You are Superwoman!" and it took me a moment to absorb what I had simply taken for granted: After years of training my body in various capacities, even garnering a yoga certification along the way, I had become mini-me Arnold Schwarzenegger. My pride was amplified in knowing there was now literally nothing a brother could have done that I couldn't. There were many times over the years when I had wished for a brother in my midst when things got difficult, like when I felt clobbered by the weight of family concerns on my shoulders, or the weight of suitcases in my slight arms. Now, years of tiny-tears and build-ups-to-get-stronger later, I was literally holding my own, and the psychological boost I felt rivaled the physical stamina on display.

Strength is power, and it can come from stress. Get out there and embrace the good kind. Build the machine of your body so strong that you can weather any challenge with fluidity, grace, and a gigantic smile on your face.

Use It in Novel Ways ("It" Being Your Strengths)

Remember the twenty-four character strengths formulated by doctors Seligman and Peterson? Those personal characteristics that allow us to perform at our best? One of the positive interventions is centered on how to "use your strengths in novel ways." You can imagine why this would be effective—true to the essence of positive psychology, it's about making the most of what we've got. Understanding and using our strengths means "focusing on the things that come most naturally to us and that we love to do."[27]

Take one of the strengths assessments that can be found online to determine what your top five ("signature") strengths are. Write them in the space below.

1. _____

2. _____

3. _____

4. _____

5. _____

Whenever you need a dose of positive emotions, try using your strengths in novel ways. In other words, put one of those strengths into practice in a new way each day. Try this for one week. For example, if one of your signature strengths is "humor," you might sign up for a story slam and tell a funny tale. Several studies have shown that this exercise increases happiness, reduces depression, and boosts self-esteem and vitality.[28]

Drink the Backwash

I drink a daily green smoothie, a blend of superfoods and powerful antioxidants that ensures a robust start to my day (the recipe can be found in the Appendix). I often take my smoothie cup (one of those hard plastic reusable ones with a metal straw inside) with me to work, and sip on it throughout the morning. After I bottom out every last drop through the straw, I pour a little peg of water into the cup and swish it around. This dislodges any residual molecules of the viscous liquid into the water base, and then I down it. It's not the most pleasant ritual, chasing the erstwhile tasty smoothie with its diluted backwash (particularly as it takes on the appearance and consistency of dirty rag water). But it's a habit I'm compelled to continue.

I inherited this little idiosyncrasy from my father, the ultimate conservationist. He is hyper-conscientious about not wasting food, likely a result of growing up deprived of the abundant sustenance so many Americans take for granted. He is also extremely eco-conscious, down to those molecules. He did his graduate studies in chemical engineering, and he's aware of fuel at the micro level of its tiniest components. They all get imbibed to maximize resources and minimize waste. I've watched him wipe many a plate with a piece of bread and eat it, or rinse serving bowls with a bit of water, and drink it down.

Alas, somewhere between guilt and maturity, I began to save my molecules, too. Guilt because if I didn't, I'd miss the look of happiness on my dad's face as I aped his well-intentioned conservation attempts. Maturity because at some point, I realized his efforts were effecting positive change and I adopted the practice to be that change, too.

One of my work colleagues, a young woman in her twenties, is charmingly keen to adopt positive habits. When she noticed I brought a green smoothie into work every day for breakfast (and that I would not need to eat again for hours), her curiosity was piqued. She asked for the recipe, and within a few days, was bringing her own green smoothie to work. Sometime later, she remarked on my backwash ritual, admitting she had tried to do the same, but just couldn't seem to take down the watery liquid. An intern had seen her wince as she tried, and while overtly asking why she was doing that, probably inwardly questioned her sanity. She was simply trying hard to adopt the good principles she was observing, and I was touched.

You never know who's watching, or who might be positively influenced or inspired by your pro-social behaviors. Commit to effecting mass positive change in the world, one molecule at a time. I am quite conscious of every action I take, though I don't always nail it in the "best self" department. It can be exhausting to try to act in the highest when you're tempted toward defaults of anger or irritation. There are also potential side effects like embarrassment or feeling singled out and lonely as you go against the grain. But, if you can handle being thought crazy or odd at times, if you are brave about your ideals, imagine the impact you could have on your world.

Gandhi said, "Be the change you wish to see." I have many wishes, including that my fellow human beings revere food, not waste it with abandon. I wish to see us change our priorities so we gauge success on how business efforts contribute to Mother Earth's thriving, not solely selfish desires or a financial bottom line. I wish for human beings to abide by the tenet that we are all part of one energy, and operate as a collective rather than the prolific ego-driven interpretation that the self matters most. And finally, I wish to see love become the over-arching currency on this planet, not money.

I am committed to making the changes necessary to realize these wishes. As you read this book, and start working with the beneficial practices contained within it, I hope you'll become the positive changes *you* wish to see. If each of us did as much, that would be the greatest intervention of all.

Using the space below, reflect on the following questions: What changes do you wish to see in the world? How are you showing up to support them? How might you create novel opportunities to be these changes?

SECTION II
The Body

The doctor of the future will give no medicine, but instead will interest his patients in the care of the human frame, in diet, and in the cause and prevention of disease.
—**Thomas Edison**

I am watching the Olympics with a new sense of amazement and wonder. My observation is that the athletes consistently outdo their own and each other's excellence to reach unprecedented heights of achievement. How do they do it? That is, embark on the journey to become the world's best, knowing what daunting odds they are facing? In the words of "Desire Mapper" Danielle LaPorte, the key is to "dream like an eagle [and] plan like a mouse." You get to the top not just by focusing on the end game, like winning a gold medal, but by devoting the majority of your time and energy to the tiny, seemingly boring details along the way. I heard *Superbodies* author Greg Wells speak at a conference recently (he was actually at the Olympics, patching in via video-link). Dr. Wells works with some of the world's finest athletes, and one of his "peak performance secrets" is that the little things add up to big wins, and the simple things make a huge difference. If you constantly focus on the macro, global, way-out-there picture, you'll paralyze yourself before you even take a step forward.

I've been a victim of this kind of mentality many times. I think big, and know what I really want to see myself and the world become. And then I get overwhelmed, because the chasm between what I want to achieve and the realm of realistic possibility seems impossibly wide—just as an Olympian might focus too much on the gravity of the context, like not getting another shot for another four years, and then choke under the pressure. The key to success is to place your focus on the small increments that add up to the larger win. Get mindful about each stroke of your paintbrush if you're an artist, your voice inflection if you're a radio announcer, your alignment cues if you're a yoga instructor. These are the subtleties that add up to greatness, the mouse-like actions that translate into grand leaps in your level of ability.

There's a powerful scientific explanation for why the tiny tweaks add up to the big wins: myelin. Myelin is the fatty substance in the brain ("white matter") that is responsible for how quickly impulses are conducted. Myelin gets thicker and thicker the more a certain skill is practiced. The more you work on perfecting the small actions, the more you fire circuits in your brain around them, and the thicker your myelin builds.[29] In other words, more myelin, more "it" factor. Steph Curry, arguably the best player in the NBA, is a prime example. Just watch some of his practice videos (in fact, take a minute right now and Google it), and you'll begin to see how his superhuman level of ability is fed directly by an unwavering commitment to discipline and repetitive action. Make the small steps—not the grand leaps—your inspiration to progress. Eating a fully regulated set of meals, adhering to robotic bedtime schedules, supporting a teammate who is simultaneously a competitor—these are the elements that take an athlete from champion to Olympian. Be the Olympian of your own life and focus on refining the details.

Creating a network of practitioners who you see regularly (not just when you're sick or in acute distress) will help you take the small steps toward balance and health that add up to the big leap of flourishing. After all, disease (dis-ease, a lack of ease or comfort) just implies that there is some disturbance in the body that needs correcting. We can't get to the work of flourishing before we correct these imbalances. Having practitioners available before imbalances get too far out of whack is key to staying optimally healthy.

I see an acupuncturist regularly. Her stealthy needles keep blockages open and chi flowing, so nothing builds up into a larger problem before we nip it in the bud (or nerve). I have a massage therapist on call in case my chronically sore neck and shoulder, the result of a car accident many years ago, start acting up. When I am particularly prone to holding tension in those areas, like while hunched over my laptop during tax season, I make sure I see her with more regularity. One of my friends is a Reiki master, and in times of emotional disturbance, I call on her to help me quickly rebalance my energy before those disturbances spiral out of control and manifest as physical problems. I also have a very active mind, a left brain that is constantly questioning and turning over ideas. It gets super busy up there, sometimes so much so that it overshadows my other intelligence systems, the gut and heart. These sessions help to pull down some of the energy in my head so that I can interact with my world using an approach that's more level, easeful, and ultimately, more impactful. I have a gynecologist for routine checkups and the occasional not-so-routine event, a dentist for twice-yearly cleanings and screenings, and a primary care practitioner who is part of a women's wellness center focused on holistic and integrative health. I've also outlined a preferred emergency room to go to should the need arise. I'm blessed to have a best friend who is a practicing physician and can be reached via text for an immediate prescription call-in for those rare but emergent situations like strep throat or UTIs.

I've coalesced together a little army of soldiers so that I can stay healthy and well, or bounce back quickly when I succumb. I highly recommend you do the same. Put a great deal of thought and care into who your practitioners are and what purpose they serve in the holistic sphere of your health. There is no greater use of your time, I assure you. I only remind you of this because somehow in the race to make those dollars, nurture our loved ones or pursue our dreams, our health is the first place we compromise. Until we fall ill, and then we lose precious days, weeks and months. Don't wait until that happens to prioritize your health. Remember that Olympian behavior is being conscious of the small daily actions that will contribute to your health and well-being, and then being disciplined about integrating them into your life. Your body needs you to care for it in order for it to care for you. Remember I alluded to the idea that we are spiritual beings having a human experience? We can only have that human experience if we have a well-functioning vehicle. Your vehicle will wear down without proper tune-ups and care.

3
Mindful Fuel

The food you eat can be either the safest and most powerful medicine or the slowest form of poison.
—Ann Wigmore

Are you someone that lives to eat? Try eating to live, instead. Mindless imbibing of foods that are high in calories, sugars, chemicals, and fats is the reason America is infamously riddled with preventable diseases like hypertension, diabetes, and heart disease. (A caveat: When I say *preventable*, I am referring to folks who have chronic conditions as a product of lifestyle.) Hypertension is high blood pressure, likely a result of too much salt. Diabetes is related to elevated sugar levels in the blood. Heart disease generally indicates that you're chowing down on foods high in saturated fat or cholesterol.

Now, before you go getting all down on yourself for any unhealthy choices you've been making, let me point out that our genes compel us to crave those kinds of foods.[30] It wasn't that long ago that we were roaming the planet on foot, foraging for plants and hunting for meat. This was the "hunter-gatherer" era of our existence, and to date, it represents the majority of our life on this Earth.[31] Meals were few and far between, and starvation was a very real threat to our survival. When we found extra fat, we could store it in our bodies' adipose (fat) cells and go longer without a meal. Predators were also a very real threat. Foods high in sugar gave us a quick rush of energy, as it is metabolized most easily by the body and, therefore, floods straight into the bloodstream.[32] When out on those plains and vulnerable to the likes of lions and tigers, access to a quick burst of energy to outrun a predator was a solid advantage.

And then the Industrial Revolution (late 1700s to early 1800s) happened, and all of a sudden, our lifestyles changed drastically.[33] The advent of technology sparked a massive shift in how much effort we now had to expend to get our food. Cars replaced walking, and by the middle of the next century, we had packaged and processed foods in lieu of foraging and hunting. For the majority of our existence we had to traverse miles on foot to score our next meal. Now, the more likely path is to hop in the car and look for the golden arches. We don't really have to work (in an embodied way) for our food, but we still have some deep programming as if we do. Are you beginning to grasp the picture? Our bodies have developed positive reinforcement around fatty and sugary foods over eons of being rewarded in the highest way—i.e., not dying. We're now caught in the trap of craving those foods, so much so that we are facing a major health crisis.

Compounding the problem is that we have become sedentary creatures, sitting in front of laptops all day, or at desks in office buildings, hemmed in by concrete jungles not conducive to walking. This is unnatural for our bodies, which are designed to move. Again, the reason probably boils down to our evolutionary history. Finding food necessitated movement. Now, sitting on our butts does. We have to burn off all of those extra calories we're consuming by virtue of *not* having to work for our food or we end up overweight, unhealthy, and riddled with disease.

The Food "Is a Drug" Administration

Our cheapest and most insidious drug to overdose on is food. Like anything else we put in our systems, food can act as a drug if we develop addictions to it and dependencies on it. And we are, for the aforementioned reasons, and because chain restaurants and fast food establishments need you to keep coming back so they can continue making those dollar bills. They cater to your cravings and provide fixes to your addictions in the form of salt, sugar, caffeine, and alcohol. These are all drugs in their own right, as they activate systems in the body that ask for more.

As I mentioned before, it gave us a survival advantage to recognize those foods that would give us the most caloric bang for the buck—like fats and sugars—and stockpile them. Over millennia, that truth in our genes kept getting reinforced. It's only now, in a flash of a millisecond relative to our time on Earth, that the whole game has changed. Our great calorie stockpiling is now our demise. Our genes are slow to catch up after eons of "winning" the other way. We must use our intellect to override these tendencies and start doing what our bodies need but don't quite realize yet: smarter calories in much lower quantities. Given that we're more sedentary than active now, we don't need as many calories to function. We want to aim to have the calories we do eat be nutrient-dense and highly rewarding for our cells' functioning. Thus, instead of large portions of nutrient-poor food, we want small portions of nutrient-rich food.

The Paleo diet is a good example of such an approach. Short for "Paleolithic," this philosophy focuses on foods presumed to have been available to our early ancestors in the cave-dwelling hunter-gatherer era of our existence. It focuses on meat, vegetables, fruits, and nuts, and excludes pretty much everything else (dairy, caffeine, refined sugars, salt, grains, legumes, etc.). The idea is that because we evolved for hundreds of thousands of years around this sort of diet, our genes, which have changed little since then, are well adapted to it. The advent of most of our "modern" food happened relatively recently with the Agricultural (beginning in approximately 10,000 BC) and Industrial Revolutions. Since our genes have not caught up to modern styles of eating, Paleo logic concludes that returning to more archaic food habits will return us to health.

I don't necessarily advocate for going strictly Paleo, as such restrictions can take away from the joy of dining out and sharing meals with friends, and can also be quite arduous to follow. I give you this example to underscore how we might tweak our diets to balance some of the consequences of life in modern times, including eating foods our bodies' genetics may not yet have caught up to, and, therefore, don't know how to metabolize effectively. There is also the problem of a lack of movement that compounds the sticky or sluggish metabolism. When we're eating mass quantities of salt, sugar, or fat, without the accompanying activity to burn it all off, the body's systems go out of whack. And then we have the myriad diseases alluded to before; too much salt leads to hypertension; excess fat deposits in the liver suffocate its functions; cholesterol goes and hangs out in the arteries of the heart, clogging them; elevated sugars in the blood aren't processed effectively, throwing the sensitive pancreas off-kilter. The results are inflammation, liver disease, heart failure, and diabetes, to name a few.

4
Pro-Active

It is exercise alone that supports the spirits, and keeps the mind in vigor.
—Cicero

Physical movement of the body is one of the most effective ways to keep some of those gnarly diseases in check, if not reverse them altogether. One of the main reasons is weight management. Your body uses energy to move, and when you exercise, you expend energy from the food you eat. If you are eating more than your body needs, or consuming excess amounts of sugar or fat, you can metabolize it through ramped-up movement. If you expend more calories than you take in, you lose weight. Less fat in your bloodstream means your liver won't have to work as hard, or become stifled by fat deposits, which keeps it running smoothly and efficiently.

Being active boosts HDL (high-density lipoprotein), which you may have heard referred to as "good cholesterol." HDL acts like Drano for the blood, clearing it of unhealthy fats that would otherwise deposit themselves in your arteries. If plaques deposit in these blood vessels, you end up with blockages that prevent blood flow to the heart. The heart muscle is starved of oxygen and what results is a heart attack.

My father had a mild heart attack in his fifties, the result of a diet that was exacerbating a naturally high blood cholesterol. Having been raised vegetarian, he learned the allure of a good steak when he immigrated to America. "Surf n' turf" dinners became a weekly ritual with his former wife, and ultimately led to spiked blood cholesterol levels and mild heart disease. He has effectively reversed any damage by changing his diet to a primarily plant-based one. My sister and I keep a close eye on our own cholesterol because, like our father, we both have slightly elevated levels at baseline. We stay vigilant about not ingesting cholesterol-heavy foods to keep our low-density lipoprotein ("bad cholesterol") in check, and we use exercise to ramp up our HDL.

When it comes to diabetes, one of the most prevalent and widespread diseases on the planet, exercise is a powerful antidote. Extra fat in the body decreases its ability to properly use the hormone insulin, which is how it regulates blood sugar. Exercise burns fat so that your body's ability to regulate insulin is not disrupted. I've had my own experience with high blood sugar levels, mostly a product of hidden sugars in my diet that I wasn't even aware of. Tweaking what I was imbibing corrected the imbalance.

We're all one step away from dis-ease in the body, and it's simply a matter of having the right tools, information, and a good dose of discipline to keep your system in balance, or, bring it quickly back to homeostasis if a problem occurs.

Exercise can also prevent hypertension. When you exercise you increase the fitness of your heart muscle. As a result, the heart doesn't have to work as hard to pump oxygenated blood through your body. The force on your arteries, therefore, decreases, lowering your resting blood pressure. This is what we want, because higher blood pressure causes strain on many organs of the body, including the heart, the brain, and the kidneys, which can lead to heart attack, stroke, dementia, and kidney disease.

My father, now in his early eighties, recently discovered his blood pressure was higher than his doctor felt comfortable with. He quickly researched what foods contribute to low blood pressure, and found that beets were all-stars in this category. He has since incorporated beets into his daily diet, and is watchful about his salt intake. My mother also prepares separate low-sodium dishes for him when we all dine together. The crux of two salient examples in as many paragraphs, my father is a great case study for using "food as medicine"; he has kept himself out of hospitals and away from prescription drugs by staying informed and disciplined around his diet and other health-promoting factors.

This is a good time to talk about inflammation, because the link between exercise and inflammation is important—and often misunderstood. Inflammation has made its way into our everyday vernacular as a "dirty" word, but not all inflammation is bad. In literal terms, it refers to redness, swelling, heat, tenderness, and disturbed function in the body. More generally, it means the body is reacting defensively to harmful agents threatening its health or balance. This is the "inflammatory response" and constitutes a life-saving part of a healthy immunity.[34] Imagine your body throwing its dukes up, gloves on, steadying for a fight against the aggressor. Just as in a boxing match, redness, swelling, and pain are par for the course when going head-to-head with an opponent.

The inflammatory response is a vital adaptation to protect us against "acute" stresses like bee stings and broken ankles. Our bodies respond to acute stress by initiating an immune response to begin the process of healing, which is characteristic of a well-functioning system.

Where we get into trouble is when inflammation becomes "chronic." This means the swelling characteristic of a healthy immune response sticks around. Stress is one of the main drivers of chronic inflammation in the body because it triggers the release of cortisol, also known as the "fight-or-flight" hormone (so named because it is released when a threat is perceived and we must decide to either stay and fight, or flee). Cortisol dilates blood vessels so that all of the organs get a rush of fresh, oxygenated blood to prepare us to either confront the danger, or run from it. As you can imagine, this is very adaptive to our survival, and was especially relevant when lions, tigers, and other human aggressors were a consistent and persistent danger. With our rapid evolution in the last few thousand years, such threats are no longer as relevant. In general, we're not walking outside of our homes worried about getting picked off by tigers, but we exist as if we are.

As with the foods we crave, our genes haven't yet caught up to the rapid change of our environment. Ultimately, this means we aren't very good at discerning the difference between a real threat and a perceived one; an angry boss can cause the same stress response as a tiger if we aren't careful to check ourselves.

The reality of our modern lives is that we have many potential stressors—like the angry boss, income and job insecurity, traffic and road rage, deadlines, and relationship and family pressures. We end up in a constant state of hyperarousal. Our bodies are flooded with the stress hormones cortisol and adrenaline, and what results is a chronic stress cycle. Because cortisol regulates inflammation in the body, the consequence is chronic inflammation. Cells of the immune system can't effectively respond to hormonal signals (like from cortisol) when under stress because they get desensitized given chronically high levels of cortisol in the bloodstream. Inflammation gets out of control, hitting levels that promote various infections and diseases.[35] To make matters worse, our bodies sacrifice systems that are considered "non-essential" to fighting threats in order to keep us in the stress cycle. That means altered immunity, and suppression of the digestive system, the reproductive system, and growth processes.[36]

Imagine a beautiful, well-manicured lawn covered in plush grass. A gardener tends to the lawn, regularly feeding it quality seed and showering it with water. It's healthy and verdant, not a weed in sight. Now imagine a pack of squirrels moves into the neighborhood and starts making a daily snack of the seed, depriving the grass of its nutrition. To make matters worse, the gardener's green thumb is turning as brown as his grass, his attention diverted as he hatches schemes to keep the squirrels out of his garden. He neglects to water it, and it starts to die.

Your body is like this story; you only have so many resources to keep yourself healthy and in balance. When you introduce a variable, like chronic stress (or squirrels), some of those resources have to go to keeping you hypervigilant. It's an expensive proposition, not just in terms of the resources you have to use to stay in fight-or-flight mode, but in the areas that get sacrificed as a result. Over time, the body's ability to repair and recover are severely compromised and ends up susceptible to dis-ease, just like the poor grass whose caretaker was too busy fending off squirrels to have time to water it.

Exercise is a key component in warding off the stress that keeps us trapped in the chronic stress cycle. There is a wealth of research to support the idea that physical activity reduces inflammation in the body.[37] The level of a substance in the body called C-reactive protein (CRP) increases when inflammation is present. When you exercise, levels of CRP go down. Just be careful not to overdo it. As I mentioned, there is good stress and bad stress, good inflammation and bad inflammation. In general, acute types, one-off spikes from a resistance training session or a burst of cardio, or a response to a bee sting or broken ankle, are healthy. Chronic forms like running marathons or not getting recovery time between workouts can be harmful. Use exercise wisely so that you're not contributing to the chronic inflammation you're trying to stave off.

Earlier, I gave you a few of the most common examples of the diseases that plague us, and how effective exercise can be in remediating them. There are many others, including various cancers that seem to wither and fade in the face of exercise. Research abounds on these subjects, and it would take me thousands more pages to even begin to do it justice, so I leave it to you to explore further and in more detail depending on what you are drawn to. (Spark is one of my favorite references on this subject; it is listed in the Bibliography section at the end of the book.)

For now, just take it as fact that exercise is a key component to keeping many of the most common illnesses at bay, and prioritize giving the body a work up and a work out. Go see a doctor for a full check-up, assess where your physical and mental health is, and then chart the appropriate course accordingly. You may have health limitations that prohibit certain forms of exercise, but the trick is to just stay at it, even in small doses, in ever-increasing increments, so that over time you turn your body into a lean machine of flourishing.

Getting High

Just as your body realizes some incredible benefits from exercise, so does your psyche. There is nothing like movement—especially of a sweaty, high-octane heart-pumping nature—to pull you out of a negative emotional state. In fact, exercise is a powerful remedy for a whole host of psychological ailments, including depression, anxiety, stress, and attention deficit hyperactivity disorder (ADHD). We just went through an explanation of inflammation and its underpinnings and how destructive it can be when chronic. Scientists have known for some time about a correlation (think of correlation as two things going hand-in-hand) between inflammation and depression; that is, in bodies where you find depression, you also find inflammation. Now, there is research to show that the relationship is also causal (a direct link between the two, where one *causes* the other). It appears that inflammation in the body actually leads to brain changes, which can result in depression. A potential consequence is that anything that triggers the inflammatory response—like infections—could also trigger depression.

The last time I had the flu, I was in bed for about a week. I fell into a depression so acute and unexpected I could've sworn I had a lobotomy. I slowly clawed my way out, getting into the gym as soon as I had the strength to do so, but it was intense and traumatic. Had I known about this research, I could have saved myself some suffering by dumping turmeric into my chicken soup. Turmeric is a powerful anti-inflammatory and might've made my flu episode more forgiving. Something to consider next time you get sick and feel the blues coming on.

This research also alludes to the fact that if you're already depressed *and* have high levels of inflammation in the body, you could be in for a double-dose of darkness. How's that for adding insult to injury? The good news is, we've already talked about the many interventions that exist to combat inflammation *and* depression, so no matter what the causes, we can put measures in place to remediate them.

Exercise is a convenient and formidable two-fer. Beyond the anti-inflammatory effects, it's also a potent mood elevator. On my darkest days, endorphin-infused a**-kickers are my saviors. My sister and I talk often about our propensity for feeling stuck or sad. It's in our genes. My father is very vocal about feeling "depressive" sometimes, and because asthma limits his ability to exercise, he ups his ante of meditation, caffeine, and naturally derived serotonin from banana peels[38] to recalibrate his mood. My mother feels large dips herself, and when I look at her lineage, and the preponderance of mental illness in her family (replete with young deaths and incidents of violence), I know that I've got to build a strong foundation for my well-being if I am to not succumb where genetics compel me to go. It used to shock me how I could feel so dark and awful before a workout, yet afterward, so uplifted, happy, and light. As if by magic, I couldn't even relate to what depression felt like once I got that exercise. When you're scaling the walls of your mind's abyss, the pitch-black obscuring a way out, you need a light to shine into the darkness. Exercise flips on that light.

There were a couple of years straight when I would wake up every Thursday morning at 6:30 a.m. to work out with one of my closest friends. In those early pre-dawn hours, when it was still dark outside, my mood would match the sky. Mornings had always been rough for me, and I would inevitably awake awash with heavy feelings, compounded during periods of acute sadness or grief. Needless to say, it took immense effort to stay committed to this weekly regimen, the lead cloak of negative emotions trying to restrain me as I endeavored to lift myself out of bed. Being accountable to my trainer (at fifty bucks per session) and friend (bailing on friends is never cool) kept me going, and it was a foundational experience in my life. I was my own best experiment in the journey out of depression via exercise; I'd struggle out of bed feeling ultra low and slow, and by the time I got back upstairs an hour later, flushed and covered in sweat, I was on a high. It was like life had its arms outstretched, waiting to embrace me and usher me through another beautiful day. What a contrast to the foot-dragging hopelessness that greeted me upon waking.

The Electricity in the Light Bulb

What exactly is it about exercise that turns that light on so bright? As we discussed before, it triggers a stress response in the body. Exercise represents a healthy form of stress because it causes tiny tears in your muscles that your body then repairs and builds up stronger as they heal. In response to the tiny tears, your brain releases painkillers in the form of neurochemicals called endorphins. Structurally similar to the drug morphine, endorphins block feelings of pain and contribute to that post-workout euphoria. They are opiates made in-house, and the dealer is your own "sweat equity." You also release a stress-buffer called BDNF (brain-derived neurotrophic factor) during exercise. This is a protein that has a protective and reparative effect in the brain, like a reset button, clearing out gunk and helping recycle and rejuvenate tissues.

I hope you're are beginning to see how exercise fortifies you on virtually every level, making you more capable of enjoying the varietal bounty that life has to offer. Remember my suitcase story from Chapter 2? How I lifted my father's heavy bags into the car with surprising ease? The sheer power of my muscles to execute a difficult task, especially with respect to assisting a loved one, was in and of itself a win. And that's to say nothing of the positive effects on all of the other organs of my body. As a result of my continued efforts in the gym and on the mat, each is performing ever more capably and efficiently. I'm able to jump higher, run faster, and go longer every year that goes by. This is in large part due to a "heartier" heart muscle, conditioned over time by lots of investment in cardiovascular activity. It doesn't have to work as hard to pump more oxygenated blood to my muscles. A stronger ticker also means my resting heart rate is slower. That equates to a lower blood pressure.

My lungs are also more fit. Their capacity to take in oxygen (oxygen demands can be up to fifteen times higher when you are exercising than when you are at rest) has increased because the muscles around them can move faster.

And then there's my brain. The increased blood flow to the dome as a result of a workout allows it to function better almost immediately—I can think more sharply and clearly. This effect is amplified as exercise also helps grow new brain cells, giving a boost to learning and memory. When you feel sluggish, slow, or even a little less than sharp before an important event, a little exercise can be a very effective intervention to up your game.

I once asked Dr. John Ratey, author of *Spark* and one of the masters in the field of exercise and the brain, what he thought would be the best test preparation I could employ before the GRE (graduate record exam). He replied, "Go for a run about thirty minutes beforehand." I had never run right before an important or nerve-wracking event, much less an exam. *What about the sweat factor?* But then I thought, *What's the worst that can happen? My smell bothers the other test-takers? Maybe that's a competitive advantage . . .*

On the morning of the GRE, just before leaving the house, I strapped on my kicks and did a light jog on the treadmill, just enough to get the blood pumping and the sweat beading. I arrived at the test center feeling armped (amped + armpit sweat), clear, and ready to go. Dr. Ratey's strategy may just have whet my acumen, because I ended up with higher scores on the real thing than any of the practice tests I had taken in preparation.

Dr. Ratey's advice brings up a good point about the importance of context when deciding what type of exercise is best. A healthy jog is by far one of the most effective ways to boost mood ("runner's high") and increase mental clarity. In addition, it's one of the quickest ways to tone up and trim down—you burn right through fat and it melts off the body. It's also cheap and accessible; all you need is a pair of kicks and the great outdoors. However, running is quite hard on the body.

I personally can't rely solely on running to get my exercise kicks (#sneakerpun). I find the repetitive high-speed action and pavement (or treadmill) pounding very taxing on my joints and muscles. If I have any injuries in my body (and I definitely have a few), a juicy run will exacerbate them and make them angry. I save running as an SOS for special circumstances, like when I need an amplified calorie burn (e.g., post-Thanksgiving), or require an added boost of endorphins (e.g., post-breakup).

The key to optimal functioning is to know how to work your body and its chemistry into the right balance and maintain it there. It's also about exploring different types and styles of exercise to find the formula that works for you. Do this with wonder and enjoy the ride without pressure. Try a variety of situations and even cultures to broaden the horizons of your experience. Zumba, for example, can give you unbelievable insight into the rhythm and culture of South America, opening a portal of enlightenment and cultural fascination through movement. Bhangra can expose you to a whole subset of music and dance specific to Punjab, a place about which you may never otherwise have heard. This can also be an avenue that implores you to question preconditioned judgments or subconscious resistances.

I remember when I first learned of pole dancing classes. The notion conjured up words like "stripper" and "dollar bills." I thought it was just a means to an end, women taking off their clothes and titillating men for money. I also wondered what all the fuss was about. Fans seemed to revere it for the level of skill involved, but really, how hard could twirling around a pole *be*?

And then I saw a video of a close friend performing a dance as the final exam for her pole class. It's okay if you're smirking—I myself was shamefully dismissive about the whole thing. Like c'mon, a *final exam* for pole class? Way to set the feminist cause back a few paces. Well color me *schooled*. She had me entranced by her routine, the grace of her maneuvers like watching a slinky descend stairs. There was this intense sensuality to the whole thing, a feminine grace infused into her movements that was so alluring. I was an avid dancer in my youth, and studied all manner of forms, from ballet, to jazz, to Indian classical. Whenever I got on a stage to perform, my graceful genes clicked on and expressed as something so lithe and nymph-like. When I saw my friend's pole performance art, I wanted to know that feeling again.

Within the week, I signed myself up for a month of unlimited classes at a studio that had just opened up mere blocks from my apartment. During that first month, I got many questioning stares and looks of intense concern from my friends and family courtesy of the bruising all over my legs and feet. The Spartan-level core strength required for pulling most pole maneuvers left my abs aching and sore. I walked around a bit hunched over, like I had impending diarrhea or had just been punched in the gut.

Boy did I stand (albeit hunched over) corrected from my initial assessment of "How hard could twirling around a pole *be*?" This pole dancing business was grueling. And I was loving it. I felt such a huge sense of accomplishment every time I left that studio—each maneuver we learned at the beginning of class would be sewn together in a mini-routine that we'd memorize and execute by the end of the hour. Watching my body spin and contort in that mirror with strength, grace, and mastery was such a rush.

It was amazing to witness all of our reservations, body image issues, and sources of self-doubt dissolve as we grabbed our femininity by the balls and danced our power. Each and every body type—from fleshy and round, to bony and thin—had its place on the floor. There were many heavyset women in the class who I envied for the way their booties undulated when we twerked. I had always had a decent trunk myself, and came to appreciate it on a whole new level for its inherent value in pole currency on a whole new level. Spins on the pole looked sublime on the long-legged ladies. Pole climbs and inversions seemed effortless by those in the class who were petite in stature.

Even hair textures got new ways to shine, as I observed tight curls held light beautifully and never got in a dancer's eyes, while silky long hair always got in dancers' eyes and, therefore, made it a sultry addition to the dance, especially when whipped around with sexy flair. All of these natural feminine features we're usually so quick to diminish, wishing we had it different or "better," were suddenly the perfect accessories.

The freedom engendered through pole dancing captured my attention and admiration. I couldn't get over some of the moves these women brought to the floor, so raw and uninhibited, the fiery looks in their eyes as they expressed their individuality, sexuality, and independence through this admissible channel. We keep sex so tethered to connotations of shame, guilt, and sin, ultimately even condemning abused women for inviting assault and rape simply for being feminine. I can't help but think of how some Islamic women are covered head-to-toe in dark cloth, implicitly placing the onus of responsibility squarely on them to keep men from succumbing to lower animal instincts. We all give off pheromones, which are organic creations intended for the exact purpose of attracting a mate. Are we ignorant enough to think they can be masked with some cloth? I see a world of women desperate to embrace that sexual feminine side, simultaneously full of fear of the consequences. The pole studio seems to be a rare space where oppression is washed away and a woman can be the fullest expression of herself.

Given years of effort and practice, trying new things, and leaving some behind that didn't suit me, I'm now fairly well attuned to my body chemistry and how to serve it best. This generally looks like a pupu platter of cardio, strength training, yoga, meditation, dance, and the occasional off-roading when on vacation or in a new scenario.

I have a favorite class I go to twice a week at a university gym here in Philadelphia. I do my best to plan around this workout because it pushes me to sustain a high level of athleticism. The instructor, Johanna, is super fit and hard core, unrelenting in her quest to make sure we end the hour spent and soaked in sweat. I won't lie, there were plenty of times I dipped my toe in the pool of resentful thoughts, my mind yelling "sadist!" as she forced countless rounds of burpees and sprints out of us. But I stayed with it, and have now developed the balance, flexibility, and endurance to keep up better than the majority of the class, which is comprised mainly of undergraduates. Again, you can achieve a surprisingly high degree of fitness—age notwithstanding— just by showing up and putting in consistent effort. Johanna combines intervals of cardio bursts (called "plyometrics," like those burpees I mentioned) with repetitions using weights to localize different muscle groups. Two of these a week and I find my heavier aerobic needs are well met.

I described earlier how I worked out once a week for about two years with my close friend and a trainer. This was a similar workout, though a little less heavy on cardio and geared more toward pushing the boundaries of our abilities in strength, flexibility, and reflexes. It was such a vital supplement to my life to ramp up my fitness capacity in all of those areas. It gave my self-esteem a huge boost as well. There were things I simply didn't think I could accomplish in that gym, like jogging on an incline at max tilt for several minutes at a stretch, or twenty-one burpees, followed by fifteen, followed by nine, with reps of dumbbell snatches in between. And yet, I did it. Holding a two-minute plank didn't seem viable given that at the one-minute mark, my abdominals were trembling fiercely and my back was bowing in. But, in the tug of war between mind over matter, my mind was a fierce competitor who ultimately showed my abs who was boss. Don't get me wrong, there were times I thought I'd actually pass out, but somehow, I never did and I found my way to the other side.

This effort spilled over into the rest of my life in the most beautiful way as I found courage in trying new feats—like speaking in front of crowds of thousands—simply because I knew the boundaries of my capacity were only in my mind. It takes getting to the point that you just don't think you can go beyond, and then traversing that line, to know you are limitless. Intense workouts are a beautiful way to access this truth.

Yoga is another. I completed my 200-hour yoga certification in two phases and two countries. The experiences were profound for many reasons, beginning with the convergence of how I dropped into the certification in the first place. I was shooting a television pilot at the time, and though I had years of yoga practice under my belt, I was not officially "certified." One of the descriptors for me as host of the series was "yogi," and I felt uncomfortable with the label since I didn't actually have the certification credentials. That was about to change.

 I knew of the Amazing Yoga teacher training from a promotional email I had received several months before. It planted a seed of curiosity that grew into a yearning for the experience. I loved the program structure: Each hundred hours was acquired over a span of nine days straight, in either Costa Rica or Mexico. Intimidating, but also highly potent and efficient. Being in such beautiful natural surroundings among others in the same "boat" sounded like the perfect immersion. Somehow, getting certified over several months in a city setting surrounded by concrete just didn't feel as . . . natural. So, excited that such a structure existed, I went back to my emails and realized the next Level I training was a mere two weeks away. They had one spot left. I asked my executive producer for that week off, and we just so happened not to be shooting those days. Check. I looked at airline tickets, and though they were astronomical given the tight window of time, tickets were available on miles and my father had loads. Check. I confirmed that the spot available was still free (of course it was) and filled it with my energy.

I remember that first day in Costa Rica I was filled with anxiety bordering on panic. The instructors announced that we'd have two practice sessions a day, each between one-and-a-half and two hours in duration. *Two* practices?! The knowledge that I had never in my life practiced more than an hour-and-a-half in a single day filled me with dread, and I confronted the possibility that I was in way over my head. I hadn't even considered being unable to hack the physical rigors of the program. I began to feel like an impostor who was about to be exposed.

That first practice wasn't as bad as I thought it would be . . . it was worse.

Being in Costa Rica in April meant ambient daily temperatures hovered around ninety degrees. The instructors sealed off the room so that our own body heat would increase the temperature even further. I managed to get through the first hour okay, but I was feeling fatigued and desperate going into the second hour. My muscles were shaky and aching and I prayed for relief, my arms threatening to give way as I lowered into the umpteenth chaturanga of the practice. Somehow I made it through that first class without face-planting, but my mind quickly screamed at me all manner of admonishment, "*Why did you come here?! How will you make it through the day, let alone the week?!?!*" Within an hour, I had one of the worst headaches I'd ever had, partly a result of the intense detoxifying effect of the yoga and heat, partly because of my mind's unrest.

 I swallowed some ibuprofen, and, despite some embarrassment and fear of missing out around skipping the second practice, I went to my room to sleep it off. By the time I awoke, dusk had fallen. I spent some time journaling about the experience, and through that writing, was reminded of the many forces that had aligned to bring me the gift of this experience, including my own hard work and effort in getting all of the logistics sorted out. I knew deep down that I was meant to be there, that it was all guiding me somewhere higher if I just had the courage to receive it.

By the next morning, I was deeply committed to staying the course and finding my evolution though it. The headache had subsided, and I began to appreciate the process through clearer eyes. I approached the arduous practices with renewed vigor, helped along by the organic, high-octane food at the resort. I ate mountains of it to replenish the calories I was combusting, and noted how it seemed to translate directly into building the key muscle groups that I needed to get through all that practice. I also gulped down three to four liters of water a day to keep up with the hydration loss from all of that sweating in hot practice rooms.

Within a couple of days, it was like I had morphed into a halcyon version of myself. Never before had I looked as strong or glowy. I was dancing a beautiful harmonious routine, balanced between heavy effort and rest, fuel and hydration, and yet only muscle and strength, not fat, were the by-products. I was fully satiated and yet consistently rising higher.

I remember vividly when, midweek, something shifted inside me, and I knew I had walked through a portal of growth, leveling up like in a video game. We were nestled in the Cliffside Mountains of the resort, perched in a glass-encased studio overlooking the beach. Rounding the bend on the second practice of the day, dusk was quickly giving way to dark and a blanket of solemn stillness unfurled over us. Suspended there in frog pose (a deep and very intense hip opener), Sarah McLachlan's song "Angel" began to play. I could feel the tectonic plates of my being moving . . . .

By this point in the training, we were fatigued and humbled enough by the rigors of the practice to recognize our own fragilities and shortcomings, and yet far enough along that we inherently understood our immense strength and capacity to endure. Hip openers are notorious for exhuming deep emotionality, and I could hear scattered sniffles and sobs around the room. Warm, briny tears dripped silently from my own eyes as I acknowledged how hard I had worked to find myself in that moment, how quickly time had passed in that practice, and how my asanas seemed to melt one into the next without added thought or force. For the first time ever in a yoga practice, I had found flow.

*****

To lose yourself in physical meditation like that is a gift, and I'm so grateful to have found similarly potent flow through yoga many times since. I recently discovered Bikram Yoga (for the eponymously named yogi who formulated a certain sequence of postures into a specific discipline; the style is coming to be known simply as "Hot Yoga"). It appears to provide a triple-threat of all the standard benefits of yoga alongside cardio *and* mindfulness. Hot Yoga takes you through ninety minutes of practice in a room heated to approximately 105 degrees. The first half of the sequence, called the "standing" postures, challenge your strength, balance, and flexibility. The second series of postures are "seated," involving twists, backbends, and forward folds. Each posture in the second series is followed immediately by a full outstretched lying down posture (like savasana, or final relaxation pose, in vinyasa yoga). The seated poses essentially create tourniquets that constrict blood flow, and the lying down actively releases it. What you end up with is rapidly and effectively circulating blood throughout the body.

When I leave that room, I am on a high similar to what I achieve after an intense bout of aerobic activity. It's also a commensurate amount of effort. I've noticed that practicing in such a hot room with unwavering discipline for that duration scares even the most gung-ho yogis away. But man, is it worth the effort. Not only do you get the benefits of cardio without the impact, you get traditional benefits of yoga like balance, flexibility, and strength. The cherry on the sundae is that it's also a super salient mindfulness practice. Movements are slow and deliberate, giving one ample opportunity to rest in a posture for some duration without the distraction of quickly moving onto the next. You have to hold the mind steady and still, reining it in even as it is screaming at you to come out of the challenging pose or to run from the inferno.

It was only my second time ever practicing Hot Yoga, and I was down to the wire. I tumbled through the studio's entrance doors, rushing to get in before they locked them (standard operating procedure at this studio given the rigors of the practice, and a consequent adherence to strict discipline). My coworkers were all converging there, and the commute in rush hour traffic had left me scrambling. The doors were locked promptly at 9:00 a.m., and if I missed the class, I'd be waiting around for the next hour-and-a-half for them to finish. Luck was on my side because I made it with just about a minute to spare. My mind was at a frenetic pace, no time to take a breather between the madness of the drive and the intensity of the impending workout. This instructor happened to be unusually strict; she allowed only two water breaks at specified intervals, and insisted that we not leave the room until class had concluded. How fortuitous that I would drop into Miss Army Drill Sergeant's class on the day I felt least in control of my mind and faculties.

The first half of class passed fairly fluidly, as I threw what little mental bandwidth I had left after traffic and other troubles into the undertaking. The second half was less forgiving. The heat felt like it might suffocate me, and sweat dripped into my eyes, a cloudy film covering my contact lenses and obscuring my vision even as I repeatedly blinked to clear it. I felt desperate. My mind screamed for relief, and I hallucinated about running to the door and escaping the torture for just one, sweet, cool gulp of air. But I was compelled to stay put. I had never seen anyone actually leave the room, not even the older practitioners in their sixties and seventies. I fought to rein my mind back in, breathing in and out slowly in even swells through my panic.

I made it to the ninety-minute finish line, one challenging, focused, moment at a time, and for the next several hours after, I was on a towering high. There was an accomplished pride transfused into the post-practice euphoria that felt so sweet. I had never hooked this intensely or deeply into mindfulness through yoga, and it was profound how much control I had—once I was forced to exercise it—over my mind and its travels. I had stayed present and stayed the course.

*****

Sometimes you have to be pushed to the mental edge in order to know that you can plow through, and do so without freaking out. Yoga instructors often talk about the potency of the practice "off the mat," alluding to the way its positive benefits spill into the rest of your life. Pushing the mental edge is a great example of this phenomenon. When you are used to holding still and steady in a place of great discomfort, you achieve a heightened ability to weather storms. This is why practitioners and meditators are much more placid, imperturbable people. They are the last folks to turn violent, aggressive, or lose their cool. This is because they're cultivating such skills on the mat, and bringing them back to life in fruitful, productive ways. It's often an unconscious process, more like an energetic shift of frequency to something more elevated.

Imagine a world where we could steady ourselves so well in moments of flux that we all took time to comprehend and process before reacting. We'd give ourselves the chance to throw smiles instead of punches, show compassion instead of selfishness. The total tonnage of positive emotions on Earth would increase, and ultimately that's what we all want, for it simply does not feel good to be angry, frustrated, resentful, or unkind. It also feels pretty icky to be around people who are in that sort of space because it rubs off on us. It's called "emotional contagion." Ever notice how quickly the mood of an entire room can sour when just one person's energy is negative or toxic? Or how uncomfortable it feels to be in the presence of a couple that is sparring? It's hard enough getting through life's challenges in a healthy frame of mind, without some oblivious and unaware creature adding misery sauce to the pot. Not to judge the Debbie Downers too harshly. It is challenging to be the vision of grace, kindness, and compassion in a world that often gives out negativity and meanness—but it *is* a choice. We can be energies that either illuminate a room, or cover it with darkness. We have to fight for light.

It's going to take accountability from all of us together to create an upward spiral. It can be done; it just takes concerted effort and practice. I invest a great deal of energy in doing just that, as do many of the wonderful human beings I know. I also know many who don't. Those folks (and sometimes "those folks" are our own selves) deserve compassion and honest communication when they are doing a disservice to themselves and the energies around them by being angry, negative, gossipy, or toxic. Be brave enough to speak the truth, and then have enough integrity to hold out your hand and help them reach for something higher. It is your choice every day how you want to show up in the world, good guy or bad guy. I hope you'll choose good, the world needs that from you.

5
Sleep

Sleep is the golden chain that ties
health and our bodies together.
—Thomas Dekker

In Section I, I talked about mindfulness as an avenue to improved sleep, because sleep is essential to well-being. Unfortunately, the majority of us get far less sleep than we require, and we're suffering immensely as a result. According to the National Institutes of Health (NIH), adults need between seven and nine hours of sleep a night.[39] That basically means we are designed to spend about a third of our lives sleeping. Those extra hours may feel like a waste of time, or an opportunity to "get more done," but I assure you, that is dead wrong. Literally, because lack of sleep causes increased risk of death across many measures, including car crashes, heart disease, and learning impairment.

Huffington Post co-founder and editor-in-chief Arianna Huffington wrote a book on sleep deprivation called *The Sleep Revolution*. After a scary incident wherein she passed out and hit her head on her desk, breaking her cheekbone, she felt compelled to warn others about the perils of not getting enough sleep. She argues that sleep is a gateway to all other measures of well-being in our lives. Adequate sleep—or lack thereof—has huge consequences on our functioning.

Sleep is when our bodies go into "repair and recover" mode. It is the time, for example, when the heart and blood vessels are healed and mended. It should, therefore, come as no surprise that sleep deficiency is linked to heart disease, high blood pressure, and stroke. Lack of sleep also throws hormone and chemical levels off-kilter. Take ghrelin and leptin, for example, the hormones that tell us when we are hungry and full. When we don't get enough sleep, ghrelin levels go up, causing us to eat more than we need (the hunger gremlin, ghrelin, is roaring). We spend so much energy regulating what we do or don't eat, and obsessing over diets and calories. Perhaps we should devote some of that energy to the more obvious culprit: sleep. We're also a nation that's struggling with hypertension and diabetes, both of which are linked to obesity, a strong correlate of sleep deprivation for the aforementioned reasons. Sleep is one of the most overlooked and underestimated factors in maintaining a healthy weight.

Without fail, if I get sick, it's after a night of inadequate rest. No surprise that sleep plays a major role in healthy immune function.[40] Since I learned of this correlation, I've been particular about getting the rest I need, even if it means making other sacrifices. After all, the alternative is far more costly. If I get sick, days of productivity are lost, and there's a high likelihood of getting others sick, which in turn compromises their productivity. The pursuant depression is also inevitable, and I'm not keen to invite that in if I can help it.

Note that staying out late and drinking is a double-whammy because sleep is short-changed *and* of low quality. Alcohol disrupts the rapid eye movement (REM) stage of our sleep cycle, a restorative phase where most dreaming occurs.[41] While researchers are still trying to learn more about why we dream, some theories point to dreams being the way we process emotions, information, memories, and stress. In addition, if your REM sleep is disrupted even one night, your natural body clock is thrown off.[42] Given that we spend about twenty percent of our sleep time in the REM phase, you can understand why alcohol-induced disruptions to this stage are a pile-on of destruction to good sleep.

In something of a triple-whammy, alcohol also suppresses immunity. One drink does not seem to bother the immune system, but three drinks—or any amount of alcohol enough to cause intoxication—does. High doses of alcohol reduce the ability of white cells (the "soldier" cells in our bodies that protect us from invaders) to multiply and kill germs. It also inhibits the body's ability to fight cancer and tumors. It appears that damage to the immune system increases in proportion to the amount of alcohol consumed,[43] so just be mindful about these truths the next time you engage in a night of heavy drinking. Limit quantities of alcohol to one or two drinks, especially in the cold-and-flu season, and give your body what it needs most: adequate sleep.

For children and teens, sleep requirements are even greater, averaging between ten and eighteen hours a night in childhood, and between eight-and-a-half and ten in adolescence. Deep sleep triggers the body to release hormones that promote normal growth and development. When I went through my depression as a teen, psychological distress stopped me from sleeping healthy amounts and my growth slowed way down. I was slated to be at least three inches taller, and a lack of sleep (and inadequate fuel because of the corresponding hunger hormones being whacky), short-changed me, especially in the torso. It's noticeable to me in yoga postures, like when I try to stretch my relatively shorter torso over the longer length of my legs and my palms don't touch the ground in a forward fold. This makes inversions like a handstand immensely difficult to get into, and after a certification and a decade of practice, that pose still eludes me. This is so salient for me now because although I can fully embrace my beautiful body for all that it represents and all that it allows me to do, it also acts as a reminder of depression's consequences for a growing body. Pay heed, young teens!

Beyond growth, also beware of how lack of sleep can short-change the brain. The adolescent brain is a fast-growing one, on overdrive as it absorbs and retains new information. Sleep is when learning from the day is *consolidated*, which just means that pieces of new information are formed into memory. Recall is strengthened to be able to use later, like when it comes time to perform a routine for an audition or remember facts for the SATs. Don't get enough sleep, and you don't get very far in storing information and recalling it for later use. That's bad news for anyone trying to do anything productive in their lives, worse for teens trying to ace exams that will determine the course of their future.

Premature aging is another unfortunate consequence of not getting enough sleep. Have you noticed how haggard someone looks after a night of inadequate rest? You might as well take a pill to age you faster if you're going to compromise on sleep. A UCLA study showed that just *one* night of not getting enough sleep activates important biological pathways that promote aging.[44] I remember when my cousin was a medical school resident, barely twenty-five at the time, and she already had a tuft of gray hair at the top of her forehead. Frequent nights on call and being awakened several times during a shift (if she even got to sleep at all) was taking its toll on her body, which was rapidly and prematurely going into aging mode. Obviously the life of a doctor may necessitate a less-than-optimal sleep schedule, but treat it as the exception, not the rule. Next time you're tempted to sacrifice sleep for the myriad other things attempting to keep you awake, envision your cells aging rapidly as a consequence. The expression "I'll sleep when I'm dead" strikes me as so ironic now, given how much faster not sleeping seems to get you there. I don't mean to scare you into slumber, just don't labor under the misapprehension that in your hectic life, sleep is the place you can find more time for your "to-do's." Simply become more mindful about ensuring you get enough rest and this will help you handle the rest.

I realize that the mandate to sleep more might seem like a case of "way easier said than done" given the majority of us suffer from sleep problems. But it's no wonder, considering the hyperstimulated environments we live in. We have glaring lights from our devices—smartphones, laptops, navigation systems, and televisions—in our faces constantly. We have coffee shops springing up everywhere, ready to serve us legal addictive stimulants until we're doped up and hopping. We must, therefore, empower ourselves to become mindful of the consequences and pitfalls, and self-regulate accordingly.

When I drink any caffeinated beverage after about 4:00 p.m., falling asleep is a painful process. I toss and turn in fitful agitation; it takes me far too long to finally drift off, and I awaken several times over the course of the night. The inevitable consequence is that the next day, I feel tired, cranky, and a bit sick.

I am very conscientious about my caffeine intake now, and limit doses to those I know my body can tolerate without sleep disruption. I have also gotten rid of the television that used to sit in my bedroom. Not only was the bright screen making it hard for me to want to sleep, my mind would become flooded with images and thoughts that were stimulating (usually in a negative way), engendering anxiety, panic, envy, or sadness right before bed. I'd have scary dreams and wake up freaked out. That simple change has led to a massive improvement in my quality of sleep.

Alongside external stimuli like television and caffeine, our internal worlds can also rob us of good sleep. We have minds full of anxieties, stressors, and worries. Take heart, however, because the struggle *is* real, but so are the solutions! There are many things we can do to buffer ourselves. Also called "sleep hygiene," there are habits and practices we can put into place that are conducive to sleeping well on a regular basis.

Take the following Sleep Hygiene Quiz to see where there might be room for improvement:

1. Do you sleep less than seven hours most nights of the week?

2. Do you have a television in your bedroom?

3. Do you have and/or check your tech gadgets in bed?

4. Do you have caffeinated beverages within four to six hours of going to bed?

5. Do you find it hard to fall asleep because you are ruminating over thoughts, worries, or other concerns?

6. Do you take any sleep aids (besides melatonin)?

If you answered "yes" to one or more of the questions above, you're a good candidate for ramping up sleep hygiene.

Cultivating Good Sleep Hygiene

Get rid of any electronics or devices in the bedroom. It's meant for two things: sleeping and sexing (I said sexing, *not* sexting). When you allow too much of the outside world into the bedroom, distractions infiltrate the sacred space meant solely for rest, relaxation, and procreation.

Shut off all devices about an hour before bed. That means anything with a screen, including the television. Digital devices give off blue light, which has been shown to suppress the production of melatonin.[45] Melatonin helps regulate the body's natural circadian rhythms around day and night. When it is not released, your body doesn't get the proper signals that it's time to sleep. In addition, what's on those devices, like work and social media, keeps the mind running and ruminating. Your brain needs time to de-stimulate and power down. In lieu of electronics, try journaling, which holds the added bonus of cataloging worrisome or agitating thoughts so you don't have to hold them in your mind—like cleaning house. Taking a hot bath or sipping herbal tea also have soporific qualities.

Try to avoid napping during the day. It'll just keep you up later, and it disrupts the body's wakefulness and sleep cycles.

Avoid caffeine (and, if you are especially prone to sleep disturbances, any chemicals that interfere with sleep, including alcohol) later in the day. In general, caffeine has a half-life of four to six hours, meaning it takes your body that amount of time to process half of what you've consumed. Gage your caffeine consumption accordingly. I won't sip coffee after about 2:00 p.m. so I can ensure this particularly potent source of caffeine has completely cleared my system by midnight. With tea, it seems to be slightly later, about 4:00 p.m.

I think of it like a zero barrier: when 4:00 p.m. hits, no more coffee or tea (unless it's herbal).

Also bear in mind that decaffeinated coffee retains some caffeine,[46] so it can still keep you up if you have it late in the day.

Exercise early or at least three hours before bed. Remember Dr. Ratey's advice to go for a jog to rev up the brain? Use your exercise medicine wisely so you're not inconveniently at your sharpest while trying to fall asleep.

Inhaling the scent of lavender before bed seems to act as a mild sedative, triggering a drop in heart rate, blood pressure, and skin temperature, which are all physical signs of relaxation.

Melatonin is a hormone secreted in the brain that regulates sleep. It is also manufactured in pill form and sold over the counter. If you're struggling with inadequate sleep, you can try taking melatonin to help you regularize your circadian rhythms. Lots of travelers use it for jet lag and swear by it. Since it's naturally manufactured in the body, it's generally considered a more benign option than pharmaceuticals and other chemical compounds that are foreign to the body and have side effects.

I know I said no phones or devices in the bedroom. There's one exception: Use of a meditation app can be an immensely helpful tool. There are several styles of meditation that work well in this department, particularly the body scan, but there are also some specific to sleep since this is such a common problem. You might want to explore those to help you relax and quiet your mind. Just make sure that you download an app that will filter out the blue light on your device over the course of the day (they actually exist!) so that your circadian rhythms aren't interrupted while using your phone in the evening.

6
Your Network Is Your Net Worth

The first wealth is health.
—Ralph Waldo Emerson

I began this section with an ode to the various practitioners whose contributions keep me balanced and healthy. They comprise my holistic wellness network, and the majority of their work is dedicated to helping me *prevent* illness and dis-ease. It's of the highest importance to emphasize your wellness initiatives as much as your sickness protocols; explore and commit to the various ways you can bolster your health. One of the most salient avenues is by keeping your immunity strong with as much dedication and determination as you do to getting well when you are sick. People tend only to realize the true gift of their health when it is compromised. And then the many detriments that accompany illness—suffering, the drain on resources, loss of quality of life, the negative impact on family members—all become so painfully apparent. Yes, folks who suffer such traumas can receive those experiences as gifts, and find meaning and purpose in them, but that's a way to make a life well-lived out of one that is in peril. Why wait until you get a wake-up call to wake up?

One of the most useful ways to "wake up" is by visiting an integrative health specialist. "Integrative health" just implies a trained physician who specializes in looking at the whole, or "holistic" picture of you—body, mind, and soul—and assessing your health from that perspective. Normally, doctors are trained to look for what's broken and try to fix it, much like the traditional pathology-focused approach of psychology that we talked about in Section I. Integrative health practitioners are as focused on prevention as they are on cure, and might assess your physical, emotional, psychosocial, and spiritual needs all at once. The body's natural healing abilities are placed at the forefront, and conventional medicine is used to complement. It's not unusual for an integrative health practitioner to recommend a comprehensive panel of blood work to assess your health from the inside out. This can highlight imbalances or areas of concern so they can be corrected before they snowball into major health issues. It's a good idea to do these panels with frequency and regularity to keep things in good form and balance instead of waiting for symptoms to tell you something is out of whack and in need of correction.

My first visit to an integrative health practice was happenstance. I discovered it driving by the storefront one day, my interest peaked when I saw "threading" advertised in the window. That was my preferred form of eyebrow maintenance, so I pulled over and stopped in, surprised to see that aside from de-hairing, vitamin injections, health consultations, and botox injections were among the many other offerings at the "medical spa." Around the same time, my mother was dealing with some pretty serious insomnia, plagued by many of the symptoms and side effects of sleep deprivation that I described earlier. She was suffering and in need of urgent help.

We had tried following the channels dictated by her health insurance, but they were failing her. The sleeping pills prescribed by her general physician caused her to hallucinate and suffer fainting spells. A psychiatrist prescribed a medication that numbed her to the point where she was barely a shadow of her former self. Given my familiarity with the integrative health approach, and the discovery of a med spa in our area, I scheduled an initial consultation for my mom. At an hourly rate rivaling most expensive lawyers, Mom was hesitant to say the least. It was a tough pill to swallow, plunking down a few hundred dollars extra on top of all of the money she already shelled out for insurance premiums. But, she was desperate for a solution and running out of options. My mother agreed to the visit on one condition: that I accompany her and consult with the doctor about my own health. That's a mother's love; she saw the merit in getting preventive feedback on my health even more than she saw the value in having a cure for her own troubles. I had no acute issue for which I was being seen, so the doctor recommended I get a full blood workup before coming in so we could focus on health optimization.

My mom and I found ourselves sitting in a cozy patient room just a few days later. The doctor listened intently as my mom described the details around the onset of her insomnia, and the subsequent erosion of her quality of life. She had been the victim of an armed robbery some years earlier (more on this incident to come), and the trauma of the experience had settled itself deep in her psyche. The doctor quickly put together a theory based on a holistic appraisal of my mom's psychological history and physical symptoms. She posited that my mother's quick weight loss, a result of the macrobiotic diet she had adopted some months before to alleviate symptoms of arthritis, had depleted her estrogen stores. My mom was post-menopausal, and her body was no longer producing estrogen. However, the hormone is stored in our fat cells, and as she was losing weight, she was also losing vital estrogen reserves. There is a strong correlation between estrogen and sleep regulation, and given a mind disturbed by PTSD, insomnia was inevitable. *Shizam.* No one in the bevy of psychologists, psychiatrists, general health practitioners, and specialists that my mother had already seen had been able to draw the link between her acute trauma, her weight loss, and her insomnia. They were screening for illness in the various categories of her symptoms, but lack of attention to how each fed into the larger picture had left us grasping for answers. We had been stuck in the realm of trying to treat symptoms, when the source would lead us to a solution.

My mother looked at me in relief and amazement, her tense shoulders relaxing in response to the doctor's assessment. It's horrible when your health is in jeopardy, worse still when you are suffering and have no idea why. Finally, we had something to work with. After a long discussion about options, the doctor determined that my mom was not a good candidate for hormone replacement therapy as her body was no longer making estrogen and might reject it, leading to very elevated cancer risk. Instead, she prescribed a protocol of foods containing naturally derived sources of estrogen, like soy products. She also recommended trauma counseling for the PTSD, and blood work to validate that we were on the right track.

The focus of the conversation then shifted to me. My blood work showed elevated levels of inflammation and sugar. I was also extremely deficient in vitamin D. I was surprised. I took pride in my healthy diet and exercise regimen, starting each day with a fresh-pressed vegetable juice and a yogurt parfait, and getting a workout of either cardio-and-strength training, yoga, or some treadmill action in at least four days a week.

"What's in the veggie juice?" she wanted to know. "Carrot, beet, celery . . ." I rattled off the comprehensive list with pride. She interjected, "That's a lot of sugar straight to the bloodstream first thing in the morning." *What? Who said anything about sugar?!* I was about to correct her misunderstanding that I was not actually adding extra sugar to my juice when she continued, "Carrots and beets have some of the highest sugar content of the vegetables." I was stunned. I guess I had always assumed fruits and vegetables were good for you in any context, and it was a net win as long as you were ingesting them.

Not when it came to optimal health, and not when you were juicing them and taking all of the fiber out, giving you several carrots and a large chunk of beet's worth of sugar all in one shot. I realized that this excess sugar and inflammation lurking in my blood might be interfering with my immunity, among other things. You may recall from earlier in this section the correlation between chronic inflammation and a lowered ability to fight infection. I was extremely prone to sore throats, and now we were getting clues as to the sources. She was helping me draw correlations I had never considered. She also offered me alternatives. "Try a morning smoothie instead, and replace the carrots and beets with a high-nutrient green base like kale or spinach. The extra fiber will do you good, too. You're losing that when you juice. Also, adding blueberries will give you antioxidants without all the sugar."

We moved on to the yogurt—Greek with fruit on the bottom, walnuts— she stopped me again to explain how much sugar those fruit compotes had. "Try replacing the flavored yogurt with plain yogurt." I told her she was taking the wind out of my parfait sails, but that I'd rather go "plain than pain." *Ba-dum-dum-tchhhh.* She then asked if there was anything else going on in life that I wanted to share. Having heard how significant a role my mom's psychological state was playing in her health predicament, I contemplated the breakup I had just been through, and the anxiety, depression, and loss of appetite I was suffering . . . .

All breakups are hard, given the process of separating from someone with whom we've shared time and intimacy. But this one—given my age and the stage of life I was in—had been particularly difficult to reconcile. Following an untenable marriage in my twenties, and a heart-wrenching, star-crossed love through my early thirties, I thought I had finally hit the love lottery.

I got a text about a month shy of my thirty-fifth birthday from an old college friend. A major crush really. He was a senior when I was a freshman, and his easy charm and good looks made him the object of lots of female (and sometimes male) attention. He was popular, athletic, and president of his class. Unbeknownst to me, my sister had given him my number some years before when my marriage had faltered. He, too, had been through a marriage and divorce, and she thought we might have that—and more—in common. When he eventually reached out, my stomach flipped and my mind screamed "fate." I'd had a vision not a few days before of a dusky man in scrubs, with dark salt-and-pepper hair, coming into my life.

And here he was. We had all of these shared memories and points of commonality, creating a deep resonance that felt like magic. Both first-generation Indian, we were literally speaking the same language. We laughed a lot, and truly enjoyed each other's company. We also fought a lot, as his strong surgeon ego and my willful independent spirit struck against each other as flint on rock. It was becoming increasingly clear we wouldn't last, yet I couldn't bear the thought of a breakup. Giving up the hopes and dreams I had around him, indeed the idea of him, forced me to acknowledge that I might also have to give up on all notions of following a more traditional path—including having kids. When the end finally came about six months later, I woke up most mornings in the aftermath in a panic.

Talk about life stress. No wonder inflammation levels were high in my body. What a gift that I found my way to a physician who could help me gain control from the inside out. She suggested cutting way back on sugar, to keep inflammation levels at bay. Given all I now know about the links between depression and inflammation, her assessment strikes me as particularly astute. She also recommended scaling back on caffeine, which would only worsen my anxiety. Finally, she proposed I begin a meditation practice to help me focus my mind and stay calm. I told her I had recently signed up for a year of unlimited yoga to help ease the depression and anxiety I was feeling post breakup. She was impressed and praised my efforts to balance out the negative emotions with a physical outlet.

Much of the credit actually went to my parents, who had given me a generous cash gift for Christmas several weeks earlier. On New Year's Eve, the yoga studio I frequented was advertising a year of unlimited yoga for the exact amount that my parents had gifted me. Talk about convergence. I signed up straight away, deciding my initiative, which I called TYP ("The Yoga Protocol") would be my broken heart's greatest ally. I was taking classes almost every day and felt TYP carrying me through the darkest phase. As I gained power in my muscles, my mind was naturally fortified through what I was accomplishing in the studio, another example of the "off the mat" benefits of yoga.

You have to focus your mind to find ascendancy in yoga postures; balance is achieved through an unwavering commitment between mind and body to collaborate. As such, the mind tends not to wander off because that translates to wobbling, shakiness, and spills out of poses. This strength of mind parlays itself into other areas of life because if you can hold it steady in poses, you can hold it steady on healthy initiatives of your choosing, like self-care, professional growth, and hope, rather than ruminating on loss or regret.

As my mind gained traction (it gets especially slippery when it comes to love and heartbreak), I was able to apply that essence to my life and career. The physical strides I was making in the yoga studio, as a result of sheer consistency of effort, were incredibly empowering, and gave me renewed confidence in my ability to level-up in life. Within a few months I was slayin', making it to Philadelphia's "Sexiest Singles" list and shooting a pilot for a reality TV show. I was resilience in action, bouncing back from adversity with alacrity and strength. I also enjoyed some sweet post-traumatic growth, embracing my singledom, and the freedom that goes with it, to create a life that contained far more joy than the one I was living before. Adding to the post-break-up upsides was a renewed faith in the power of integrative and holistic health care. I wouldn't have been so aware of the toll my psyche was taking on my body without this wonderful doctor to help me connect the dots. From that knowledge came the power to tweak, heal, rebalance, and reboot. A stronger physical self fed directly into a stronger psychological self. I was growing more powerful in every regard and moving forward with increased momentum and drive.

*****

That's evolution; our survival depends on our ability to adapt effectively to change. Do that, and it's a win. If we can adapt with flourishing, well, that's a win-win.

In that spirit, as life opens me up to opportunities to create a more evolved self, I embrace them with gusto, though they often come with a good dose of discomfort. A car accident back in college left me with chronic pain in the lower left part of my neck and trapezius muscle. During one period of particularly acute agitation (attempting headstands with my trainer) I found my way to a massage therapist to help alleviate the soreness. Notice I said *therapist*. This was no spa massage with aromatherapy and candles. It was a straight-down-to-business WWF-style smack down. It was incredibly painful and uncomfortable, but the work that was happening deep in the muscles and tissues resolved the problem of the acute flare-up almost immediately. Massages that you find on a typical spa menu, like Swedish and deep tissue, can definitely confer benefit in keeping your muscles and tissues limber and unkinked. But for more serious and acute challenges, it may be worth exploring therapies specific to your issue, like sports massage for athletes and runners, physical therapy for injuries, and so on. These avenues are not always pleasant and certainly not painless, but in the interest of a more flourishing (read: evolved) self, they are worth the effort. Find empowerment around your health by focusing on preventive maintenance, and try to stay open to all manner of treatment modalities that might get to the root of your (t)issues.

Over the long term, the benefits of my own massage therapy seemed to plateau as the acute pain was resolved but the chronic pain persisted. The therapist suggested I visit an acupuncturist—there was a talented woman working in his practice who might be effective in moving some circulation through that consistently knotted and tense section of my neck and shoulder. I had never tried acupuncture before, nor did I really know of anyone who had (unless you count that episode of *Sex and the City* where Charlotte visits an acupuncture specialist in the hopes it will give her fertility a boost). It is still considered an "alternative therapy" that many people—including my own doctor and surgeon friends—are fairly dismissive about. Without empirically validated studies and concrete facts, modern medicine is averse to consider alternative therapies. This is logical and protective, but not comprehensive. Remedies with far fewer side effects often slip through the cracks, even if they're validated by the school of life. Further, we don't want to just mask symptoms of pain through drugs and pharmaceuticals. This can skirt over the root of the problem and put us in a cycle of addiction. I'm so grateful I found my way to acupuncture—it is a staple of my health care.

 Acupuncture is an ancient practice widely acknowledged to have started in China about a thousand years ago. The Chinese describe it with the character "Chen," which literally means to "prick with a needle." That sort of sums it up. Acupuncture involves the insertion of thin needles into the skin to stimulate different points on the body, depending on the problem for which you seek treatment. In traditional Chinese medicine, acupuncture is described as a technique for balancing the flow of life force energy, known as *Chi*, which courses through the body along pathways called meridians. By inserting needles into specific points along these meridians, energy flow—which gets blocked—will rebalance. The Western philosophy leans more toward acupuncture as a way to stimulate nerves, muscles, and connective tissue, which in turn stimulates blood flow and boosts your body's production of natural painkillers.

Though acupuncture is not widely recognized in Western medicine, many people swear by it. My experience with it has been convincing to say the least. In a few short sessions, the literal pain in my neck began to subside. I felt the whole area unwind for the first time in years, and the philosophy behind acupuncture seemed rather befitting—the blocked energy in my upper left neck and shoulder was being released, loosening stagnation and tension and returning blood flow to the region. Over time, I became more aware of how stress—and holding tension in the area—would exacerbate the ache. As soon as I felt it take hold, I'd actively release my neck and shoulder and step away from whatever I was doing (usually hunched over a laptop in a state of deep concentration) to breathe, relax, and practice mindfulness. I say all of this in the past tense deliberately; I can't remember the last time I had soreness in that area.

My acupuncturist also serves as something of a psychotherapist. Ascribing to a holistic model, Caroline attends as much to the workings of my mind as those of my body. We spend at least a third of each session talking about what is going on in my life, what my emotional state is, and what, if anything I have on my mind (which is always a lot). She takes as fact that what is going on psychologically will inform what is manifesting physically. In other words, imbalances in my psychology will manifest as imbalances in my physicality. She also keeps me in constant touch with my spirit, helping me in my quest to be a more evolved, authentic self. As such, she does not shy away from reminding me when I am straying from that truth. She will devise treatments accordingly, to open heart channels that will aid me in making growth leaps or fortify my ability to stay attuned to spirit. The approach is always sensitive to source, and this keeps me deeply connected and attuned to the root of all of my imbalances. I'm, therefore, much better equipped to find solutions and opportunities for evolution.

 Like acupuncture, Reiki is a healing modality that involves movement of energy. I mentioned it earlier as a treatment I employ to help me rebalance and reboot in times of acute emotional distress. The word "Reiki" comes from the Japanese root words "Rei" (meaning "Universal Life") and "Ki" (meaning "Energy"). "Universal Life Energy." Reiki is based on the principle that the therapist can channel life force energy into the patient (through direct touch and/or hovering their hands above the body) in order to reduce stress, promote relaxation, and activate natural healing processes. Physical and emotional well-being can thus be restored.

I was barely a week into ending the relationship that had been my summer bliss, and my heart was in tatters. My publicist had set us up, and as ever, she was an ace at making connections. Walking into our first date "blind" (I had seen his picture on Google, of course), I had a powerful and immediate reaction. His smile, crooked and sheepish, was disarmingly pure and kind. Born to Indian parents, a doctor of optometry and raised in Georgia, he had a dogged sense of familial allegiance, a strong protective instinct, Southern hospitality and charm, and a penchant for serving others. I melted for how he would walk around to my side of the car and open the door to help me out *every single time* we took a ride. I loved the way his arm instinctively shot out to harness me whenever we came to a hard stop. No wonder I fell hard, even if it was imprudent given his impending move to the West Coast and a recent heartbreak that kept him fearful and guarded. He was convinced from the beginning that I, too, would break his heart, a fear lending itself well to our eventual end, a self-fulfilling prophecy.

One evening, barely two months into our relationship, I felt a microscopic but perceptible shift in our dynamic, that of connection giving way to alienation. We had just been apart for two weeks, I to explore a PhD program on the West Coast, he to attend a friend's wedding in Canada. We barely spoke the few days he was away, given wedding festivities and spotty international cell reception. I was stressed by the radio silence, my insecurity exacerbated by an inherent awareness that the clock was already ticking on the relationship. I was angry at his inattention, and told him as much.

When he returned from the wedding, all of those days apart had taken their toll. It was like trying to fit two jigsaw puzzle pieces together that are deceptively well matched but just don't quite snap into place. He felt pressured by my attachment, I felt alienated and anxious by his reaction. And this is where the self-fulfilling prophecy hammered down: He was just waiting for validation on his initial belief that he wasn't good enough for me, and given my deep unhappiness at his efforts to stay in touch, I had inadvertently given him that validation. We had talked a few times before about the different directions in which our lives were moving, and now, it was clear they were forking apart. We simply didn't want the same things. I awoke several times that night, my spirit calling my attention to that truth.

The next day, I ended the relationship. If I have learned anything from my experiences in partnership, it is that I am looking for a level of resonance, fluidity, and commitment that I simply cannot compromise on. Setting a high bar means you also commit to keeping it high, even when it's utterly painful to do so. I chose to end the relationship as soon as I felt the bar drop a fraction, rather than wait for it to wane or become something so entirely different from how it began that it was sullied in our memories. An ideal move in theory, but I don't think I was quite prepared for the intensity of upset I would endure in the days following our parting. I felt awash with anxiety, my stomach pitching as I grieved the loss of this relationship in my life. That's the challenge inherent in ending a relationship on a "high" note—you don't have any ugliness to remind you of why you left. My mind was a hamster in a wheel, doubt about my choice to end things perpetually spinning around. Adding to my distress was the fact that despite my posthumous attempts to stay in touch, he stayed out of reach. Eventually, I would see what a big favor he was doing me, but in the moment, I was inconsolable. Knowing he was in the same city, carrying on with life and having an ostensibly good time (at least according to Instagram) was torture. I had to get away. Luckily, I knew exactly where I needed to go.

The Omega Institute is a place of immense beauty and peace just a handful of hours' drive from Philadelphia. I called to inquire about space and found out they were nearly at capacity as it happened to be a weekend of "ecstatic chanting" at the institute. Some of the most talented and beloved musicians and spiritual teachers of our era would be gathering for three days of music and discourse. Among them Grammy-winning phenom Krishna Das, whose music had always had a profound effect on me. I could hook into the sounds and lose myself in them, thought and worry relinquished to the powerful melodies and devotional chants. That such an event would be taking place right when I needed it the most felt like divine timing. The congenial woman at the reception desk inquired if I wanted the last single room in a shared cabin. Heaven yeah I did. I planned to hit the road first thing in the morning.

I usually looked forward to long drives, especially to upstate New York. Once past Manhattan, the roads opened out to soul-filling, breath-stealing, mountainous vistas. This time, however, it was hard enough to find my breath without the beauty of the drive taking it away from me. I was anxious and dreading the time alone with my distraught mind.

That evening, one of my besties paid me a visit, and we soon found ourselves at the home of a mutual friend. She was on her way to becoming a Reiki master, and upon hearing of my emotional distress, offered me the gift of a session. I agreed, grateful for any help in taking the edge off of my suffering. I lie down on the massage table in the cozy and candle-lit room, and closed my eyes. With Reiki, it's as if the practitioner tunes in to a radio station that plays "atoms and molecules," and since that's what's playing in the room, that's what you sing along to. I hooked quickly into her energetic frequency, and became acutely aware of my thought-filled mind as an intense buzzing sensation in my head. As she hovered her hands slowly around my energy field, maneuvering it, I felt relief for the first time in days. The buzzing in my head began to dissipate, and

I was able to access a place of deep peace. It was like dropping easefully into a meditation without the barrage of thoughts I usually have to expend so much effort to release. At one point, I felt light like chiffon gauze, and experienced the sensation of floating toward the ceiling like a ribbon on a wisp of breeze.

As the session drew to a close, I experienced a level of groundedness and calm that was nothing short of miraculous given the distress I had been steeped in when I arrived. Caitlin shared what she had experienced during the session, including feeling intense energy pooling in my head, and a raw and open heart that she worked to put a protective cover around. She also mentioned that at one point, she felt my body become feather light, as if it could levitate. I was floored (so to speak). We had exchanged no words during the session, but our unspoken, energetic experience was ostensibly a shared one, and this validated powerfully the essence of Reiki as a treatment modality. I went to bed calm enough that night to sleep soundly, and woke up feeling surprisingly strong, ready to make the trip to Omega.

*****

The work was not done after that—Reiki didn't "cure" my broken heart and make me forget my pain, a la *Eternal Sunshine of the Spotless Mind*. On the contrary, this relationship would continue to serve as a mirror for my own growth and healing, taking me to incredibly powerful and evolved places through the pain. What Reiki did was get me to a place of balance so that I could take the next step forward empowered, rather than paralyzed, by my grief.

It is a magical thing to tap into the physical manifestations of a mind slowing down and becoming free of attachment to thought. Generally, in mindfulness meditation, this access point is more cerebral. You realize steadiness when your mind-wandering abates. Reiki is a portal of connection between mind and body—steadiness means balanced energy. In this case, my mind was freeing itself of attachment to painful thoughts as the Reiki work dispersed the energy; the commensurate liberation manifested as a floating sensation, a total weightlessness of my body.

Like Reiki, there are scores of other healing modalities out there that alone, or in tandem with others, can provide the optimal prevention-and-cure combination for your particular energy system. I've described just a few of here, which are among those I've gravitated to or magnetized based on my life's unfolding. I encourage you to look into others, many of which

I've also tried, like Body Talk and Tapping, Spiritual Clearings and Hydrotherapies (e.g., Floating Chambers), silent meditation retreats and diet-based approaches.

My mother effectively eradicated her issues with arthritis by going on the macrobiotic diet, eliminating foods that were causing inflammation (e.g., "night shade" vegetables like potatoes, tomatoes, and eggplant), and ingesting foods that fight inflammation, like turmeric and tart cherry juice. Of course, in doing so, she also lost a good deal of weight, which depleted her estrogen stores and caused other issues. Let this serve to underscore the fact that your body is a complex system, as sensitive as it is resilient, and requires a holistic and conscientious approach. Having a primary care doctor on your team who has a practice grounded in integrative and holistic health care (who you can consult with first on any changes you want to make) will serve you well. Simply stay open and receptive to the wealth of possibilities out there, and try not to limit yourself to any one system, philosophy, or practice. Sometimes the offerings of modern medicine are vital and life saving, at other times dauntingly linear, toxic, or addictive. By the same token, the alternative therapies are potent remedies in certain contexts, and in others, dangerously ineffective. The key is to find a balance between them. Like being disciplined about preventive care every day to keep your immunity strong, with exercise, sleep, herbs, and supplements, and then taking the antibiotics when you get the occasional bug or bacterial infection that needs to be quashed. With cancer, and the rapid way in which it spreads, you'd be taking a potentially lethal risk going the route of alternative therapies. However, most cancer therapies involve killing off cells—both diseased and healthy—with chemo and radiation. As you may imagine, this can decimate the immune system, leaving the body highly weakened and susceptible to infection. Giving the body the best chance at healing in a case like this might mean availing of cancer-fighting drugs, and then feeding your body solely pure and organic foods that are nutrient-dense, as with an Ayurvedic or homeopathic diet, and avoiding extra salt, sugar, unhealthy fats, and anything that will amplify imbalances and distract the body away from the healing work it needs to do. Unfortunately, we tend to see patients being fed the exact opposite. Someone coming off of knee surgery is served Jell-O and pudding on their hospital tray. Sugar = inflammation = slow healing.

I listen closely to what my body tells me, and take action as soon as I sense an imbalance or issue. If I feel it can be resolved with alternative therapies, I will try those first. I had recurring ear issues following an infection some years back. I was averse to taking antibiotics each time a flare-up occurred. Instead, I consulted a health practitioner who suggested garlic drops for my ears, and fire cider, a piquant blend of vinegar, garlic, onions, horseradish, lemons, oranges, habanera, turmeric, and ginger (#immune-boosting ingredients), to drink every day. This formula has been my natural go-to since (it helps that it's actually pretty tasty), saving me from unnecessary doses of potent antibiotics and their side effects, among them killing the healthy gut bacteria that keep systems running smoothly.

The prescribing and imbibing of antibiotics is also creating noxious new strains of bacteria, as our overuse renders them resistant. The price to pay—illness with no cure—is catastrophic. It is, therefore, vital to pay close attention to your particular diagnosis or problem, and use modern medicine expertly and deliberately. Exploration and curiosity around other healing modalities will keep you enlightened to alternative or supplemental therapies, so that you, the person that knows your energy system best, can make the most informed decision and find the optimal way forward. Knowledge and information are your best friends in the quest for health.

The day I wrote these words, things were ear-wry. I had woken up that morning with a scary, high-pitched ringing in my left ear.

The evening before, I attended a dinner party at a friend's place, and her stuffy nose indicated that she was getting over a cold or infection of some kind. My suspicions were solidified when I saw her husband give their ten-month-old some amoxicillin before they put her to bed. To warrant antibiotics, they were obviously fighting some pretty intense germs, and as my right ear began to grow hot and inflamed, I knew my body was reacting. I felt like the agar in a petri dish, the prime target for gnarly parasites looking for a new host. As my generally less-than-robust immunity threw up tiny dukes to steady itself for the fight, I felt my left ear clog up.

This was not a new sensation for me; the ear infection I had suffered a few years prior, the first since I was a child, had left me prone to blockage and fluid. The thought had crossed my mind more than once that all of these attacks may eventually lead to permanent ear damage and hearing loss—the fatalistic thinking characteristic of highly analytical minds. We absorb information, our love of learning then showing its fangs when it creates a database from which to pull all sorts of doomsday diagnoses. In my photographic mind, I could see the results of a former Google search, yielding alarming consequences of ear infections, among them deafness.

I didn't stay at the party long, excusing myself to rush home to try to fight whatever germs were trying to take hold. I checked myself into the Pax Clinic and laid out a buffet of home remedies and prophylactic measures.

First, I gargled. This is such a simple and highly effective way to stave off throat infections and irritations. Trust the girl who used to get strep or tonsillitis once or twice a year from the age of ten until about thirty. I was just prone. I have learned first and foremost that one of the most potent remedies for a burgeoning or already-sore throat is to gargle with warm salt water.

Next, I filled a neti pot with salt water and poured it through one nostril, followed by the other. This is not the most comfortable procedure, feeling somewhat like jumping into a pool and swilling chlorine water through your nostrils. But, it works magic in the early stages of fighting a cold or sinus infection. It also helps alleviate symptoms, contributing to a speedier—and easier—recovery.

I followed the sinus-clearing with a spoonful of fire cider, two echinacea pills, and dropped some garlic oil into both ears. I also popped two "cold snap" pills. ("Cold snap" is a blend of Chinese herbs available over the counter at most health food stores. When you feel the first sign of imbalance, like a slightly sore throat or runny nose, start regular dosages of cold snap. It's a miracle worker.)

I went to bed feeling more than hopeful that my organic arsenal would incinerate any lurking germs, and I'd wake up with a clear ENT area (and maybe some garlic breath). That I did (on both counts). As my eyes fluttered open, I spoke some sounds out loud and discovered that my hearing was balanced and unobstructed. I felt immense relief as I fell silent, getting ready to rise from bed and start a new day. My relief was short-lived, however, as the silence was eclipsed by a persistent ringing in my left ear. I waited for it to subside, but it held steady. After ten minutes or so, I calmly began to panic. My mind was going straight to the feedback loop I had already created around my doomsday scenario of "What if all of these infections lead to ear damage? Hearing loss? Deafness?!" My father lives with tinnitus, a persistent ringing in his ear, and I was afraid I might have the same.

I swung my legs over the bed, already moving toward the soft decision I had made in my subconscious to go to the ER to get it checked out. I showered, hoping the steam might alleviate the inflammation in my ear and take away the ringing. No such luck. I meditated, knowing full well the need for equanimity through this (as with all of life's challenges). My years of practice were meant to serve me in exactly such situations, so that no matter what din existed around me, the calm and placid space deep within could always be accessed. I completed my twenty minutes, and opened my eyes, feeling quite peaceful and grounded, a refreshing state of being, under the circumstances.

I got into the car, and drove over to the emergency room. I suppose Sunday mornings are not a very popular time to be in the ER, because not ten minutes after arriving there, I was being checked out. Though there was no sign of ear infection or wax buildup, to my relief, but there was also no sign of the cause of the ringing. Chagrin. The nurse had me swallow some high-dose Sudafed and Tylenol, with a "that's the best we can do." The hope was that the combination would reduce the inflammation in my ear, dry out any lingering fluid, and stop the ringing. Given my $400 co-pay for the ER, I quite expected something more than the world's most expensive decongestants. Insult to injury. I felt alarmed leaving without a firm prognosis. What if this ringing in my ear was permanent, my brain's grating next-door neighbor for the rest of my life?

The irony was that simultaneous to this ear drama, I was having serious issues with my next-door neighbors, whose early bedtime schedule, lack of a social calendar, and the extremely flimsy walls between us left them consistently disturbed by my hi-tech sound system and robust circle of friends. They complained of constantly having my sounds in their ears. Now I had this ringing in mine. Karma?

My folks were waiting for me when I emerged from the ER, and I almost cried at the sight of them. In times of uncertainty and upset, when our health is in question or we are in physical pain, our connections are the glue that keep us from falling apart. They buoy us so we keep our heads above water until we can swim again.

I gave my parents the diagnosis (or lack thereof), and my father was a quick-draw with his customary positive outlook (as you read the following words, picture a sprightly older gentleman, Indian but with skin like a tanned Caucasian, sporting a long white beard, clad in cargo pants and sandals, speaking in a whipped and airy accent, Anglicized over years of living in America), "Vell now, I've had this rringing for sawm tie-um. And I use it to brring me closerr to the sownd of the Cawsmos, to Gawd." Using the ringing in my ear to get closer to God felt like a stretch, but I sure did love how my dad could receive any of life's woeful traumas as wondrous dramas.

What a delightful case study in positive psychology he is, and one of the predominant voices in my head when I am confronted with choices around how to find a higher way. Luckily, I didn't really have to put that notion to the test; the ringing eventually subsided some hours later. But not before I truly imbibed the words of my father, this great teacher of mine, and felt, through the whole experience, that the one thing I really took from it all (besides next-level Sudafed) was reverence for these love connections in my life.

I had a chance to feel that deep reverence again a few days later. I was just getting back on my feet after a day in bed with fever following the ear troubles. I was showered and ready, all set to go to work, and felt quite weak. Despite my mental gusto to be productive, my body was telling me that I should conserve energy and not exert myself. I paid heed and decided to stay put. Within a few minutes, one of my besties texted to see if I was home. He was in the neighborhood and could pop by for a visit.

He came over with my favorite coffee indulgence—a lavender latte with soymilk—and as we sipped, I went over my health fluctuations from the last few days. He immediately asked if I had explored what Louise Hay had to say about the psychosomatic underpinnings of ear challenges. I hadn't, so he looked it up and read aloud, "Anger. Not wanting to hear. Too much turmoil. Parents arguing." I couldn't believe how spot-on it was given my life the last few weeks. My parents and I were trying to execute a complicated real estate transaction, part of dissolving our family business now that they were retiring. The deal was a vehicle to preserve the value of one of my parents' assets by exchanging it for another investment property. We were on a tight timeline, and I had been searching high and low, bringing all of the info back to my parents to consider before the time window closed. I was growing increasingly weary and overwhelmed as my parents argued more than they agreed over their preferences and opinions. Turmoil was pretty much the exact word I would have used to describe my current state of being. Good ol' Louise Hay had nailed it. Thanks to my buddy Louis (add an "e" and you have "Louise" . . . #convergence?!) for ushering in this enlightenment.

*****

The moral of the story is this: Surround yourself with good people, good practitioners, and good remedies. Put a plan of action into place for when things go off-kilter. Formulate a strong connection with a physician who can prescribe in a pinch. Consult with non-traditional practitioners for alternatives, and make sure they know your patterns of health and illness so they can view your system as an integrated whole and help you design a wellness plan accordingly. Keep your body healthy and strong with exercise, pure fuel, and meditation. Leverage resources that will help you make connections between your environment, life stressors, and your psychology. Don't feel you must always look to modern medicine for the cure. Sometimes it works to save your health and your life. But sometimes it amounts to drugs that deal with symptoms without regard to the source. The key is for you to be in the driver's seat of your own health. You know your body best because you've lived in it your whole life. Who else can say the same? Trust your intuition (which you'll hone more and more with mindfulness), and work with health practitioners to get yourself to flourishing. Use it all to build a wellness and resilience fortress, of which you are in command.

7
Tune Into Intuition

The intuitive mind is a sacred gift, and the rational mind is a humble servant.
We have created a society that honors the servant and has forgotten the gift.
—Albert Einstein

When it comes to our intuition, most of us are "sleepin' on it." That's a phrase I learned not too long ago from a spirited and spunky friend of mine. I had to ask her to repeat it a few times, so bemused was I by this way to describe something that is underrated or under-appreciated. "Sleepin' on it" is how people generally approach their intuition.

Our intuition is that strong knowing deep inside that holds powerful wisdom. We all have this "inner voice," we just have to cultivate enough silence to hear it. As psychologist and NPR personality Daniel Gottlieb describes it in his powerful book, *The Wisdom We're Born With*, "Beyond the racing mind, beyond the intense emotions, we know. Beyond what we fear or fantasize or wish for—inside, where it's quiet, we know" (p. 149, 2014). He's getting at what it means to trust the essential truth sitting inside all of us, and how a practice—like mindfulness—that helps us quiet our racing minds and detach from the intensity of our emotions is how we tap into that truth. The wisdom contained in that knowing is as righteous as anything our brains may conjure up, if we just allow it to shine forth.

One way to do that is by "going with your gut." The gut is often called the "second brain" because it has around one hundred million neurons (nerve cells specialized for information transmission and communication). That's a lot of intelligence. While the high-level thought processes, like religion, philosophy, and poetry, are the domains of the brain in our heads, the enteric nervous system, as the gut's neuronal system is technically called, has its own reflexes and senses.[47] This allows us to literally *feel* the inner world, giving us a "gut instinct."

Learn to pay attention to it, because it can also be faster than the brain, which is designed to make conclusions based on analyses, rationalizations, and processing work. Think about (or, feel into) that all too familiar sensation of butterflies in your stomach. This is signaling in the gut that is part of our physiological stress response, and we *feel* it first, before we set about processing its causes.

Our intuition is a sadly underutilized asset, sometimes with tragic consequences.

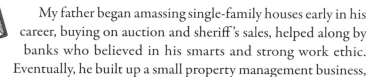 My father began amassing single-family houses early in his career, buying on auction and sheriff's sales, helped along by banks who believed in his smarts and strong work ethic. Eventually, he built up a small property management business, which my professor mother joined him in nurturing, the both of them working diligently to keep it running. For many years, before the now-common online systems of ACH and automatic debits, my father accepted tenants' rent payments in cash. He would leave a healthy sum of it in the office for the contractors, who required advances before they began work. Cash meant they didn't have to wait for a check to clear the bank and could access the resources right away, for materials and other expenses. Dad liked to employ folks who really needed work, and I think it resonated with his own story of folks taking a chance on him when he was on the come-up. The trouble was, if they were desperate for work that meant they were also often desperate for money.

The office had rested unalarmed for decades. Over the years, my mother had prevailed upon my father many times to have one installed. He resisted, prioritizing freedom for the contractors to come and go at will over that added security. Ceding control in any capacity, including shedding your armor to be free, requires a great deal of trust, and I think my father wanted this to be the foundation of his world. He, therefore, had no compunctions pulling out cash from the drawers and counting it in front of those in his midst. This included the son of one of our most established contractors, who had begun helping his father on jobs, and often accompanied him to the office. Coincident with his appearance in our world, we had a spate of burglaries in the span of weeks, wherein the cash that sat in all of the contractors' folders—thousands of dollars worth—was cleaned out. Though we wanted to believe it was random, all signs pointed to this being at the hand of someone with inside knowledge of our business operations. My father's rationale was, "We are all related in this world, one family of humanity and descended from common ancestors, so the money has gone to one of our cousins." My mother, however, wasn't so forgiving. She had sacrificed and toiled for that money. What kind of evil troll of a cousin would steal it from her?!

An alarm was promptly installed, and all was placid for a while. Alas, that peace was not to last. A few weeks later, while traveling abroad, I received a distressing phone call. My mother had been the victim of an armed robbery at our office in West Philadelphia. It was a violent and traumatic ordeal, and as I listened to the details surrounding the event, I was shocked and heartbroken.

My head swam with questions and alarm bells clanged, my stomach churning and sick, tears spilling from my eyes as I pictured my mother being bound and gagged, pistol whipped, kicked, and pushed to the floor by the thieves.

My mother was by herself at the office when it happened. That my father wasn't there was no accident. This was a calculated scheme. The robbers had an accomplice place a call to the office earlier that day to figure out his whereabouts. Learning that my mom would be there alone set the plan into motion.

Two men rang the doorbell that warm September afternoon, white males in their thirties, dressed in heavy, oversized jackets. My mom didn't recognize them when she arrived at the glass door of the porch entrance. "Yes?" she inquired, as she assessed them through the clear pane. They told her they were Drexel University students looking for an apartment. My parents rented mostly to students seeking off-campus housing, and this demographic was a staple clientele of their business. The men told her that they were desperate to find a place as the semester had already commenced. Having been a college professor herself, my mom had a soft spot for students. In addition, as the rental season was winding down, inquiries for apartments were dwindling and a few were still vacant, meaning thousands of dollars of lost revenue.

As she slowly unlatched the door to let them in, she said, "You seem like nice boys. You wouldn't hurt me, right?" Even as their words appealed to her rational mind, my mother sensed that something was off. Her intuition had been speaking to her, receiving incongruences like their clothing—one was in an overcoat and the other in a heavy leather jacket—which was eerily inconsistent with the balmy September weather.

As my mother walked to her desk and sat down, the men continued to stand. She invited them to take chairs, but they remained still, silent. Then, suddenly, they turned their backs to her and she knew she was in trouble, the rush of fear shooting through her stomach as she began to process their inconsistent and bizarre behavior. When they did an about-face moments later, the need for such heavy coats in September was chillingly apparent. Both had hidden weapons under their bulky exteriors, and they drew them now, aiming directly at her.

Over the next several minutes, they abused and tormented my mother, demanding to know where the money was. She told them there was no money in the office, and repeatedly questioned them with, "Son, why are you doing this?" They bound and gagged her, dragging her to the back of the office where they left her as they ransacked it. They went straight for a tower of filing cabinets where cash for the contractors had historically been kept. They ripped file folders out of the cabinets, dumping them upside down and hurling them to the ground in frustration as they found nothing but documents and receipts. The rampage continued until the sound of the doorbell interrupted their onslaught. They panicked and scrambled to escape, though not before taking my mother's wedding band off her finger and leaving her with a menacing threat, "If this had happened at 425, things would have gone very badly for you." These men had just called out the numeric address of my parents' home in the suburbs. They were referencing the fact that in the suburbs, no one would have come to the door and interrupted what I can't even imagine they intended to do. Though they left without the heap of cash they had set their sights on when devising this heinous crime, they had just successfully robbed my mother of much worse: every place she actually felt safe and comfortable in the world.

*****

I will delve into this story further in Section III—the *why* of what transpired on a meta level. For now, take to heart (and gut) the importance of intuition. You see, my mom lives with PTSD to this day, yet her deepest intelligence had tried to forewarn her. We all have it inside of us, and often either don't know how to hear it, or we squelch it even when we do. Sometimes other concerns override it, like society's needs or expectations, or the reasoning of the analytical mind. We attend to others' voices or opinions above our own inner knowing, we over-think the obvious, second-guess that which is clear, or become paralyzed by too much choice. I just gave you an example of how very absolute a consequence not honoring your inner voice can be in your life, and how powerful a tool the intuition is in living a more fluid and easeful one.

Stay Triple A

It takes a great deal of effort and practice to stay attuned to our inner truth, and to keep fighting to protect that truth. I've been working at mine for quite some time, through mistakes and practices that act as asymptotes toward self-awareness. Even when life is brimming over with blessings, I am alert to areas of need, to the feeling that something is remiss and warrants attention. It's like a little button that gets pushed somewhere deep inside that signals *more*. This is particularly relevant when it comes to purpose and fulfillment, because I know there's so much more

I want to do before I leave this Earth. That knowing keeps me reaching deeper, wider, and farther to a higher self. Toward more peace, satiety, creativity, and fulfillment. It keeps me growing in the direction of my True North.

It took me quite a long time to get to the place where I could recognize my soul's calling and abide by it no matter what—or whom—came into my life. I've often used romantic partnership as a distraction from the hard work of pursuing my own goals and dreams. It's so tempting to get lost in love and put your destiny on hold, but eventually, it catches up. You can't get that time back, so commit to yourself and find balance between your destiny and your distractions. Even a new exercise regiment can be a way to numb out any pain of dreams unfulfilled, albeit in a healthy way. A destiny unfulfilled will take the form of various negative states of being, like anxiety and depression. When acute, these are easily quelled by a robust workout. You have to be careful to recognize this, and not chase endorphins to cover over your feelings instead of addressing the real problem.

When I truly became attuned to *me*, my unique path and purpose, I stopped allowing myself to stall on my dreams. It's no wonder I haven't yet found "the one"; he's been waiting on me to find myself first, and the strides I've taken the last few years to project a voice that is hell-bent on effecting mass positive change on the planet, including writing this book, are putting me there.

Stay Triple A: Attuned, Aware, Aligned. Use your intuition to inform you about how to stay Triple A, so you are guided toward what will keep you safe, healthy, and happy on your path to fulfillment.

Repeat the following words, like a meditation mantra, when you need help staying Triple A:

Universe, source energy, all that is: keep me safe and protected as I uncover and follow my true purpose on this Earth. Allow me to trust my intuition to tell me when I am where I need to be, and also to tell me when I am not. Give me the courage to pursue my dreams, even when doubt threatens to pull me off course. Give me the discipline to stay that course though temptations may distract me. Infuse into me the energy that I need to live out my dreams, and bless me with the integrity to work toward that which is in the highest service of the Universe and its constituents.

8
On Fertile Ground

The management of fertility is one of the most important functions of adulthood.
—Germaine Greer

For most folks, one of their body's biggest tasks in a lifetime is to spawn new little bodies. Staying healthy is among the most effective ways to boost fertility and increase the chances of a successful pregnancy. Guys, in case you checked out just now, check back in. You are half of the equation when it comes to making babies. You produce the sperm that fertilizes those eggs, and you need to keep yourself as fit and healthy as your partner. When a couple goes in for fertility testing, the male partner's sperm is analyzed first because it's far less invasive to do so. And, I hate to break it to you, but new research indicates that men are overtaking women as the root cause of infertility in relationships.[48] Your health and habits could make or break your attempts to start a family. In addition, in whatever capacity you exist in relationship to the women in your lives—as romantic partners, best friends, sons, brothers, grandsons, brothers-in-law, step brothers, half brothers, caretakers, caregivers or colleagues—this information is just as important for you. To foster growth in these relationships, and bring light, love, and knowledge to them, takes understanding—understanding of what it means to be a woman and the predominant challenges women face. One of the biggest is fertility and childbearing. To understand the subtleties of this issue for the women in your lives will mean you can relate and communicate. This understanding and support is so vital for women. They flourish with it, whither without it. And if the women are happy, the planet is happy. She's not called Mother Earth for no reason.

Now that I've got the males' attention . . . . Women—especially those hovering around thirty—pay special heed to the words that follow. If you hope to have babies at some point in the future, this section will enlighten you to the things you can do now to give you options later. Many women are simply not attuned to these realities. For example, there are consequences to smoking and excessive drinking (which I define as the chronic imbibing of more than one drink per day) that are easier to bounce back from when we are younger. As we age, and our bodies become more susceptible to wear and tear, we must be more mindful of how our actions impact our system as a whole. I get much more depressed after drinking in my thirties than

I did in my twenties, and I ascribe this to a body that is older and less capable of removing the impurities and toxins that affect the whole system, including the brain and its chemistry. Alcohol is a depressant, so its effect on the brain is to suppress activity, giving the telltale signs of drunkenness like slurred speech and clumsiness. No wonder then that you wake up feeling low and slow after a night of heavy drinking.

We've already discussed how engaging in activities that stress your body in unhealthy ways (like poor diet leading to inflammation) makes it less capable of routine upkeep and maintenance. This includes your eggs and sperm, and the organs in which they are stored. We tend to relate alcoholism to the liver, or smoking to the lungs, but it is all one system, and these vital parts of your body are susceptible to all of the same toxins and unhealthy habits. It's widely acknowledged that women who smoke do not conceive as efficiently as nonsmokers. In fact, some research points to the rate of infertility in smokers as *twice* that of nonsmokers. This shouldn't come as a surprise given that when you smoke, more than 7,000 chemicals spread throughout your entire body and organs.[49] In my female friends who are smokers, I've noticed a high degree of fertility difficulties. If you are a smoker, and hoping to get pregnant at some point in the future, *quit*. The body is resilient and can bounce back from the damaging effects of the tobacco, but to what degree is uncertain, so the sooner the better.

In addition to avoiding unhealthy habits to preserve your fertility, it is vital to keep your body (and, therefore, your eggs) optimally healthy. Use this book, and many of the pieces of learning from it, to help you do this. Much of what we've already talked about, relative to keeping your mind and body stress-and-inflammation-free, are directly applicable here. In terms of diet, a daily green smoothie cocktail can help you get a spectrum of the superfoods you need to keep your body thriving. The one I've concocted contains a blend of greens for vitamins, minerals and fiber, walnuts and ground flax seed with omega-3 fatty acids for healthy brain and heart function, berries for antioxidants, and a banana for potassium (see the Appendix for the full recipe).

Omega-3's are a class of polyunsaturated fatty acids that seem to drastically lower inflammation and cardiovascular disease risk. In addition, imbibing them has incredibly beneficial effects on brain functioning, correlated with lower risk of depression, Alzheimer's, and dementia. Since your body can't make them, you have to get them through your diet. Salmon is one of the most powerful foods I've come across for its high omega-3 content (not so tasty in a smoothie though). There are other fishes, like sardines and mackerel, that contain high doses of omega-3's, but they are much stronger in taste. Omega-3's can also be found in plant-based foods, like broccoli and leafy greens, walnuts, and soybeans, but your body has to convert them to the right form, and they are in less potent concentrations to begin with.

Let's Talk about Stress, Bay-Bee

Stress is an important part of the conversation when talking about fertility because it suppresses a woman's ability to conceive. For our genes, a body under stress is a suboptimal vessel in which to bring a baby to term. Think again about evolutionary adaptation; stress indicated threats to survival in the environment, like potential predators and limited access to food. Getting pregnant at such a time would likely not result in a healthy new baby who could withstand the elements. Better to wait until the environment was safe again to give the child maximum chances for survival, signaled to the body as a mind that was calm and peaceful. Remember again that our bodies are not yet adept at discerning "tiger" stress from "boss" stress, so the realities of our modern world throw us into a chronic stress cycle. This wreaks havoc on our fertility. Everything that we can do to decrease our levels of stress, and the pursuant inflammation, helps us stay optimally healthy and signals "readiness" to make a baby.

As we've already discussed, exercise is a key factor in quashing stress and fighting inflammation. It also keeps cells youthful, and there is a clear and strong correlation between a young and healthy body and fertility. This may sting a little for those of us over age thirty-five, who would be considered "geriatric mothers" according to standard medical terminology—at least until the more PC "advanced maternal age" starts to become *de rigueur*. Ever seen *Bridget Jones' Baby*? Her hilarious expression of jilted surprise at being labeled a "geriatric mother" in her early forties says it all.

Nature is designed to deselect older eggs through the advent of menopause. The time limit on when we can conceive and bear children is the essence of the biological clock. With no chances of getting pregnant later in life, any babies born are from younger eggs with the highest changes of being healthy. To stay young, you have to keep your cells young, and what dictates a cell's age is its DNA.[50]

DNA is packaged into X-shaped structures in the cell called chromosomes. Each time a cell divides and copies its DNA, the ends of the chromosomes—called telomeres—get shorter. Shrinking telomeres are a sign of aging. Turns out, exercise boosts production of a compound in the body that protects the ends of telomeres from being snipped away, keeping them longer, and keeping you young.[51] Just remember that overdoing it with marathons or activities that will excessively tax your body and not allow you to maintain a certain amount of fat stores is not optimal for conception, either. Indeed, there is evidence to show that strenuous exercise can have a negative impact on fertility. So keep it in moderation. When you work out, make sure the body has the recovery time it needs to repair and build stronger. You can understand why nature would not put a baby in a body that couldn't feed it; fat stores mean mama has some extra resources to support growing a new human in her womb.

Another way to keep cells young is by extracting them and freezing them when they *are* young, putting the biological clock on "pause." Modern technology has made it possible for women to preserve their fertility by cryogenically freezing their eggs.

A few years ago, a close friend (knowing my romantic heart and unwillingness to "settle" just to settle down) wondered why I wouldn't just freeze my eggs. This way, I wouldn't feel pressured while I waited for the right partner to manifest. I was approaching thirty-five, so I decided to explore the process. I went to the initial consultation with a specialist, and decided I would go for it. I had the requisite blood work done, and an ultrasound to determine when I should start the hormone injections. All that was left to do was go to the final appointment, learn how to use the injectables, pick up the $10,000 worth of hormones, and begin. I brought my mom with me, and as I sat there with two nurses, learning how to inject the hormones into the fleshy part of my backside to stimulate release of eggs, my mother's eyes held deep consternation and doubt. Once back in the car, on our way to pick up the hormones from the pharmacy, my mother looked me straight in the eye and said, "Is this what you really want to do?"

From the time we met back in seventh grade, my best friend would say that all she wanted was to skip her early twenties—including the commensurate partying and dating—and go straight to having a family of her own. I remember thinking she was crazy. I already wanted to stay in my twenties forever, and I hadn't even lived them yet. No wonder I remain happily single, and she well-settled—such convictions are powerful. She was married by twenty-five, and had her first child before she turned thirty. My sisters also showed nurturing instincts early on; taking care of others was second nature, and they loved cooking big meals. They always wanted families, and both were married in their twenties and had children soon after.

I had no such conviction around motherhood, but I did when it came to love. I wanted to be madly in love with whomever I married, to really be seen, and supported, and I wasn't going to settle for anything less. Any babies born as a product of that kind of love would be the greatest blessing. Ironically, it took being married at twenty-five, to a partner who didn't love me in the way that I needed, to figure out this fundamental truth within. Once I did, however, I never let it go.

My mother's question was loaded with the subtext of that truth, and I knew the answer. *No.* Contemplating options to have a baby without a partner was simply not my desire. And while freezing my eggs would buy me extra time to have biological children while I waited for my twin flame to show up, the decision, though a solid insurance policy, felt less than clear. Adoption has always been on my radar, and I felt at peace with the idea. We're one family of humanity, after all, so it's part of our meta level jurisdiction and responsibility to take care of each other. That includes each other's babies. As Hillary Clinton has famously stated, "It takes a village to raise a child." To me, adoption is simply the action of one member of the village of humanity taking responsibility for a child when their biological parents cannot provide them with the nurturing and care they need. Point is, I had options that precluded me from feeling desperate to have my own biological child through egg-freezing. At least for the time being, I let the idea go.

*****

Whatever the flow of your life, receive it as a gift and find gratitude in the way it unfolds. Meantime, do what you can to ensure your dreams have the highest chance of coming true. If that means having the experience of giving birth, and/or raising a biological child, then do what you must to take good care of yourself now so that you can support life later.

Sunny-Side Up

A friend of mine, a smoker around age forty, recently gave birth to a beautiful baby girl. It was the culmination of a long and arduous journey. She and her husband had tried for years to conceive naturally before resorting to in vitro fertilization. They found themselves saddled with mounting frustration, the probability of a successful pregnancy grim as she produced only one or two eggs per cycle. After several unsuccessful rounds, they decided to try using donor eggs. They chose a young woman in her mid-twenties, a healthy non-smoker and non-drinker, who, after taking the hormones to induce egg release, produced twenty-two viable eggs on her first try. They ended up with several fertilized embryos, and once implanted, one of them took, and she became pregnant. My friend and her husband were able to use his sperm, a donor egg, and her womb to create this miracle baby in their lives. The fact that she had to use a donor egg was nothing to despair over, nor feel any less than overjoyed about. If her eggs were not taking, it was simply nature's way of ensuring healthy children as and when possible.

As an aside, my friend shared with me that her baby rarely cries or fusses, and that she is generally just content and happy. I congratulated her on the gift of such an affable child, and told her it must be the Universe balancing the many challenges she had to face to bring her into the world. She laughed and acknowledged that while that might be true, she also had another hypothesis: Babies need a fourth trimester. She had read a book called *The Happiest Baby on the Block* before her daughter was born, and it made the infant's first few months settled and happy ones—which revolutionized those first few months for her parents, too.

The book explains how, early in human evolution, babies gestated for closer to a year, more than happy to take that extra time in the womb to grow and ready themselves for the outside world. In the process, however, swathes of mothers were dying in childbirth, unable to sustain the delivery of such large creatures. Ultimately, nature found a happier balance, birthing babies at nine months. The consequence, as the book theorizes, is that it was too soon for their comfort, leading to agitated, scared, and unprepared infants. Special care must therefore be taken in the first few months of the baby's life to make sure they feel soothed and sheltered, like recreating the womb atmosphere in the nursery. I'm fascinated by this theory, and had to share it with you because it could transform your own baby's earliest experiences.

I began this section by sharing inspirations about the success of Olympic athletes, namely, that a seismic shift in achievement is the result of consistent incremental steps. The lesson is to be the Olympian of your own thriving. Add ounces of the best ingredients to your life recipe every day, with consistency, to find optimal well-being.

I've given you many examples of how to integrate changes into your life that will set you on a higher path, but it's on you to execute. When you feel too tired, weak, lethargic, unmotivated, or just plain sad to take a step forward, remember that Olympic gymnasts often take those steps on a balance beam barely four inches across. You got this.

The Spirit

Educating the mind without educating the heart is no education at all.
—Aristotle

I believe in science. That might seem a funny thing to say starting a section on "The Spirit," but the two are inextricably intertwined. I see the domain of science as the "objective" reality, that is, the world around us that we can see and measure, like the Earth, sky, and oceans. It follows repeatable traits and patterns, and we can quantify elements in it. The "subjective" reality includes the realm of the intangible, which I call *spirituality*. It is all of those phenomena we cannot see, like the mind or spirit, but have faith in the existence of. Faith in these phenomena, though they may elude our eyes, fortifies our connection to something bigger than ourselves, to a Universal source energy. This keeps us searching for meaning. Both are necessary because what science cannot often explain, spirituality can make room for, and what spirituality cannot make apparent, science can ground in proof. When science seeks answers to questions, and posits theories to make sense of those questions, spirituality keeps us unbounded and unconstrained, always seeking higher truths and questioning the "answers" we've already found. If science is decidedly logical, spirituality is nonlinear. It's like the left and right brains, one side rational and the other creative. We need both to be complete.

Science abides by the *analytic* method, meaning that any elements comprising a theory are based not on hypothesis (think "hypothetical," not yet "real") but on empirical discovery (think "evidence"). The analytic method involves positing theories based on careful and deliberate observation and exploration. Formulas are created to package these theories into something quantifiable. Take Newton for an example. He was a quintessential scientist, most famous for discovering the existence of a little something called "gravity." His theory of gravity came about as he sat under an apple tree, observing the fruit falling to the ground. He asked himself why the apple should fall perpendicularly? What force was compelling it downward toward the Earth? He realized that the same force that brought the apple crashing to the ground was also responsible for keeping the moon falling toward the Earth, and the Earth falling toward the sun.[52] His theory of gravity was born, and a corresponding equation formulated to quantify it.

The laws of thermodynamics, which define physical states like temperature, energy, and entropy (the measure of a system's disorder), adhere to the analytic method. The first law of thermodynamics, also known as the *law of conservation of energy*, states that energy can neither be created nor destroyed, only transferred or changed from one form to another.[53] Think about switching on a light. The observation would be that the light creates electricity when you turn it on. In truth, the light bulb is only a conduit, a vehicle for electrical energy (which is invisible to the naked eye) to flow through and become visible. Thomas Edison made this connection through his observation of electricity. He understood that even if we can't "see" energy being transferred, it is very much flowing and the first law of thermodynamics holds. Again, all theories begin with an observation of how something appears to behave and are then packaged into a hypothesis or formula. Until such an observation is made and a theory posited, however, we rely on the realm of spirituality to help us make meaning of the phenomenon we can't explain. It's a tag-team.

I count figures like Albert Einstein, Jill Bolte Taylor, Brian Weiss, and Eben Alexander (to name just a few) among my gurus for their unique positioning as brilliant scientists who have cemented the bridge to spirituality. Before I arrived on campus at the University of Pennsylvania as an undergraduate, I was assigned the book *Einstein's Dreams* as summer reading. During my first week of orientation, the book was a focal point for discussion and debate among cohorts of the incoming freshmen. I still remember how it made me reconsider something I took completely for granted: Time as a linear construct. Long-held facts were jiggled loose as I contemplated time as circular, or folded over on itself like an accordion. Provoked, I began to research the life and work of Albert Einstein, and came across the following quote: "The basic laws of the universe are simple, but because our senses are limited, we can't grasp them. There is a pattern in creation."[54] This experience gave me pause to consider how the human mind must rationalize events in order to make sense of them. If time is linear, there is a beginning, an end, and a finite life span during which to "exist." You get one shot—a period of roughly eighty years if you're lucky—and you do what you can before the ride is over. This is much simpler to grasp than the infinite, which comes with infinite possibilities. But, for that simplicity, we sacrifice the expansive; we tend to be myopic in our assessment of the tide of life and our place on it. A short-sighted, finite view makes us self-focused, and desperate to win, acquire, and amass before the sands in the hourglass run through.

What if we suspended our belief in reality as we perceived it, took away the hourglass and bathed in infinite sand? If we widened the sphere of possibility, what potential might we uncover? If we had faith in a divine design, discovering the unity among all things, how might our lives unfold differently? Asking these questions, and being brave enough to seek out the answers, is the work of the spirit.

9
The Spirit Trip

You have to take seriously the notion that understanding the universe is your responsibility.
—**Terence McKenna**

You may recall my description of Jill Bolte Taylor's "stroke of insight" from Section I. In a dramatic and unforeseen unfolding, the Harvard neuroanatomist suffered a stroke that suspended her ability to process linearly. The gift in it was, she gained access to the realm of the infinite. Without needing as grave an access point, there are ways to suspend logic and linearity and explore the vastness and oneness of the Universe, allowing you to bridge the ostensible gap between the objective and subjective realities. Such "cosmic trips" are controversial because they generally involve imbibing medicines containing compounds the government has deemed illegal. Among the most common are psilocybin, LSD, peyote, ayahuasca, and DMT (dimethyltryptamine).

I'd be remiss if I didn't go a bit more in-depth into DMT in a discussion about the spirit. It's frequently referred to as "the spirit molecule," after all. DMT is a psychedelic compound that is structurally analogous to melatonin and serotonin, both of which are integral to a balanced and happy brain. Though accounts differ vastly in terms of detail and experience, there is a common thread of potent psychological healing in those who partake. Given the epidemic levels of anxiety, depression, and other mood disorders we are facing in the Western world, it seems quite foolish *not* to explore the potential of DMT as a healing modality.

Indigenous Amazonian cultures have been using it for divinatory and healing purposes for centuries in the form of ayahuasca (pronounced *eye-oh-waska*), a brew made by mixing the Banisteriopsis caapi vine with the leaves of certain plants containing DMT. I first read about ayahuasca in a *National Geographic* article written by a young woman named Kira Salak, who ventured deep into the Peruvian Amazon to experience a "shamanic tour" as part of a story she was writing. It was on this assignment that she experienced ayahuasca for the first time, and her experience was profound—the major depression she had lived with her entire life vanished.

A health practitioner with some depressive episodes under my own belt, I am consistently drawn to any healing modality that might help resolve what is one of the most troubling and prolific mental health issues that humans face. Pharmaceuticals are our go-to for the treatment of depression, though they are far from ideal. They alleviate symptoms, but do little to wrangle with the source of the psychological distress before heaping a mountain of side effects onto the patient and causing further troubles. Salak describes how she had invested years in the best of what modern medicine had to offer for the treatment of depression, from extensive therapy to biofeedback, all to scanty avail. It wasn't until she found herself in the jungles of Peru for her first shamanic healing that she felt real relief from her depression for the first time. In Kira's words, "as if a waterlogged coat had been lifted from my shoulders."[55]

Powerful and life-changing as the experience was for her, Salak cautions that this complex and rigorous ritual is not for the faint of heart: "You must be brave. You will be learning how to save yourself." She's alluding to the intensity of the experience, which involves a lot of purging—literally, everyone is provided a bucket for the profuse vomiting—and metaphorically, as you work your way through the "mud" of your illness and experience visions of darkness and demons, uncovering and confronting past traumas. Kira's descriptions are so vivid, vulnerable, and self-effacing that I was primed to receive her ultimate conclusion: Where no modern medicine had been able to help her, she found her cure in ayahuasca.

My search for more information on the molecular composition of the brew led me to Ethnobotanist Terence McKenna. Through McKenna's research, I came to understand and appreciate DMT as a powerful source of spiritual enlightenment. DMT is the molecule responsible for the transformations Kira describes, and is in fact organically manufactured by the human brain. Several days in a dark room—fourteen to be exact—is apparently what it will take to engender the right circumstances for your brain to produce DMT on its own, so you can experience the spiritual journey "naturally" (with the caveat that fourteen days in a dark room seems anything but) without having to ingest a foreign substance to kick-start it. There's a chemical sequence that takes place, wherein a buildup of melatonin in the brain from the extended darkness results in the pineal gland producing a superconductor molecule called pinolene. The pinolene stage—normally activated during lucid dreaming and near-death experiences—triggers the production of a neurohormone that switches more of the brain on (as much as forty percent more of the cerebral cortex). That's when you enter the DMT stage, where you purportedly can journey into hyperspace through the "third eye," beyond three-dimensional realms of time and space. Sound "out there"? It quite literally is. But tales of ayahuasca journeys abound, and folks who have done it share some common themes and experiences, in particular that drinking this ancient brew leads to a change in consciousness—a profound shift that results in spiritual healing.

The journey seems to engender a deep reverence for the sacred nature of life on Earth, which few could deny the planet sorely needs right now. We're killing our planet with our disregard for her health and balance, and if we don't intervene soon, we'll lose our life support. Do you ever think about how much human beings produce just in the form of the contents of drugstores, supermarkets, retail stores, and restaurants? Where does all that crap *go*? We generate it, but we pay no heed to where it lands. We only care about the sale. I often wonder how that can possibly be, how we are not held more accountable to our individual contributions in polluting the Earth. The answer boils down to financial gain, which is also why certain power players on the planet deliberately keep us away from anything that can shake us awake to these truths—including ayahuasca.

Author and journalist Graham Hancock gives a profound TED Talk on the intricate chemistry involved in making the ayahuasca brew, and, like Kira Salak, forewarns to "brace yourself" for the journey. He's careful to stress that it's not a recreational trip, but rather a very serious journey to heal the spirit. In his dispassionate yet personal account, Hancock describes tales of serious drug users (he himself was a heavy cannabis user) ingesting the brew and being freed completely of their addictions.

I am fascinated and encouraged by the potential of this "spirit trip" as a healing modality. The main caveat I give here is that like with any therapy or medicine, DMT should only be taken in a controlled, therapeutic setting with the right professionals. The second caveat is that the Western definition of "professional" may differ from that in other geographical centers; each system has its own way of training. Stay open and vigilant so that you don't get pigeon-holed by ascribing only to systems you are familiar with. A shaman who has been studying plant medicine for decades and has a legacy of several centuries behind her has a degree of knowledge we may not be able to quantify against a traditional Western degree. I encourage you to research further, use your gut, follow trusted sources, and find out for yourself whether the ancient practice of taking this spirit trip could be an effective and potentially life-saving tool toward optimal psychological health and spiritual evolution.

10
The Soul's Journey

The main requirement for spiritual growth:
A yearning to know who you really are.
—Adyashanti

On the subject of controversial but powerful healing techniques in the domain of the spiritual, we should chat about past-life regression therapy (PLRT). PLRT is a technique that uses hypnosis to recover memories of past lives or previous incarnations. It's an exploration of iterations of our soul's journey in different lifetimes, eras, and physical forms, and can also be used to uncover repressed or forgotten memories from this lifetime.

I was first introduced to the concept after reading *New York Times* bestseller *Many Lives, Many Masters* by Dr. Brian Weiss. In the book, Weiss describes his experiences working with a young woman named Catherine for whom "traditional" therapy (from his training in psychiatry) was proving ineffective to alleviate recurring nightmares and panic attacks. Out of options, he decided to try hypnotherapy. Like meditation, hypnotherapy is just a tool to get you to a place of deep relaxation and focused concentration so that the memory sharpens and you can remember long-forgotten incidents.[56] Long-forgotten indeed. During their hypnotherapy sessions, Catherine seemed to recall traumas and repressed memories from other *lifetimes*. Doubtful as he was about the veracity of these "memories," Dr. Weiss was amazed at her progress. With each subsequent session, Catherine's symptoms improved, and her inner light seemed to shine more brightly. Eventually, her symptoms completely disappeared.

Weiss too became a believer when, during one of their sessions, Catherine shared revelations about his own family, particularly about a son that he and his wife had lost. His "dead" son sent him a message through Catherine, and he could not deny the truth of what was unfolding. Weiss' experience with Catherine forever altered the course of his life. He is now known for his ability to successfully cure patients of their psychological ailments and phobias using past-life regression therapy. He also trains other healers in this modality, and found himself sitting across from Oprah Winfrey recently to share his story.

I believe such situations are divinely ordered by the Universe, à la Einstein's theory that everything happens according to a larger design. When a hard-core scientist, trained to be analytical and "rational," finds a portal to the spiritual realm in such dramatic fashion, it strikes me as obtuse to chalk it up to coincidence. That seed was planted.

It would be several years after reading *Many Lives, Many Masters* before I myself would get certified in PLRT, training with the master himself, Brian Weiss. And if that weren't dreamy enough, I wasn't even looking for the opportunity. It found me.

I was on a trip to Turks and Caicos with some girlfriends, and as we lounged on the soft white sand of the beach watching the slowly setting sun trace its arc toward the horizon, we rapped about spiritual journeys. Sue brought up a seminar conducted by Dr. Weiss that she and a mutual friend had attended in New York. "He also does trainings," she said. I had no idea he even held such seminars, much less trained other practitioners in the craft. It was like being offered the chance to go on a quest to a magic kingdom. I felt called to the training, a pure conviction from deep within to explore this realm of therapy.

A handful of months later, it was manifesting. I had secured a spot in one of Dr. Weiss's coveted trainings, a wild card entry from the long wait list. I felt an incredible excitement in my body and a simultaneous peace in my heart as I coasted through the gates of the Omega Institute for the training. The drive up had been spectacular, an end-of-October bonanza of changing foliage, rare verdant pockets attempting to assert themselves amidst a sea of glimmering yellows, shiny reds and crispy browns. The trees' transitions seemed to mirror my impending transformation, and I was buzzing with potential.

Two days in, and the excitement gave way to anxiety. I hadn't yet had an "experience" (Dr. Weiss's label for an exploration into a past life), and I was beginning to wonder if I was going to leave here in five days uninitiated and disappointed, "heavily meditated" stamped across my forehead. I walked up to Dr. Weiss and expressed my consternation. He told me to roll my eyeballs upward toward the sky (a test of how receptive a patient is to hypnotherapy) and smiled. He placed a hand on my shoulder and told me I should be patient. When I was ready to "go there," I would be able to do so with ease. I let this sink in over lunch, knowing full well that although my creative right-brain hemisphere was strong and active, my left brain was as potent, talking to me often and all too aware of boundaries, scientific definitions, and limitations. During our first few sessions, almost as soon as I would relax deeply, thoughts would infringe on the space being created, conjuring up all manner of doubts . . . *What if I do see something? How can I trust it's not just a hallucination? Or a projection of my imagination? What would my dad say about all this? He'd call it "hogwash. . . ."*

We watched a video when we came back from lunch. It was a taping of a session with a prominent New York City news anchor, who, curious about past-life therapy, had agreed to be regressed and have it filmed. I watched as Dr. Weiss led her back to her earliest memories of childhood, and she began to describe the day of her birth. I could hardly believe what I was hearing. Memories of being *one day old?* She saw the hospital room, heard her father's jovial banter with the nurses, even felt her mother's disgust at the man in the adjacent room who was trying to force his wife to have sex with him just hours after giving birth to their baby. She recalled it all in vivid—and as it turns out, accurate—detail. When she later asked her parents about the circumstances surrounding her birth, they corroborated everything she had experienced in her regression. I couldn't understand how a newborn could take in details of their environment like that, let alone understand the words being spoken. Or pick up on such mature states of emotion as her mother's upset? And have it all stored somewhere to be able to talk about decades later? None of it made sense, not according to the standard rules or definitions we have regarding how infants, time, and memory work anyway. Once I accepted that, I was able to relax my mind around needing to know *why* and just began to focus on the *how* and the *what*.

Following the video, Dr. Weiss led us into a regression in which we visualized walking down endless flights of stairs, a metaphor for reaching deep into the cavernous recesses of the memory. During a regression, an adept practitioner will aim to ease you into a space of deep relaxation so that you can unhinge your hold on anything that you've repressed, opening the vault of your experience. I suppose it worked, because as soon as Dr. Weiss primed us to go back to our birth, I felt a flood of memories and feelings rush in. *I was having an experience.* But the color and tone were not what I had expected for my birth-day. Instead of sounds of joy and excitement, I was aware only of solitude, fear, and sadness. I felt detached and cold. I heard the muffled voices of doctors and nurses as they pulled me out of my mother's open belly into a too-brightly lit operating room, stark white and dim yellow throwing a pallid hue over everything.

It took me quite a while to talk about this experience with anyone, jarring as it was to try to reconcile the paradox of a baby's birth—usually associated with immense joy and warmth—as an unhappy event, especially when that baby was me. I eventually broached the subject with my mother, who, visibly uncomfortable, said brusquely, "You need to just let it go." I implored her not to cast the conversation aside, even though I could tell it hurt her to acknowledge. I knew well enough by now that this memory could be linked to unhealthy patterns in my own life, and as such might be a chance for healing and growth. I wanted that chance. My mom sighed, looked down, and reluctantly explained to me that the day I was born, she went to the hospital for the surgery—a scheduled C-section—alone. My father put her in a cab to "get things started" while he stayed home and saw to my aging grandmother and one-and-a-half-year-old sister. Ever the logical (and less-than-sentimental) engineer, this was the most efficient plan of execution as far as my dad was concerned. Efficient, perhaps, but also deeply wounding. My poor momma, a new immigrant in a foreign country, found herself giving birth—and going through major surgery—by herself. It must have been especially difficult for her given that she grew up in a family of seven, and was accustomed to having consistent help and support in her midst. It was in a processing session later with a good friend that I would put it all together and become aware of the connection between the unhealthy attachment style I took on that first day of life, and the way I always engaged in relationships, holding on so tightly, afraid to let go even a little for fear of feeling isolation from those I felt the closest to.

There are four styles of attachment, as it were: secure, avoidant, ambivalent/anxious, and disorganized. How an infant relates to their caregivers, in other words what *attachment style* they develop, can have direct consequences on their relationship patterns in adulthood. All but "secure" are problematic. A secure attachment style in infancy manifests as an adult who is comfortable with intimacy, not overly worried about rejection nor preoccupied with the relationship. An avoidant style presents as someone uncomfortable with closeness and intimacy, who values independence and freedom over partnership. Craving closeness and intimacy, while also feeling very insecure about the relationship, is characteristic of an anxious style. And a disorganized style is a combination of avoidant and anxious, those who reject intimacy *and* worry about their partner's commitment, afraid to get close to them as a result.

I seemed to have suffered some of the ambivalent/anxious style in infancy, showing up over the years as a need to cling to the prominent relationships in my life. This generally came at the expense of my own growth and progress, as I spent valuable amounts of energy feeling anxious and paralyzed by fears that I would lose a boyfriend, a best friend, even my sister. Once I finally understood this truth, I was able to begin charting a new course, actively choosing a more secure, stable style of attachment over old ways of being.

My fear of loss has given way to a confident trust that I am whole. This implicit trust has brought me closer to those I love, not farther away. I don't have to work so hard to gain their love because I know that I already have it. An initial lack of trust was the seed of doubt planted as an infant, and it took me years to uncover it. Back on that first day of my life, I was surrounded by my mother's sadness and fear, not her reassurance, as she herself felt bereft and alone. This left me desperate, and I held on too tightly. I can remember my mother telling me stories of how I used to chew on the scarves she wore around her neck, leaving them riddled with holes. I realize now what a strong indication of anxiety that was, like grinding your teeth at night. Being able to tap into information from my earliest experiences and see my life from that perspective has liberated me. I feel immensely more confident in my relationships now, my expectations of them more balanced and reasonable. What an incredible outcome of regression therapy.

Others in the training uncovered similarly empowering revelations. One participant couldn't wear scarves around her neck, they made her feel constricted and desperately uncomfortable. In a regression conducted by Dr. Weiss in front of the group, we all witnessed her discover that she had been choked to death in a previous lifetime. Once she understood the root cause of her phobia, she was empowered to release it. She wore a scarf to class the next day. Another young woman connected with a sibling she had lost too young in a previous lifetime, which allowed her to make sense of the utter fear and anxiety she now held around her brother's welfare. Streams of tears flowed down her face as she recounted what she had seen; having this rationalization for her fears allowed them to wash away.

I myself saw into several lifetimes over the course of the next few days, and even now, the images that come back are as clear as any of my other memories. I know it all sounds pretty far out, but the truth is, past-life therapy has helped me discover unhealthy patterns that would have perpetuated if not for an enlightenment to their existence. In turn, this has allowed me to make sense of the way I relate to others, and get a handle on lingering phobias and predilections so they have no power to hold me back. The ability to take real ownership of your life in this way, fully free and unencumbered, is an invaluable gift. Past-life therapy acts as a window into the soul's journey, giving us insights into where we've been, and what we carry with us. We can use this information to detach from anything that is no longer in our service, leaving it behind so we can make bigger leaps in our growth. Ultimately, it's all in the highest interest of our spiritual evolution.

11
You Gotta Have Faith

Whether or not it is clear to you, no doubt the universe is unfolding as it should.
—Max Ehrmann

To have faith is to trust in the divine design of the Universe, even when we don't have all of the answers in front of us. The thing with faith is the keeping of it, because it will invariably be tested. For so long, I failed to understand how a higher power could be at work in a world fraught with suffering. And now, as I dive deeper into my spiritual study, and into positive psychology, particularly post-traumatic growth, I am awestruck by the immense power that gets unleashed through the vehicle of suffering. Human beings can find unparalleled elevation and beauty through it. As such, it's almost as if we need to fall in order to rise to our highest height. This applies to all aspects of our lives, and for me, nowhere is it more evident than in love.

Since I have been blessed to know the very deepest kind of love, I am resolutely unwilling to compromise on feeling anything less when it comes to choosing my life mate. It's a brave move for a woman, especially an Indian one, to hold her ground and stay single, laying claim to a divine right to be in absolute love and loyalty to her partner, or be in solitude. And as men come into and out of my life, my faith is constantly tested around what it is I'm holding out for. Each time I deny a suitor, I wonder if I'm crazy. Or too romantic. Or too independent. Or too picky.

Back in high school, one of my favorite classmates told me she was sure I would marry a British man. I remember giggling when she told me, cocking my head to the side in amusement as I contemplated the prophecy. My older sister had married a Brit, and we had family there, so we felt comfortable in the land of tea, scones, and fascinators. India, after all, had been under British rule for years, and the impression left was indelible. I also break into the accent regularly, much to the amusement of many a Brit who assume I am a native until I come clean. It seemed fitting I'd end up with such a bloke . . .

 I was slated to work through the New Year on a project with my production team. Far from feeling frustration over having to work on a holiday, I was charged up, ready to access more of my creative talent and let it shine. I was deeply committed to prioritizing that exploration over other temptations, like travel. It felt wonderfully novel and satisfying to tell everyone I was staying local for the holidays to work on "scripting and designing."

On the evening of the thirty-first, the team made a game-time decision to take New Year's day off. I was dog-tired from all of the creative output, and had a new year not been ready to turn over, I would surely have stayed in. But, the idea of being alone, home-bound, and sleeping through what many consider to be the most significant night of the year was too unorthodox, even for my independent spirit. I peeled myself off of the couch and ended up at a close friend's house party, resolved to make like Cinderella and leave just after midnight.

Upon arriving, I wondered if I'd even make it to twelve o'clock, having scanned the room and realizing I hardly knew any of the other invitees. And then I noticed a handsome fellow with dark brown wavy hair standing at the other end of the room. We locked eyes and shared a smile. *A single guy around my age?* This was house party gold for a girl showing up solo on New Year's Eve. The vibe was sweet and immediate as we got to talking, like old friends reconnecting after years. His presence anchored me, and I was drawn to stay, eventually enjoying easy conversation with the other folks at the party, my midnight curfew long gone.

I had just plopped down on the couch for a breather, barely ten of us left, when the door opened. In walked three new arrivals, among them a dusky complexioned looker with a slender, toned frame. He wore a black beanie and a scarf wrapped around his neck, his denim jacket audacious given the cold outside. I noticed him immediately from my vantage point on the couch, and felt a swell inside. Objectively, I found him extremely handsome. But it was deeper than that, more visceral. My heart started to pound, and I felt a quick sweat slick my underarms. Was he even real? How was it possible that two handsome single men ended up at the same party I almost didn't go to on New Year's Eve, both within my sphere and both so enchanting? I was in some kind of flow with the Universe. I barely had time to contemplate the magic of all this before I saw the New Addition striding towards me from the kitchen.

He took a place next to me on the couch, and I couldn't tell you what those first words were, so distracted was I by his accent. *British*. The hours glided by as we learned about each other, and I discovered he was one-half Indian, and one-half black. He had grown up in London, and was now living in Philadelphia. I swear, this was the *exact* description of type I had conjured up in my imagination many times; mocha-complexioned, some mixture of races (ideally Indian and black), dark wavy hair, a British accent, good-looks that were more a matter of taste than objectivity. And each time I would indulge the vision, I would simultaneously acknowledge the absolute rarity of such a specimen on the planet.

And then somehow, like the law of attraction doing its finest work, at a house party in a neighborhood clear across the city that I almost didn't go to because I was supposed to be working, surrounded by American accents, mostly white faces, bikers, and tattoos, the embodiment of what I had been envisioning, down to the British accent and mocha skin, ended up right next to me on a couch.

We made a date to hang out at the end of the weekend as his son would be with his mom, and he had the evening free. I was buzzing with anticipation, incredulous at the power of manifestation. I could hardly wait for Sunday to arrive and witness this dream manifesting further into reality.

Seeing him standing in my doorway not two days later, my open heart gaped wider still. I was so ready to be done looking for "the one." And, well, this *had* to be *it*, didn't it? Sara's British man prophecy had foretold it, after all. Over the course of conversation and two bottles of burgundy, he shared more of his life, including the tragic murder of his brother in London just a few years prior. Tears sprang to my eyes thinking of my own siblings and what life would be like if I ever lost one of them, giving me some small window into the depths of his grief. We talked about shared experiences, including respective divorces, and, as an added bonus, discovered we were very close to the same age. When he left that evening, I immediately called my sister to gush about what had happened. Her voice was full of glee as she reveled in the joy that her little sister might finally have found her match.

Over the next two days, I heard nothing from him. My rational mind knew he could be busy with his son or playing it cool. My heart, however, knew otherwise. This behavior was not commensurate with the immediate organic chemistry we had shared, or the magic of how it manifested. I reached out to see if he was all right, anxious and deeply agitated at being threatened with its evanescence. He replied that he appreciated the concern, and apologized— sometimes he withdrew from all connections, going solitary and reclusive. As much as I hated to think it true, and how desperately I wanted to resist a faltering, I could feel the embers growing cold. His abrupt withdrawal was a foreboding sign, and I steadied myself for dejection.

Days passed without communication, and I allowed the utter disappointment to wash through me as I grappled with the incongruity of manifesting what I thought I had wanted for so long, only to have it desert me. It seemed a cruel twist of fate, and I was angry at the Universe and Her Grand Design. I felt betrayed. I knew I was playing victim, when I should be empowering myself around the positives of the experience, like knowing my powers of manifestation were robust (even if misguided), or grateful that I wasn't more invested in the relationship before he ghosted. But I wasn't ready for that resilience yet. In the immediate aftermath, I could not reconcile why this would happen. Much to my frustration, no answers were forthcoming, either.

*****

Enter faith. We must trust that in time, and due course, the reasons reveal themselves. We aren't born with a rule book or a guide map, we aren't meant to. We are spiritual beings having a human experience, here to grow as we go. To be given the gift of life and navigate the journey for oneself, seeking and finding the answers to our own, very personal questions, is true living. Along the way, we must have faith in the unfolding, and surrender to this flow in complete and abiding trust that all is happening in our highest service. It's the only way to play it if you want to enjoy the ride without all of the unnecessary suffering.

I want you to absorb what I just offered, to really let it sink in and see if you can find some acceptance around not knowing *why*, as dissatisfying as that may sometimes feel. Author Mickey Singer's *The Surrender Experiment* may help. It's a manifesto in holding fast to your faith through every twist and turn of life, no matter what it offers up. The essential message of the book is to stay open and receptive to whatever comes your way, instead of holding too tightly to your wants and needs. Following the ego's superficial preferences of "like" or "dislike" can render you stuck or unhappily off track. In contrast, when you follow your spirit's essential quest for love, connection, and wonder, and pursue experiences out of pure passion, you end up in a place of bliss, infused with a contentment most crave but rarely enjoy because they're too stuck in their heads to allow their hearts—and the gentle guiding hand of the Universe—to lead the way.

That said, I don't want to leave you hanging on the "why" of the story I shared earlier, though it might already be apparent. True, I magnetized into my life exactly what I was envisioning, down to the British accent and Indian-Black fusion, proving the law of attraction and the power of manifestation are alive and kicking. However, the learning for me centered around the realization that we can want things from the level of the ego, like a certain look, a certain amount of wealth, or an accent that makes us giddy, and manifest it right into our lives, but that won't lead to flourishing. In order for the fulfillment of a desire to truly satiate us, it must come from a place of deep purity, generated at the soul level. Singer taught me that truth powerfully through his words, and the Universe reminded me of it in the form of folks who heard the story about the ghosting Brit and essentially called me out on what I *truly* want versus what I *think* I want. This enlightenment has released me from many judgments I was holding on to around the right life partner. Turns out, I'm not so concerned with what form they come in, only that they are a match for my spirit.

And so I wait, in faith, through every new experience, every date, every relationship attempt, and every British man who comes along, knowing that I'm living my own surrender experiment, and that what I seek requires patience and growth to manifest. The more I live into this faith, and surrender to the unfolding, the more life offers me hints that what I truly seek is yet to come.

 The following is based on an exercise I learned in a training called "The Silva Method." This practice is designed to help you connect to higher realms of consciousness, where you can re-attune to what you *really* want at the soul level, versus what you *think* you want at the ego level. It has the added layer of helping you align not just with what is in the highest service for *you*, but for *all* of humanity's constituents. Do good as you do well.

If you like, you can practice this exercise every day as a meditation:

1. Close your eyes and repeat "1" to yourself three times, visualizing the number "1" in your mind. If it helps, you can imagine drawing the number "1" in the air or on a chalkboard. Then, visualize the number "2," and again, repeat it to yourself three times. Do this again with the number "3."
2. Now, count backwards from "10 to 1" in your head.
3. From this place of focus, ask the Universe to help guide you in the direction of your *True North*. Ask that everything you receive, and everything you give, come from a place of the purest intention, and that it all be in the highest service of everyone everywhere.
4. When you are ready to release the practice, count forward from "1 to 5" in your mind, and open your eyes.

When you practice this exercise, pay attention to what comes up. Any symbols or images? Surprising or unexpected desires? Use the space below to journal about your experiences with it.

_____

_____

_____

_____

_____

_____

_____

_____

_____

_____

_____

_____

_____

_____

_____

Over time, you'll gain clarity on what you truly desire, and your actions will start to reflect this more pure and aligned direction. You'll start to magnetize back (law of attraction) more of the same. As you enjoy the bliss that comes from living authentically, you will be motivated to keep doing more of what makes you feel that way, which will make you feel even happier. That's the upward spiral called "living your truth."

12
The Ebb and Flow

I am not absentminded. It is the presence of mind that makes me unaware of everything else.
—G. K. Chesterton

Back in Section I, I described flow (also called "the zone" for you athletes) as the intersection between the level of skill you bring to a task and the challenge it offers. When level of skill is well-matched to challenge, a state of complete presence and attention can be achieved. It's full immersion in an activity with energized focus and enjoyment, thus allowing the flow-er to be freed of their perception of time and lose themselves in the task.

Many people chase the highs of drugs because they crave that feeling of time suspension, creative liberation, and relief from attachment to thoughts and pain. Working to find more flow in your life can give you the same feeling, and whereas drugs numb you to your life, pure flow is in fact quite the opposite—you are fully present to your life.

You may have noticed by now some of the parallels between the hallmarks of the flow state and those engendered in meditation—indeed, meditation can absolutely be flow-like. And, as with meditation, the price to pay for the unparalleled magic of such an experience is effort. Think about any top-level athlete, like NBA basketball players. The extremes of hours they've invested into the game are commensurate with how ready they are to drop into flow when they hit the court. Flow is a spiritual journey requiring effort and readiness. It's not about chasing flow down, but being prepared, faithfully putting in the effort until the opportune moment presents itself, even when you are tired, bored, or tempted to do something else. Like staying home to watch a movie instead of going to an open mic night (I'm raising my hand right now). You have to be gritty about your growth so you can get strong enough in whatever you are drawn to—singing, writing, basketball, surfing, yoga, poker, guitar—that when you find a flow opportunity, you are ready to meet it without fear or reservation. Like when that reality TV voice competition show holds auditions in your town, and you show up, confident and ready to own your evolution.

Finding flow demands vigilance with regard to your energy expenditure; invest your energy wisely, sparing it for your true passions and those experiences that will be deeply rewarding. This is not an easy thing to do, what with difficult choices around how to prioritize your passions and immediate versus long-term gratification. But I assure you, it is worth it. Finding flow pays off huge in your ability to achieve great things (the "A" in PERMA), which feeds directly into your flourishing. One of my besties reminds me often that if it's not a "*hell* yes," then it shouldn't be a "yes." I'm going to amend that slightly to, if it's not a "HEAVEN yes," then it shouldn't be a "yes."

I've learned to temper my zest for new experiences with a mindfulness that I want to be deliberate with my precious resources. I don't say "yes" to every opportunity I am offered, even if I am really tempted to indulge, as with chances to network and expand my professional horizons. These activities are never in vain, as I have found some of the most salient relationships in my life as a product of simply "showing up." But, networking usually means small talk, and I find it extremely draining. I can real talk for hours, vibing on conversation that is soulful or philosophical, because it energizes me, and makes me feel alive and connected. But the small talk, prattle that doesn't reward me with either growth or flow, depletes me. I even get light-headed, feeling myself float skyward to escape the tedium. When I've had an evening like that, my energy cup runs bare, and I sacrifice precious resources that I could otherwise channel into the creative pursuits that give me flow. I'm mindful of that now, and assess networking based on the opportunity cost to other areas of my life. Only you know what your energy limitations are, and where you want to prioritize the finite resources you have. The point is to be mindful of this, and choose wisely. The tools and exercises in this book are designed to help you along.

Being mindful of energy conservation has been quite relevant for me over the course of writing this book. It has taken every skill I have, not just in putting words on the page, but also in mindfulness (focus), memory to recall facts and experiences, patience to not lose it spending all of that time in solitude, or hurl my laptop against the wall when I just couldn't grab the right word or phrase, and grit in staying the course over hours, days, and months to get thoughts down that are authentic and beneficial. I had to make difficult choices, like not visiting my rapidly growing niece and nephew in India, or losing thousands of dollars in missed work opportunities. But, bringing this book to fruition was following flow, in the way that I was leveraging all of my innards to create a manifesto that was the very personification of skill meeting challenge, and as a direct result of this intersection, in the way hours would evaporate when I sat down to write.

Commitment to these words has also meant that when an idea surged toward me on a wave of inspiration, I had to hold it in my mind until I could write it down and flesh it out. Inevitably, these inspired moments happened in yoga classes, while driving, or talking to my family or friends, all scenarios not very conducive to halting and writing. I, therefore, had to stay very focused in the moment, making mental notes and recording thoughts as soon as I had the freedom to do so. It took a great deal of mental energy to stay "on" like this, actively listening and engaged in order to stay inspired. Most of the success here came straight down to mindfulness. In addition, that sustained energy came from reserves I had stockpiled, conserved from other situations where I had scaled back. Only if you conserve your energy will you have enough to bring to the next flow opportunity and the commitment and clarity to execute on a level commensurate with your mastery.

Use the following exercise to help you access more flow in your life.

A. Brainstorm some areas of your life that represent flow opportunities. Remember to think not just about where you already find flow, but also where you might access it anew. Examples of where it already shows up in your life might include playing video games or painting. An example of where you might access it anew is signing up for a class in something you find fascinating.

1. _____

_____

_____

2. _____

_____

_____

3. _____

_____

_____

B. What are some areas of your life that require a lot of energy and don't represent deeply rewarding experiences?

_____

_____

_____

C. What could you eliminate from your life to free up energy for your flow opportunities?

_____

_____

_____

D. Now, list three specific action steps you can take to get you closer to flow. For example, I find flow when I sing. My three action steps could be:

1. Cut time on social media in half—limit of one hour per day. Spend the extra time practicing guitar.
2. Limit social engagements to only those that are a "heaven yes" to conserve energy. Don't GO for FOMO.
3. Commit to two weekly practice sessions with music collaborators.

1. _____

_____

_____

2. _____

_____

_____

3. _____

_____

I hadn't picked up my guitar in months when a friend texted about putting me on the bill for an open mic night that he was hosting. He had asked me several times before, and I always had an excuse. Most recently, it was a bout of strep throat. I got sick the evening before the performance, barely able to talk much less sing, and was compelled to back out. Throat problems of various sorts had plagued me since I was a child, and as I explored the inextricable connection between physical ailments and their psychological underpinnings, I had no doubt my chronic throat issues were a result of repressing my truth, a fear of putting my real voice out there and being vulnerable. I was determined to push through that fear and disable my self-limiting beliefs, so when my friend reached out to me again to ask if I wanted to play at the next open mic, I gave him an unequivocal "yes."

Another friend happened to be hosting a jam session later that evening, and I decided to drop in, hoping to get some practice in before the open mic. As I sat there listening to the other musicians, many of whom were excellent, I realized how rusty I was. I hadn't played in months and I was unprepared to "bring it." Other bands and singers were eager to grab a chance at the mic, stepping up to fill the gaps between performances as quickly as they arose. It was like double-dutch, I could see the ropes turning, waiting for me to find the opening and jump in, and I kept missing the entry. My heart was pounding, my throat went dry, and I couldn't bring myself to do it. The window of flow was open, and I was not prepared for it. I left that night not having sung, realizing the work I'd need to put in to get myself to a place of readiness.

Over the next week, I enlisted the help of a friend to accompany me on guitar, and we spent several nights rehearsing. This, of course, meant other sacrifices, like missed social events and discipline around not turning on the TV, but I had to conserve and commit.

When the evening of the open mic arrived, I got up on that stage, sat behind the microphone, and poured my heart into the music. Not only that, the friend who was supposed to accompany me arrived late, meaning I had to hold my own on stage for the first three songs. I stepped into the spotlight and gave a solid performance, the whole set flying by as if in the blink of an eye. I found the flow that night.

*****

As I mentioned earlier, I find potent flow in yoga, too, though it takes on a different tonality (#musicpun2). It's not so much about practicing to meet the flow as having practiced enough to drop into flow. I've been a yogi for over a decade, even grabbing my certification to teach along the way. This dedication to the practice has conferred on me a certain level of comfort with the asanas and their various expressions, as well as a high degree of familiarity with a typical vinyasa ("vinyasa" just means to arrange poses in a specific way) sequence. As a result, I can attempt most of what is being taught and even take it a step further to try for the more challenging expressions of poses.

My favorite classes are a "hot power" format similar to the style I described in Section II, though slightly more relaxed in temperature and structure. Ambient temperature in the room is upwards of ninety degrees, ensuring that the muscles warm up quickly and that you sweat profusely. This helps to rinse the organs and cleanse the body of toxins. It can be a challenge not to wonder how much time is left in the class when your muscles are screaming for oxygen and the perspiration is pouring into your eyes—and also that much more magical when you actually drop your hold on time and achieve the flow state.

I recently found a class that provides some of the most amazing flow experiences I've ever felt. Since I've been working at yoga for a while, and do so consistently, this teacher's deliberate yet challenging style helps me find the perfect balance between energy conservation, strength, challenge, and skill.

She begins with a meditation, and I relish this intro because it gets at the true essence of yoga. Yoga literally means "union," and is all about cultivating oneness of body, mind, spirit, and world. Meditation is essential for recognizing this union, and it is powerful when a teacher attends to it. Ling does so beautifully, with either readings or breathing exercises.

Once we begin to move, the class gets incredibly challenging, but not because it's fast-paced. We tend to think "the faster the better" with exercise, and I see this often in power yoga classes, one pose following the other quickly, almost overlapping, all the yogis frenetic and rushing to catch up. Ling is more deliberate in her style; the asanas unfold slowly, which gives me time to find that true yog, or union. I can then access a grace in the movements, a fluidity that I bring back to the rest of my life. In Ling's class, my practice is infused with *bhakti* (a Sanskrit word alluding to deep devotion). My forward folds present as if I'm bowing forward in reverence.

I've memorized the Ashtanga ("Ashtanga" is a particular style of vinyasa yoga, codified and popularized by K. Pattabhi Jois) sequence by now, and that can drop me out of flow and into boredom when the order of poses is too predictable. Ling deftly weaves postures together in a way that's so interesting and unpredictable, I have to stay present and wait for the next asana to be called instead of going on autopilot.

She often guides us into poses that require many building blocks to work up to, showing each stage of work involved, from the simple to the more complex. I have acquired much of the foundational strength required to try the deepest expressions of most poses, and it feels immensely gratifying to be just on the cusp of nailing many of them, which keeps me highly motivated.

Getting to this place of "security" with anything is simply a matter of consistent dedication and effort—when you put in the work, you unlock opportunities for flow. Because of my commitment to the practice, I often find myself in the sweet spot of intense challenge meeting preparedness.

I said *often* because I am not always in flow in the class, nor do I expect to be. I've had my moments, like showing up to the Saturday morning class after a night of partying, struggling not to swoon as I pitch my body into "down-dogs" (one of the most foundational and essential yoga postures, like a "reset" button between asanas) and all the blood rushes to my head. What you bring to your flow opportunities on any given day will depend on many factors, like: Are you well rested? Did you drink the night before? Have you been meditating? Are you warmed up? Are you well fed? Are you on the cusp of getting, or getting over, an illness?

The variability of life is why you can't chase organic flow; it'll find *you*. You just need to be receptive to the opportunities when they do arise, and be ready to jump in double-dutch style when there's a convergence.

Also remember that life is about balance; flow is seen and felt in contrast. If you were always in flow, you wouldn't appreciate being there because you wouldn't know what it felt like to drop out. Again, don't chase it, just be prepared for it, and let it find you. Chasing highs and pleasure-seeking are hallmarks of hedonism, which, as you may recall from Section I, doesn't engender lasting happiness or well-being. Instead, we want eudaimonia, to put in the work to cultivate our best selves so that when we find flow, we value and savor it because we know what it took to get there. And then we work some more, until we hit the next flow opportunity, and we bliss out on it anew. That upward spiral is how we stay alive and thriving—moving up the steps of our own growth and evolution, ever more capable and well-designed.

Note that when I say well-designed, I don't just mean physically or mentally; I also mean *spiritually*. Are you working every day to find soul-flow? That is, to be a better human being? To be kinder, more loving, more compassionate, and more connected? At the end of the day, that day being the last one you live, your spiritual work will top the list in relative importance when you assess whether your life was well-lived.

13
Musically Inclined

Music produces a kind of pleasure which human nature cannot do without.
—Confucius

Music is the singular thing humans have created that is truly universal. It is a constituent of life no matter what era, culture, creed, religion, socioeconomic status, or geographical region you hail from. Even the most isolated tribal groups have some form of music. We gravitate to it in all its avatars, creating it, performing it, listening to it, singing along with it, moving our bodies to it. We seem to need it to nourish us, as we do other basic necessities, like food and water.

Music is like meditation for me, and a potent way to hook into flow. On my darkest days, sonorous sounds give me something to which I can tether my disturbed mind while I regain perspective. On my lightest days, music amplifies my joy. It's something I share with my friends and loved ones as a staple of what keeps us bonded, like a separate language we speak through song. It has also been a way to channel my difficult emotions into something creative, which is cathartic and deeply satisfying. I write and produce songs regularly, and when I perform them, I can find complete immersion in the present moment (when I am prepared, anyway). If I am not doing the work of staying with each note or chord as they unfold, moment to moment, my music loses potency.

I performed some of my original songs at the open mic I described earlier, and as long as I was attuned (#musicpun) to my guitar, and to the chords I had to play to accompany my voice as I sang each note, I flowed seamlessly. Anytime my mind left the bubble of my music, to get distracted by a friend walking in, or to wonder how the audience was receiving what I was sharing, I felt my fingers slip on the strings and my voice lose its hold on the pitch. This isn't just about talent and craft, though performance surely gets more seamless with time and practice so that, distractions or not, one can power through without a hitch. It is fundamentally about presence, and staying locked in the moment in focused concentration. That is meditation and flow, and music is a powerful access point. It is perhaps the beginner's blessing to have to focus intensely to find it.

That said, even virtuosos always have something more to learn, a new level to aspire to, or the realization that they too can fall out of flow, drop chords, and forget lyrics. One of my editors recently told me a story about attending a solo show by Pearl Jam frontman Eddie Vedder. At one point during the performance, Vedder forgot the lyrics to the song he was singing and had to stop and acknowledge his fallibility, exposing the raw vulnerability of being up on that stage solo given that he usually had his band to bolster him (and shield missteps, as it were). I love this story, not least because it reminds me of how salient a mindfulness tool music can be—to hook us into the present moment, and to notice when we have left it. It's also a reminder that we are not robots, we're ever-renewing creatures who aren't perfect, and in fact, we find our most authentic selves in those moments where we just give ourselves permission to be human.

Music is a gift for humanity to access prayer, a word I use fairly synonymously with meditation. Meditation is rumination or reflection, sometimes with words or phrases, and prayer is usually associated with speaking those words or phrases in the context of religion and the venues in which devotees worship. To me, it's all the same, a way to quiet the mind and focus the spirit on connection to a higher source.

As far back as I can remember, I could access spirituality through music, even if my puerile mind could not quite grasp the esoteric concepts of meditation or religion. My parents would take us along to all manner of prayer expression, from the Hare Krishna Temple, to Catholic Church, to Quaker Meeting (one of the more consistent styles in my upbringing, no doubt because of the secular style of worship Quakers employ). As a child, I rarely cried, a bit of a stoic and a tomboy was I, but music could crack my hard shell, and dissolve any inclination to remain guarded or impassive. When songs were sung my heart would swell, and I remember being on the verge of tears many times. It was an antidote to my emotional walls, and I became obsessed with many of the hooks I discovered along the way, nagging my parents to buy me the tapes (back when those existed; my young millennial readers are probably scratching their heads right now). To this day, I remember all of them; they are nestled in my DNA with the rest of the code for my life's unfolding.

Those pieces of my fiber are now a strong part of the voice I project out into the world. I have a deep-seated passion for using music to help people find access to meditation and flow. It's like guiding a mindfulness session through music; I can contribute to helping someone stay with each note as it unfolds in the present moment so they find focus and respite from any concerns about the past or future. As such, music is perhaps humanity's greatest tool for mindfulness (and the consequent dissolution of boundaries). It's a way to bliss out in the *now*.

I encourage you to begin using music to engender meditation. Keep your mind and heart open to opportunities to learn a new instrument, attend kirtans (musical discourse sessions that are meditative and instructive like the ones I dropped into at Omega), and any other creations you can conjure up to capitalize on the incredible power of music to enhance well-being.

List three ideas for how you can use music to find meditative flow. Be as specific as you can. For example:

1. Go to the symphony next Friday evening.
2. Find out about a kirtan in my area and sign up to attend.
3. Hook into one of Pax's upcoming music sessions.

1. _____

2. _____

3. _____

14
Chasing the High

You're chasing the dragon, you're chasing the high.
A bird with one wing, who's still trying to fly.
—Ozzy Osbourne

It's a common phenomenon to feel unfulfilled in one area of our lives because we compromise for the sake of another. "Another" usually takes the form of society's expectations, or the needs of family and friends; our purpose work is where we then sacrifice. I myself have been in a constant state of tug of war between the care of my parents, the needs of our family business, the desire to remain close and connected to my friends, and the big dreams I have for myself that end up taking a back seat. But life is about balance, and we owe ourselves and our dreams as much love and consideration as we give to the others in our lives who matter.

Imagine giving up your career aspirations to raise a family; at best, you end up with regret, at worst, steeped in resentment. When we fail to attend to our deepest callings, like personal fulfillment or unrealized dreams, we end up in pain. That pain can take the form of depression, anxiety, and other psychological issues, or physical pain when we are processing psychosomatically. It can be tempting to use many of the flourishing practices we've already discussed—meditation, the gratitude practice, a treadmill-induced endorphin rush, a high-concentration yoga class—to blunt the acute edge of the knife that's needling us. These behaviors are objectively healthy and offer vital contributions to our well-being, but, they can simultaneously be used to quell important information about imbalances in our lives. We can end up chasing the high they give us to mask symptoms of our imbalance or lack of fulfillment, just as we do with drugs. Anything can act like a drug to alleviate pain, including basic distractions, like TV, so we must stay attuned to the "why" of our negative emotions. Psychological pain and discomfort are essential signals that something in our lives needs recalibrating. When things bubble up, instead of resisting, try embracing the information for what it's trying to teach you. Proper attention to these signals allows us to change our circumstances so that we can find more flourishing.

Use interventions and best practices to remind yourself of how blessed you are, how many resources you have, and how to keep yourself strong and psychologically upbeat so you have the *courage* to get out there and remedy the source of the pain, not numb out to it in the first place.

What "healthy" behaviors might you be using to distract yourself from discomfort? What is the source of your discomfort? Spend some time digging deep to discover places where you might be *chasing the high*, and then ask yourself why.

_____

_____

_____

_____

_____

_____

_____

_____

_____

_____

_____

_____

_____

_____

_____

_____

_____

_____

_____

"Chasing the high" can also manifest in our creative pursuits. In this case, it's not to numb out to pain, it's to grasp at more euphoria. We achieve one success and relish the high so much that we want more. We hustle to try to recreate that feeling, to oust the first success with something even more powerful, and end up competing with ourselves to stay relevant. We come to resent the very thing that once gave us so much joy.

As a society, we put incredible pressure on ourselves and each other to perform at higher and higher levels, and then are quick to judge and alienate when the creative sprint can't be sustained. We even have an expression for when an artist makes one great contribution, and is subsequently unable to recreate that same level of success: "one-hit wonder."

This phenomenon is gaining insidious traction on social media platforms. There are some high-profile cases involving Instagram stars who hit a stride of popularity, amassed scores of followers with paradisiacal images, and then crumbled under a mountain of pressure, the momentum needed to churn out that level of high-quality material unsustainable. The irony is, much of it is a depiction of "real life" that's actually completely contrived. One young woman who rose to "Instafame" with beautiful snapshots of her home (which to many viewers appeared mansion-esque from the angles) admitted she lived in an apartment, and would take shots of just one corner, buying lovely (and expensive) accessories to redesign it and create the illusion of perfection and grandeur. Her followers were buying into the fantasy en masse, though the reality behind the camera was a cramped, messy, unkempt space. Just a fraction of her world—the frame captured in the camera lens—shone, like the end of a penny that's dipped in cleaning solution on one of those TV infomercials. She ended up miserable, living a lie under a mountain of debt and unable to keep up with appearances. Ultimately, she decided to share her story publicly to tell the truth behind the fallacy.

Essena O'Neill is another example of a young woman who racked up followers posing for pictures in which her perfect body (accompanying a perfect face) was always in perfect form. She came forward to tell the truth of how mean-spirited and insecure she had become in her quest to meet the unmanageable expectations of her growing fan base.

My point in telling you all of this is to alleviate some of the suffering you may be causing yourself when "chasing the high" of your own creative pursuits. They are not meant to act as an abused drug, addictive and ultimately toxic. On the contrary, creativity is our ultimate outlet for expression and catharsis, a cornerstone of being human and one of the purest gifts of our existence. It's a birthright as ancient as we are.

The oldest art we have evidence of comes from caves and dates back approximately 40,000 years. That means we were expressing ourselves creatively long before we even had language.[57] Since we've known how to draw even before we could talk, it would appear that artistic ability is an organic and fundamental part of our very nature. Thus, allow your creative flow to be expressed equally organically, without the pressure for it to *be* something, or the need to channel it into success, financial or otherwise. And if it does lead to those places, that's just a testament to the fact that your fellow human beings are resonating with your art and it is evoking emotion or reaction. Those outcomes are not the ends in and of themselves, but beautiful side effects, and that's what we need to be mindful of. We tend to chase external validation once we've gotten a taste. We need that validation to feel, well, valid. This is highly detrimental because our self-worth is then attached to our creativity. When we're in a stride with it, we're soaring. But what about when there's a lull, when we are depleted or can't produce at the same level or volume?

We are also surrounded by depictions of celebrities enjoying copious amounts of fame and fortune, and it's hard not to feel diminished if we aren't achieving that same level of recognition. I've been guilty of the same. Once I realized my writing was resonating with people, or that my sharp wit could make folks laugh, or even that I could sit in front of a camera and instead of freezing up, talk to it as if it were my oldest and dearest friend, I began putting pressure on myself. When would that writing become a source of income? After all, if it was any good, surely someone would want to pay me for it, right? When would I get my next on-camera gig? Did a lack of attention mean I wasn't as capable or talented as I believed myself to be?

The pressure around those questions was quickly beginning to suck all of the joy from expressing my natural skills and abilities, and I had to check myself. I was being stymied around present-moment bliss because I was focused on external sources of validation. Relishing the awesome creative potential sitting inside me as it manifested in the world around me was, in and of itself, the gift. Once I began to release the choke hold I had on my creative potential, staying present to how *it* wanted to manifest, I began to seriously enjoy myself (as an aside, fame and recognition have a great deal to do with marketing and PR in addition to talent and ability).

Taking improv comedy classes has helped tremendously with this, because the work involves generating scenes live and in the moment, without scripts or plans. As I get further along in my improv training, I'm more and more liberated from the pressure to create for any reason other than finding the present-moment joy from it.

Summary? Stay super conscious of when your creative gifts are wanting and needing expression, and honor that flow with integrity. In equal measure, be as conscious of when they cease to bring you relief, joy, ease, or balance. Realize that all creative pursuit is magic, a gift of our humanity, and let it be enough to simply enjoy its expression. When you feel stress around your creative flow, back off and allow yourself to recalibrate. Learn to appreciate the difference between when it's time to walk away from a project for a little while, and when it's time to walk away for good. Art is art, not science. It is fluid and imperfect and commands constant inspiration. It does not warrant being contained, commanded, or demanded of. It wants you to love it, nurture it, and feel passionate about it, because those are the purest qualities of our existence. When those virtues are present, you may just get lucky enough to have bliss show her face.

Are there any creative pursuits in your life that you feel pressure around? If yes, what do you think is the source of that pressure? What is one action step you can take to diminish that pressure—e.g., can you redefine your relationship to that aspect of your creativity? How can you buffer yourself against feeling pressure from your creative outlets or expressions? For example, for every ten paintings you make, you donate one to charity (it hangs in a Children's Hospital ward, or a nursing home).

_____

_____

_____

_____

_____

_____

_____

_____

15
On Being a Unicorn

It is the duty of each one of us to be a holy woman.
We shall have elevated aims, if we are holy women.
—Eliza R. Snow

A Unicorn is a female of the highest quality, a rare breed of strength, integrity, kindness, and independence. She is uncompromising in her growth and extraordinary by all measures.

A Unicorn is beautiful (because she believes it *and* works hard at it), educated (even if just by the school of hard-knocks), self-assured, professional, and doing life for herself by standing on her own two feet. And sometimes hands. My favorite yoga teacher has a physical deformity wherein her left hand is underdeveloped. It's essentially just a palm, with tiny buds for fingers. No one really seems to notice nor care, they're all so absorbed in the skill and dedication she brings to classes—which, in a testament to her bad-assery, are always packed. She's the teacher I described earlier in whose classes I find my most immaculate flow. She can also execute the most challenging postures I've ever seen, from handstands, to side-arm balances, to backbends. She does so with such grace, strength, and fluidity that I almost can't believe the human form is capable of that kind of mastery, much less with a handicap of five fingers. I almost hate saying "handicap," because far from holding her back, it seems to inspire her to ever-increasing levels of difficulty in her own practice. She's straight up Unicorn status.

If we all aspired to be part of the Unicorn club (#UniSquadGoals), I'd feel confident that our humanity was headed in a righteous direction. If for no other reason than because, barring extenuating circumstances, moms exert the single-greatest influence on their children's lives. They set the bar and the examples. Unicorn moms breed Unicorn children, and the planet sorely needs conscious constituents of integrity if it is going to survive and thrive.

So, how do we achieve Unicorn status? I'm about to drop knowledge on what a Unicorn lady's defining characteristics are, so you can cultivate more of them. But before I do, a note to all of my readers, no matter what gender you identify with: Though I've used the word "Unicorn" to specifically encourage women around my version of "feminist" ideals, everyone can, and should, aspire to these qualities. In addition, a deep understanding of Unicorn status will mean that you can truly appreciate such a creature when you are in her presence. Learn to revere her, protect her (she's an endangered species, after all), support her, and love her, and relish how the magic of her Unicorn-ness directly nourishes your own happiness and evolution.

Unicorn Qualities

Good Will Hunting

A Unicorn is invested in work that is in the highest service of her fellow human beings. She's conscious of how her own goals and dreams impact others, and is careful not to hurt or harm anyone in the pursuit of her success. I know many such women and make every effort to be in their company so that their Unicorn-ness can rub off on me. I also know women who wound or crush others in the stampede of their self-interest. It may often be unwitting, but it is no less damaging. Consciousness around how our energy affects others is a hallmark of a Unicorn woman, and a quality the world sorely needs more of. I strive every day to be in the highest service with my own thoughts, words, and actions, not least so I may be a positive influence in someone else's quest for the magical Unicorn horn.

Girl (Un)interrupted

A Unicorn is self-sufficient in work that does justice to her highest potential. This is not to say she can't be a homemaker—on the contrary, being present for one's children is up there with the most significant and selfless jobs that exist. But, she must not fulfill that role at the expense of her own happiness, else those around her, especially her children, will be unhappy, too.

Now You See Me

Her beauty is not about perfection, but owning her real self and embracing features that give the finishing touches to her unique character.

I've got a bump along the bridge of my nose that I often considered "fixing" with plastic surgery. I used to have conversations with one of my best guy friends around the pros and cons of a more "perfect" nose. His main argument against it was that the bump gave me character. Did I want to be just another "pretty face"? I was quite self-conscious about my side profile, an insecurity fed by moments where my nose became a source of jest. My wasband once ran his finger along the crest of my nose and simultaneously along his own with the other hand. He said no words, the drunken smirk on his face a tacit decree of his own nose's perfection. On a different occasion, one of my closest friends, also inebriated (alcohol is called "truth serum" for how it emboldens people to say things they otherwise wouldn't dare utter) observed that I had a "Derek Jeter" nose. She was referring to Jeter's distinctive peaked schnoz, and adding injury to insult was the fact that we were in the presence of my crush. Granted, we were all young and immature, and I didn't hold what was meant in jest against the snout snobs, but it nonetheless left me deeply self-conscious. I also wondered what effect this feature might have on a career in front of the camera.

Well, I have yet to notice it's held me back at all. I also recently received such awesome validation on this feature from one of my best friends, the comment made that much more special because it was inadvertent. We were talking about how she had a "nose" thing, preferring men with prominent sneezers and side profiles. I jokingly commented that she obviously preferred this in her best friends, too, and she matter-of-factly proclaimed, "Of course. I *love* your nose. It's such an asset to your face." She wasn't trying to be complementary, she was stating an objective fact, therein also validating that beauty is indeed in the eye of the beholder. What a cool accentuation (#nosepun) of the proverb.

Over time, I've understood how to recognize such qualities as precious gifts. My nose is distinct. It gives my face recall, and I'd rather have a singular horn (hello Unicorn!) than blend in with the masses. It's also an heirloom. I got this feature from my father, who is a seriously awesome human being. I would not wish to erase this souvenir of a great man from my face, also a reminder of my Greek heritage—genealogy lovers in the family tell me the aquiline nose comes straight from Greek presence in India circa Alexander the Great.

Besides, I want to formulate real connection with my fellow human beings, not alliances that are based on appearance or extrinsic value. If our identity is based on superficial factors, what happens when they cease to exist? Like the fading of youthful beauty as we age, or the ebb and flow of wealth in life . . .

So many young women in Hollywood take advantage of the spoils of plastic surgery and create new faces or bodies. Clinically beautiful (who even decided what that is?) as they are, something of the soul ceases to project through that plastic once it is formed. Jennifer Grey rose to super-stardom acting in blockbuster hits like *Dirty Dancing* and *Ferris Bueller's Day Off* with a distinctively "imperfect" schnoz. Then, she got rhinoplasty and her career took a nosedive. So to speak.

Kylie Jenner—though gorgeous—projects a completely different persona post-work. She had many fans who related to her edgy, raw style. Now, it's Banal Barbie. I wonder how they feel? Did they lose an important role model? Or did they buy into the notion that such changes make one more desirable?

These are the real pressures we face as a society, and they are not easy to confront. I give the Unicorn merit badge to people everywhere who have the courage to prioritize their inner light, and cultivate *that* over their physical appearance, so that it shines brightly through their natural physical form, even when society—including those closest to us—makes us insecure. The spirit's beauty has little to do with appearance and everything to do with action.

A Rebel without a Cause

A Unicorn thinks, lives, and feels outside the box. She's not about "business as usual" just because it is convenient or the majority opinion; she takes the road less traveled, is intrepid in her quest for authenticity, and prioritizes growth over fear. She constantly seeks to live as a more evolved self, spends precious resources to do so, and helps those in her world do the same.

Miss Congeniality

A Unicorn understands the merit of graceful and honest communication and employs it as her default. She listens thoughtfully and nonjudgmentally, receiving as much as she speaks, never shouts or yells in anger (except maybe at sporting events), and responds in an active-constructive way to others' good news.

Love Actually

She doesn't settle. She is looking for a high-quality mate to evolve with, someone who feeds her spiritually, intellectually, and physically, in that order. She is only in partnership when it has the potential to make her a better version of herself compared to when she is flying solo. Otherwise, she risks becoming a lesser version of herself, and that is not an option for her, because she's got her skin in the game of growth.

Can't Buy Me Love

The bottom line is not her bottom line. She doesn't make decisions solely based on how much money she'll make, or marry a partner because of their net worth; she won't risk her integrity for financial gain. Her bottom line is love. That is her preferred currency, and she uses it to guide her decisions.

How close are you to Unicorn status?

Scan back over the descriptions of Unicorn qualities, and use the space below to reflect on which ones you embody and how. Also think about where you may not be showing up in full Unicorn glory. How might you change those behaviors to merit your horn?

Guys, use this exercise to reflect on which Unicorn qualities you feel you embody. Which ones inspire you to be a better self? Which ones do you resonate with the most? Which among them would you like to help the women in your life cultivate more of?

_____

_____

_____

_____

_____

_____

_____

_____

_____

_____

_____

_____

_____

_____

_____

_____

_____

_____

_____

_____

_____

_____

_____

Shoe Game

You probably thought this section was going to be about how a Unicorn is always on point with her shoe game. Not exactly. I felt compelled to write a little bit about what a Unicorn is *not*, because I've had some very real experience navigating my own bouts of non-Unicornness in order to get to a place of understanding what it *is*.

To put it plainly (and to be *pun-ny*), a Unicorn is *not* a woman who trades her soul for soles. You see, until fairly recently, I held the belief that I needed a man to give me stability and security. Having a career of my own and contributing meaningfully to the world warmed the bench until the starting team of getting married and having kids hit the field. No doubt, cultural mores (e.g., an Indian father who reveres life and believes a woman's top priority should be child-rearing) played heavily into my philosophy.

And then I began to see a different truth.

The lesson began in my marriage, when I realized that financial wealth and security were not enough to make me happy. For as much as we had, it couldn't compensate for the emptiness of a partnership that wasn't supportive.

When I left that marriage, I fell in love with a man with whom I had absolutely no security, financial or otherwise. Working in our family business became a necessity to subsidize the frequent international travel needed to sustain our long-distance relationship, especially as my parents rejected the union on ideological grounds. It was my first real taste of standing on my own two feet—my own two *soles*, if you will—to subsidize my soul-level desires. Sure, I had lived independently and worked to support myself after graduating and moving to New York City, but I also knew the safety net of my parents' protection was always there (as when I was married).

My protectors' desires ended up either becoming my own, or trumping them. If I wanted to deviate outside of that system, I needed their permission and support to do so. I had to find my way to a place where I didn't need anyone's permission to live my life on my own terms.

How powerful to realize now that independence, liberty, and an ability to exercise my will and use my voice are the *real* right and privilege, not being taken care of by someone else.

 I practiced flexing this will for the first time when my sister started working. She gave me a chance to explore a life beyond the realm of the "secure" by lending me money for acting training when I moved to New York City. I was simultaneously readying myself to apply to medical school to realize my parents' dreams of my becoming a doctor. Problem was, I had cold feet that wouldn't warm to the idea of a pathology-focused system of medicine, wherein we try to "fix" the broken, rather than emphasize health.

My reservations were stoked during my first semester at Penn, in a healthcare management class at Wharton. I began to understand the changing nature of the medical profession, how the "business" of medicine was ousting clinical practice in relative priority and importance. Doctors were spending as much time filling in forms and charts as attending to their patients, and I couldn't understand how to be a part of such a system without losing my faith in it.

Meanwhile, I had already gotten a taste of the power of television to effect positive change. As a teenager, I had a recurring role on a major network series called *Rap Around*. The premise of the show was to give a live, unscripted forum to teens from various socioeconomic backgrounds to "rap" (as in talk, although spitting rhymes in that format would have been eight-mile cool) about issues of importance, from bullying, to eating disorders, to racism. As a season regular on the show, I was recognized often, and though I must admit it felt really good to get a small taste of celebrity, it was so much more than that. I was hearing powerful and touching feedback about how much a certain episode—and my voice in it—had helped another teen through a difficult time. A potent seed was planted around what I could do with my voice and how impactful it could be given the right forum. A career in medicine was slowly being eclipsed for that dream.

No wonder I moved all the way to India and got married—it seemed a viable reconciliation between my dreams and my parents' wishes. To see my sister and I go into medicine was my parents' ultimate wish, second only to seeing us both married and well-settled. Deeply ingrained in the Indian culture is the idea that girls will go straight from their parents' home to their marital home. It is, therefore, a parent's duty to their daughter to get her betrothed and transfer the responsibility of her care and protection to her husband.

That I had checked at least that box was no doubt a relief to them. And it gave me the chance to pursue my dreams without their worry weighing on me or weakening my resolve as I fought to carve out a place in the challenging and often unforgiving ecosystem of entertainment.

I was twenty-five when I got married and settled in India. Alas, having traveled halfway across the world for newfound freedom, I once again found myself restrained. Though many of the plum television opportunities were in

Bombay (including the MTV headquarters—back then I was obsessed with the idea of becoming an MTV VJ), Delhi was where I had to be. My wasband's family lived there, he was focusing on building a business there, and his plan was to settle there. Bombay was simply out of the question.

Being the capital of the country and the seat of government, Delhi's offerings were mainly news-network focused. I landed a coveted anchor seat at CNBC—a gift that I was so blessed to have—but it was already apparent I wasn't as free as I'd thought I'd be. In retrospect, it was naive of me to think I'd adjust well; just because I looked the part didn't mean I'd be able to play it. Priorities were misaligned as I attempted to focus on my work, and ended up failing to meet expectations in my role as a daughter-in-law (serving tea on a tray to relatives and that kind of thing). I was a bird with a cuffed ankle, flapping my wings to fly but never getting very far. Ironic that I'd come here to be free, and have to return to the "land of the free" to be liberated.

Several years unfolded as I found my way to independent thought through independent means—*real* freedom. Along the way, I had one final test of the temptation to sacrifice my inner truth for a life of security and lavish leisure. This came in the form of a family friend, who, as it turns out, had been holding a torch for me since we first met back in college. When we reconnected nearly a decade-and-a-half later, his interest was swift and intense. He made it clear that he wanted to marry me, and that he was just waiting for my assent to "put a ring on it." I wanted desperately to be able to love him. I was thirty-three and vulnerable, a divorce notch on my belt, a severely broken heart under said belt, and a biological clock tick-tocking in my ear. A kind, loving, wealthy, and generous man was waiting to take a knee, and I was reminded by more than one family member how silly I'd be to turn down a proposal from him. Overtly, the comments were of a *why would you say no?* nature. The subtext was something closer to admonishment. I can imagine what they were thinking—*someone up there must love you! A thirty-three year old divorcee and this wealthy bachelor comes a-calling? Snatch him up silly girl, and guarantee your future!"*

Within a few weeks of us dating, whatever he lacked in the traits that I needed to feel physical lust for him, he compensated for with designer gifts I lusted after. Complicating matters was the fact that he treated my friends and family with the same magnanimity with which he treated me, and I was a sucker for this kind of man. He checked many boxes, but elusive was the one needing ticking the most. Some souls just provide the activation energy our hearts need to set alight, to spark the kind of love we can only receive from our "twin flame."

That activation energy was undeniably absent. I was in a vortex of hedonism, where eudaimonia was being edged out of the ring. Every month that I stayed in this vortex, my heart's truth bought out by money's purchasing power, I took a major hit physically.

A few months into the relationship, I lie in bed with a heating pad on my nether regions to ameliorate the unabating torture of the burning urge to pee. Knives stabbed my throat with each swallow. My spiritual agony over being in a relationship with a man I wasn't in love with pronounced itself as a particularly unpropitious bout of strep throat coupled with a UTI. I was not vocalizing my truth and my throat was taking the hit. I was increasingly irritable and frustrated, and it was manifesting as a searing pain when I urinated.

I was sacrificing my deepest layers of integrity by accepting his lavish gifts, almost coming to expect them to keep my attention piqued. It was a blackmail of the heart in the guise of Manolo Blahnik, Alexander McQueen, Roberto Cavalli, Chanel . . . yet none of them could sufficiently distract me from the truth that I had stayed in the relationship far too long, allowing myself to be entranced by designer labels and the allure of a hedonistic life. I knew what being in love felt like, and I knew I didn't feel that kind of love in this relationship. I also knew I did not want to settle for less in this short life I'd been gifted. My body was screaming this truth at me loud and clear, and given the blistering physical toll it was taking, I had no choice but to pay attention. I ended the relationship soon after.

Not a year later, I was waiting in baggage claim at the Philadelphia International Airport, fresh off a trip to LA. In a perfect full-circle act of karmic balance, my bag failed to appear on the conveyor belt. I waited around as the very last passenger picked up their luggage and went on their way, and felt uncannily placid knowing mine was not going to materialize. I had been in LA for a mixture of media industry meetings, on-camera work, a conference, and a presentation at said conference, so as fate would have it, the bag was loaded with swag. There were the silver Manolo Blahnik's my sister bought for me as a thirtieth birthday present (ironically the exact ones Carrie wears in *Sex and the City,* that—spoiler alert—get stolen). My first Chanel pearl necklace, which I bought after nailing the audition for a huge media gig. The beautiful rose pink Dolce and Gabbana leather jacket with gold detailing made of the most buttery soft leather I'd ever touched, a thing of beauty *and* comfort (and all fashionistas know what a rare combination that is). In aggregate, it was all worth about as much as all of the gifts I had been given by the wealthy Indian suitor.

When that suitcase failed to drop onto the conveyer belt, I knew I would never see it again, and I knew exactly why. Based on my last relationship, I had not yet learned how to appreciate beauty in the material without attaching to it. This needed reconciling before my spirit could soar. And now, here was a forced lesson in the form of losing many of my most prized material possessions.

Don't get me wrong; though I embraced the unfolding with acceptance, it was an agonizing process letting go. Each time I remembered a piece in that bag I would never see again, I was bereft anew. My sister was almost angry at my interpretation of the incident, frustrated that I didn't go into "the zone" and call it back. She was well aware of my ability to effect change from that place of pure intention, just as I had on that trip to Ireland, and many times since. It wasn't for lack of trying, but I just couldn't *connect* to the suitcase to call it back in. When I would enter a place of mediation to try, the purity of intention was decidedly absent. In its place was a stronger intention for spiritual growth. This was a lesson I had to learn, and if this was the form it was going to come in, so be it.

Suffice it to say, the bag never found its way back to me. And through its disappearance, I felt a potent sense of freedom from the material. I was forced to detach from my most prized possessions, and I carry that with me now. My inherent value has nothing to do with these objects, so whether or not they are around, I am still rich in the ways that really matter.

Have I renounced my love for material things? Heck no. Do I still adore fashion, style, and all the beauty and fun that come with them? Heck yes. After all, it's fun to be a girl in a material world, with all the makeup, accessories, nail art, hairstyles, and glamour that go with it. Expressing my unique style and identity in these ways can be immensely satisfying. But my relationship to it all is different now. I own them, they don't own me, and that liberty is a far more valuable thing than the things themselves.

*****

I hope these truths of mine inspire you to take a good, hard look at your own lives and areas within them where you may be compromising your inner truth for outer gain. If on an analytical, cerebral level, we understand how vital eudaimonia is to well-being, the anecdote I just shared is the manifestation of that knowledge on a spiritual level. Your body will come to speak the truth your mouth won't. The Universe will guide you back to yourself through signs, signals, and eventually straight-up bitch slaps if you aren't listening yet. You will continue to get the information you need until you pay heed.

Using the story I just told you as inspiration, take some time to conduct a little spiritual hygiene of your own. Get practiced in knowing how to release your soul from the allure of soles.

List five of your most prized material possessions (e.g., shoes, laptop, favorite pair of jeans, expensive accessories like diamond earrings or an heirloom watch, your car, etc.).

1. _____

_____

2. _____

_____

3. _____

_____

4. _____

_____

5. _____

_____

Now, one by one, take stock of each of the items you listed, savoring its beauty and reflecting on any meaning you have attached to it. Saturate yourself with love and lust for these possessions. Maybe you want to close your eyes and relive memories associated with them, relishing each experience by coloring it with as much detail as you can, immersing yourself in the joy you've felt over each item . . .

Now let them go. You don't literally have to throw them out or give them away, just commit to releasing their hold on you by imagining your world without them, and being totally okay with it. This may not come naturally or quickly at first. All good. Keep up this practice like a meditation until you feel free of attachment to your material love affairs.

16
The Mind Says Unicorn, the Body Says P(h)ony

Deliberate choices are the only sacred things in the universe.
Everything else is just hydrogen.
—James Alan Gardner

I just wrapped up something of a manifesto on what being a Unicorn is not, and how to set about owning your inner wisdom and the truths it speaks to you. But becoming a person of deep integrity is a process involving difficult choices. What do we do when the mind really wants Unicorn status, and the body is tempted back into pony rides? In other words, how do we navigate Unicorn-ness in a body that is tempted into hedonism, in particular, sexual gratification?

We seek out pleasure, because pleasure feels good. It feels good because we have deep genetic programming around attracting a mate and procreating so that we can carry on the species. If falling in love and having sex didn't feel as good as they do (and they're up there), no one would do it, and we'd die off within a generation. This of course also tempts us to settle into scenarios that are conducive to procreating, but not necessarily in alignment with our spiritual compass.

The first step is to see this process for what it is, and be compassionate toward yourself while you try to reconcile any disparities between what you are compelled to desire and the direction in which you want to evolve. I know many strong men and women who defy the systems (and bodies) they were raised in, along with the inherent norms and expectations, to live in greater alignment with their truth.

This is especially relevant to the norm of marriage and kids. Make these choices because you really want to, not because you think you're supposed to. Navigating marriage and rearing children are among the most rewarding—and commensurately challenging—life scenarios that exist. It's not fair to you or the loved ones you enter into these partnerships with to give anything less then your all-cylinders-firing commitment.

Again, as with unhealthy food cravings or negative thought patterns, begin to discern the difference between where your genetic programming compels you to go, and where you want to go to be in the highest service. Get deliberate about your decisions and get happier.

Equally important is to recognize that sometimes the mind wants to race with Unicorns, but the body can only handle the pace of a pony. Before good ole Edison discovered how to convert electricity into "artificial" light, the natural rhythms of night and day were our sole circadian compass. Women cycled according to the moon (which is why menstruation is often referred to as the "moon cycle"). This meant that in general, women across the planet were all on the same cycle. Before you go jumping to thoughts of "holy crap, that's a lot of PMS," wait for it—one common cycle meant women could support each other through what was a very vulnerable and trying time. Beyond the physical symptoms of menstruation, like cramps and bleeding, the psychological implications of hormonal fluctuations (irritability, depression, sadness, hypersensitivity, and a host of others) are real and acute.

I have one or two days in the month where I feel such high irritability as a product of the hormones surging through me, it's like Dr. Jekyll turning into Mr. Hyde. Miss Mindful Positive Psychology morphing into Miss Misanthrope. I wish I had license to stay in solitude and not interact with other humans during this time, so as to avoid hurting or offending anyone with my short temper. I am aware of it happening, and equally aware of how little control I am able to exercise over these feelings.

It's sad to me that we all cycle at different times now, so we don't have the solidarity in the experience that we used to. We take drugs to numb the pain and diminish symptoms. There are even forms of birth control that override our periods so we get them only sporadically. In effect, we can scale down to almost zero any evidence that the cycle even exists. Ironic, because it is also the hallmark of what makes life possible. The fact that we try so hard to deny and defy it strikes me as the most despondent phenomenon. But, to do so levels the playing field with men so we can come in on more equal footing, without the handicap of some days out of the month where we are bleeding and in pain, or feeling emotional or volatile. To ensure equal opportunity seems to necessitate repudiating any signs of vulnerability or weakness. And with that denial has come desensitization to a powerful physiological need: to take rest and be nurtured during those sensitive days.

We're entering into an era of such independence and fortitude, we're neglecting this biological piece of ourselves that needs attention. If we were to conserve energy during those days, and allow ourselves the rest required to honor our female biology, the root home of all life on Earth, we'd feel immensely more joyful and balanced. The first law of thermodynamics applies; energy is being expended to allow us to cycle through menstruation; we must expend less during that time to stay balanced.

I observe women running themselves into the ground, trying to be June Cleaver at the expense of self-care. Whether during our monthly cycle, or listening to our inner voice and honoring our spirit essence as it guides us along the path that is our True North, we must take responsibility for our health and vitality, be deliberate about our choices, and honor them with resolve.

17

On Purpose

*The two most important days in your life are the day you are born,
and the day you find out why.*
—Mark Twain

We all have a purpose to live out, a role the spirit is called to play while embodied in the human form. We must honor that calling above all else and stay in integrity to it—else we live incomplete lives and suffer over regret.

 *"What are you going to do with another girl? Should I drop her in?"
he jeered as he dangled my infant mother upside down above a well.
"No!!" shrieked my panicked grandmother in protest. She lurched
toward the baby and grabbed her back.*

During a past-life regression, my mother recalled this memory of her life being in peril when she was just a baby. Whether her uncle really meant to murder her remains a mystery, but the sinister subtext is clear. His behavior was a barbaric substantiation of the misogyny that existed in her world in 1944. Boys were encouraged to get educated and pursue careers, ultimately returning home to take care of the family. They were an investment, ensuring a family's security and future. As such, they were prized and revered. Rearing girls, on the other hand, was an expensive proposition with no hope of any ROI. Their fate was to leave and never come back, with the ensuing heartbreak adding insult to the injury of a dowry—a girl's parents were expected to compensate her new family for the "burden" of taking on another body in the household with cash and gifts.

When she was a teenager, my mom remembers my grandmother asking my grandfather what the point of educating their daughters was, when they would just end up in the kitchen. It's no wonder why my mom went on to top her classes at the university, and sweep all of the gold medals in academics. She was proving her worth to a society that consistently doubted it, a world that sought to displace it elsewhere, to a realm more suitable, like the kitchen.

It became her soul (pun intended) purpose to do everything a man could do and then some, taking a position as a professor at the nearby college, becoming head of the department, being selected for the single PhD spot the college offered to the most brilliant mind, and taking care of the family estate when her father passed away, something that none of her other siblings, including two brothers, could handle. She was her own woman, self-assured and living by the hand of her own means. She was a pioneer, and from the way she has always described that time, she felt content and fulfilled.

And then she met my dad. He was visiting from America, irresistibly charming and handsome, and keen to win her hand. She had a rich, purposeful life, and wasn't necessarily looking to give all of that up for marriage. In retrospect, I'm certain she wouldn't have. But as previously discussed, we're all driven strongly to find a mate. This pressure was amplified by my mother's age—she was already into her thirties and quickly moving into "old maid" territory by the standards of the culture in which she was ensconced.

She left everything—and everyone—she knew, and moved to America with my dad.

*****

It hasn't been an easy life for her, and I know how much she misses her teaching days, what it felt like to have such strong purpose, and how she gave it up for marriage and kids. I once asked her whether she regretted the decision to leave India and move to America. I urged my mom to answer truthfully, assuring her I would not be hurt or offended by the response. Her resigned sigh and the crestfallen look on her face told me what I already knew to be true, and though I sure am grateful she birthed me, I was deeply pained over her unhappiness at not feeling fulfilled in her life.

My mom and I have worked hard the last few years to uncover more meaning for her, including ways she might turn her trauma from the armed robbery into renewed purpose. Together, we're using the science of positive psychology to move toward post-traumatic growth. It's working, and her spirit shines brighter every day. But, her essential avatar was as a professor, and that she gave it up continues to be a painful reality for her to confront.

Take a vital cue from this story, and realize that if there is something in your life that lights you up, that gives you flow opportunities, and makes you feel like the best version of yourself, you must prioritize it. Of all the life-thriving information contained in this book, the importance of cultivating and nourishing your purpose is perhaps the most essential for your spirit. You must do the work your spirit is called to do and not relinquish that quest to anyone, or anything, including fear. Else you can be sure that the fissure created in the wholeness of the spirit will only grow wider as time goes on and purpose is left unheeded.

I have seen many friends and loved ones live days of suffering because they are unfulfilled, including yours truly. The discomfort is visceral, constant and nagging, unwilling to leave you until you do the work to uncover your calling and honor it.

In moments when I commit deeply to my soul's calling, and work hard to stay on a path of authenticity to it, my inner light shines the brightest. Those are the days I feel truly gratified, purposeful, and blissed-out. It's a filling of my cup that no other facet of my life can replenish on its own.

I want those days for you, too, because if there is a key to the magic kingdom of joy, a cherry to top the sundae of life and true holistic flourishing, it is to live your purpose. If you haven't yet found it, keep searching until you do. Your mindfulness practice will help you tremendously here, not just to get clear on what it is you came here to do, but to stay attuned to it. And mark these words of mine: As you align with your purpose, the Universe will conspire to help you in unimaginable and magical ways.

This process won't be without its challenges; you'll have your days. Your purpose may come into direct conflict with the world around you. Maybe you'll have to make seemingly selfish choices between your path and that of family and friends. Moments of paralysis, doubt, exhaustion, fear, or loss may arise. Allow those feelings to wash through you, acknowledging that they exist to keep you "safe" and free from harm. But the real harm is to deny your purpose, so to those emotions say, "Thank you for trying to get my back, I appreciate you. Now, if you'll excuse me, I'm gonna get back to doing what I came here to do."

I recently saw a video that validates beautifully the importance of purpose and fulfillment. In it, Willow Smith interviews her grandmother and actress mom Jada Pinkett Smith.[58] Just as I've tried to highlight the life-giving nature of staying committed to purpose through the matriarchs in my family, these ladies show the power of the same through the matriarchs in theirs.

In the video, Jada first explains how women are inundated with the messaging that to be a good mother, you have to "completely sacrifice everything." Women are taught that attending to themselves "is a problem." She then articulates in such a raw, passionate way the real secret to being her best self in her various roles as mother, wife, daughter, and actor: *self-fulfillment*. "You have to take care of yourself in order to have the alignment and power to take care of others, at the capacity that we do, because it fills the well. We have to be *responsible* enough to take care of ourselves *first*." She's making the point that fulfillment is not selfish, it is responsible.

What happens when we aren't responsible for our fulfillment? Imbalance ensues. And then we look outside of ourselves—to those we love—to fulfill us and make us happy. That doesn't work, because it strains our relationships and leaves us feeling emptier than ever. Conversely, the more we work on finding our own fulfillment, the happier we are, and the happier our families are, too: "Each year I get more and more and more in balance . . . more and more in alignment . . . and each year, you know what? I get more and more happy . . . and the very thing that I thought would make [the family] unhappy? Is actually fulfilling for you as well." Preach!

You know the quippy adage "happy wife, happy life"? Jada nails the essence of it, making a cogent case for fulfillment the likes of which I'm not sure I've ever seen. The video went viral. Go watch it as a positive intervention around purpose.

With the help of Willow and her matriarchs, and me and my matriarchs, we've got a pretty solid case for the importance of purpose in finding fulfillment, the most fundamental component of your flourishing.

So, how do we find the path to purpose? Truth is, we're all on it somewhere, even if that manifests as us being lost and trying to find our way back. If you take space to listen to your inner voice, as in meditations, you will begin to uncover what you are destined to be. Pay attention to what draws you in, to what energizes you and fuels your inner fire, and seek out more of it. Following the lead of that good juju will guide you in the right direction.

Figuring out your purpose and honoring it requires real gumption and sweat equity, but it is the most worthwhile work that you will do. Ready to put in some effort?

Let's start with an assessment of where on the path you are. Use the following exercise to gage your "satisfaction with life."

The Satisfaction with Life Scale (SWLS)

Using the 1–7 scale below, indicate your agreement with each item by placing the appropriate number on the line preceding that item. Please be open and honest in your responses.

1	2	3	4	5	6	7
Strongly Disagree	Disagree	Slightly Agree	Neutral	Slightly Agree	Agree	Strongly Agree

_____ In most ways my life is close to my ideal.
_____ The conditions of my life are excellent.
_____ I am satisfied with my life.
_____ So far I have gotten the important things I want in life.
_____ If I could live my life over, I would change almost nothing.

_____ **Total**

The Satisfaction with Life Scale[59]

If you scored a "5" or less on any responses, take stock of why that might be the case, and journal about it below. Can you think of anything missing in your world? Be totally honest with yourself. What steps will you take this week to get closer to finding fulfillment? What can you pursue that lights you up inside? Be specific and action-oriented.

If you scored above 5's, your satisfaction with life is robust, and the work for you is to maintain those scores. Journal below about why your life is "close to ideal." What contributes to that? What important things in life have you gotten, and how will you ensure you keep them around?

_____

_____

_____

_____

_____

_____

_____

_____

_____

_____

_____

_____

_____

_____

_____

_____

_____

_____

_____

_____

You can always return to this exercise, every six months or a year, to take stock of your satisfaction with life, and reflect on potential areas of improvement.

I recently heard "spirit junkie" Gabrielle Bernstein recite a prayer that I found extremely powerful for engendering purpose and aligning with it. You can recite this like a mantra, anytime you need renewal of purpose. Use the counting practice I taught you in Chapter 11 to prime you, then repeat these phrases for a quick download of guidance:

> *Universe,*
> *What would you have me do?*
> *Where would you have me go?*
> *What would you have me say?*

18
Love Connection

Without friends no one would choose to live,
though he had all other goods.
—Aristotle

Other people matter. This was the tagline of the late Dr. Chris Peterson, my graduate school advisor, and a great mentor. The phrase has become something of a maxim in the positive psychology community, as much for its objective humanitarian appeal (like "love thy neighbor") as for its absolute relevance when it comes to the fundamental role connection plays in our lives. All beings rely on connection to other beings to survive. That need rests right alongside other basic necessities.

I don't think there's an illustration of the concept more formidable (or controversial) than psychologist Harry Harlow's famous 1950s studies of rhesus monkeys.[60] Harlow wanted to probe the nature of connection, as a fundamental need, both physiological and emotional.

He set up an experiment where he separated infant rhesus monkeys from their mothers just a few hours after birth. He arranged for the little monkeys to be "raised" by two types of surrogate mothers, both inanimate: One was a bare wire mesh monkey that dispensed milk; the other was covered in soft terry cloth, but dispensed no milk. What he discovered was astonishing. The tiny monkeys spent a far greater proportion of time clinging to the terry cloth "mother" than drinking from the cage wire machine, even though that's where their physical nourishment came from. Even more compelling, the monkeys that could go back to the terry cloth mother for soothing after being exposed to loud noises or frightening stimuli developed normally. Those that didn't have this option threw themselves on the floor, screamed in terror and rocked back and forth. They were socially and emotionally stunted and pathological—illuminative given our close genetic connection to monkeys.

Through his experiments, Harlow demonstrated the importance of contact and connection to healthy development. It's not a big leap to infer that we humans need the same, and indeed, there have been many studies since comprising a wealth of research that demonstrates how fundamental a need social connection is to our well-being. When this need is satiated in our lives, we thrive. In its absence, we wither and fray.[60a] That is why it is so vital to attend mindfully to our connections, and invest energy and resources into keeping them strong.

19
The Power of Love

*My efforts now turn from trying to outrun suffering
to accepting love wherever I can find it.*
—Mark Nepo

My older sister met who was to become her first great love mere weeks into her freshman year of college. It was a beautiful and pure love, and I saw it fall to pieces over clashing religions. Hearts were broken, and many tears spilled, including my own. I felt like I was losing a member of my nuclear family.

Seeing their love falter like that, I chose a very appropriate man to marry. He was my classmate at Wharton, three years my senior, and of the same religious background as my parents. He also came from the Northern region of India, just like my family. Perfect.

Until it wasn't. All those points of commonality did not a successful marriage make. We didn't want the same things on a fundamental level. I wanted us to spread the wings of our potential and soar, where ever the wind took us, like a pair of power-couple eagles. He wanted to stay grounded, living with his parents and safely ensconced in the nucleus of the familiar. He couldn't support my big dreams and lofty ideas, especially if that meant leaving his family. I couldn't stand knowing I wasn't the priority in my marriage, much less ignore the stinging thorn of unrealized potential in my side. It became untenable, and just over two years in, we got divorced.

In the year following, I was dangerously close to becoming cynical about love, not sure it even existed. And then, in the way the Universe does when you really need it, I got the antidote to my suffering. Beyond checked boxes and resumes, indeed, to prove the truth of the aphorism "love is blind," it came in the form of a Sudanese Muslim man almost six years my junior. (Just in case you're thinking, "Another one? This girl really has a type!" Nope, same relationship I alluded to in chapter 1.)

Now, if there exists an absolute-value unfeasible choice for an Indian girl in terms of a man, it would be an African Muslim one. The cultural and religious divides are so great, endeavoring to bridge them is to cross between two mountain peaks on a tightrope. I didn't choose this man for "easy," or "rightness," quite the opposite. I resisted his attempts to get closer to me for months. Coming out of a marriage, I didn't think my heart could handle what turned out to be the exact thing it needed: to be consumed by love.

It was pure and potent, divinely ordained given how the Universe conspired to bring us together. You could see it in the way we looked at each other, recognizing one another's spirits and wanting, as one does in love, to feed the other's soul and elevate it higher. For that kind of love, and no less, we'd fight hard, through endless tears, broken hearts, and screaming matches.

He didn't see a way for us to be together; being with me meant defying his family, and this was not something he could do. Besides, he would eventually have to move back to Sudan, and I must admit, the idea of living in a place so foreign and potentially hostile without any of my family around petrified me. Flashbacks of *Not without My Daughter* come to mind.

More damning was the reality that conversion was the only way I would even be allowed to enter his family. It seemed insane to contemplate converting into a religion I neither believed in nor espoused the values of. In fact, I bucked at dogmatic ways of approaching God.

It is a cruel and agonizing torture when you've finally found a love that you want to hold onto forever, and you're forced to let it go. Worse when you've been married, and had your quota of having to "let go" quite filled. The stress of it was overpowering, and I suffered fainting spells and seizures.

Once, on the morning of an impending departure to Ireland, my mother gave me an ultimatum: If I left one more time, I would not be allowed back. My parents would sever their connection to me, and I'd be on my own without my family. As if being awake to this pain was too hard, I completely lost grip on my consciousness and I seized, my body shaking and my eyes rolling backward into my skull. When I came to, I saw only the intense fear in my mom's eyes, pleading with me not to go. But go I did, because our souls' connection pulled at me like a magnet.

Sitting my parents down one day, I went to battle for our love in one last desperate attempt. I explained that his family had finally exhausted of fighting with him, and wouldn't stand in the way of our being together as long as I converted to Islam. I have never seen my father go so white or look so alarmed. It was searing and unrelenting. As he sat there, dead quiet, his fiery eyes belied the frosty chill permeating the room. Such a proposition went against some of his deepest-held beliefs, including the rejection of any faith that wasn't inclusionary or Universalist. He could not tolerate my being forced to espouse the tenets of a religious system for love. Still, I knew my father's love for me, and I loved this man, so could he not make the leap to love this man, too?

Ultimately, we would make the mutual decision to part ways. I could not convert into a religion I did not embrace the ideals of, much less raise my children in it, and he, wanting to raise a family in Islam and in accordance with his family's wishes, could not be with me if I didn't.

Living that love story was one of the most challenging and painful experiences of my life. It was also one of the most rewarding and self-affirming. In loving someone against every odd, contrarian opinion, and voice of dissent, I got closer to my real self—a self, as it turns out, that is committed to love above all else. I literally put my money where my mouth was in that relationship, spending every last dime I earned on plane tickets to visit him. Like a parent for their child, nurturing the love was automatic and reflexive. My heart expanded in a way that it will never again shrink back from, my desire to prioritize love now magnified in every context, whether with my family, friends, or in partnership. Indeed, we can never know our limits, or our potential, until we endeavor to test it. Anytime I contemplate a time in my life when I felt I was at my best, this experience still ranks among the highest.

*****

We are brought into this world to learn the lessons of love, the main ingredient of our spirits. We are pushed to extremes of pain to show us how to make love our baseline, even when it feels impossible, like forgiving those who commit the greatest transgressions upon us. To be able to do this is to evolve in the highest as a spiritual being having a human experience. The spirit soars in love, it crumbles in hate.

Where were or are you being given opportunities for growth through love? Do you prioritize opportunities to give and receive more love, even when it's hard or it hurts? In other words, are you making sure that love is the primary currency in which you deal?

_____

_____

_____

_____

_____

_____

20
Rocky Terrain

The beginning of love is to let those we love be perfectly themselves,
and not to twist them to fit our own image. Otherwise we love only the
reflection of ourselves we find in them.
—Thomas Merton

The landscape of relationships is changing rapidly. The modern era affords most of us the freedom to explore our sexuality and relationship preferences in a way humans have never before enjoyed, the greatest leaps, perhaps, by the female gender. I'm reminded of the movie *Suffragette*, such a powerful depiction of how hard some women fought to win us the privileges we now enjoy. The right to vote, the advent of birth control, and the repeated cracks and heightening of the glass ceiling have all contributed to women being able to stand apart from a male counterpart and still be financially secure, and raise children. Denmark, where the ratio of single mothers is among the highest in the world, is a prime example. The culture is very accepting and supportive of single motherhood ("solomor"), and women feel quite comfortable in the role.[61] Incidentally, Denmark is also one of the happiest nations in the world—as of the most recent "Happiness Report," it ranked #2.[62]

The rise of social media and technologies that put the possibility of new connections in the palm of our hand with just a few keystrokes or swipes is another example of this changing landscape. It's all too easy to find an alternative when something (or someone) in your life isn't working. Don't have a partner to help build that IKEA armoire? Get instant help on an app where you can outsource such tasks. Not enough time to pick up groceries for dinner? No problem. A few clicks and a bag of ingredients arrives at your doorstep.

It's a quick-fix era, down to the way we are relating to each other romantically. When we are unhappy in our romantic partnerships, we can hop online and begin flirting with a new love interest on any one of a number of dating apps (lots of which are "hook-up" specific; talk about instant gratification). Or, we can use the same to avoid commitment completely.

You know the expression: "Why buy the cow when you can get the milk for free?" It's one of the most annoying and yet apt expressions for the baseline relationship dynamic between men and women. Men have a strong evolutionary drive to spread their seed as often and into as many females as possible. Watch an episode of a nature show with wild animals mating and you'll see the truth of this. During mating season, the male's main objective is to ensure his seed produces progeny that carry on the species. The female's objective is to pick the strongest, most powerful male to impregnate her so her offspring will be genetically superior, have access to resources and protection and the greatest chances of survival. These are respective genetic wins.

Males and females of our species have the same drives and instincts, and it's no wonder we're seeing the sociological and anthropological trends that we are. There are cows everywhere, searching for strapping bulls. The milk is prolific as the cows search, so why wouldn't the bulls be tempted to partake and satisfy this deepest of genetic and biological cravings without having to commit to just one cow? Indeed, monogamy and marriage are primarily human constructs, and many argue they are against males' fundamental biology. As such, when my married female friends advise me on how to successfully court a male, advice usually includes giving men "the chase," meting out "the kibble" (to connote the slow doling out of attention, including waiting on having sex), and feigning reserve even when your heart is swelling with love.

As a recovering romance addict, I myself am figuring out how to best address this new reality. My favorite movies include *300*, *Gladiator*, and *Avatar*. The reason these movies are my favorites (aside from being cinematic marvels with next-level acting and endlessly quotable one-liners) is because they are epic love stories. Oh yes, look beyond the violence and gore and you've got incredibly romantic tales. (Spoiler alert! If you haven't seen the aforementioned movies, presumably because you've been living under a rock, and you don't want me to ruin the endings for you, skip ahead to the next paragraph.)

At the end of *300*, as Leonidas falls to his knees, about to meet his demise, what does he scream? Not "Curse you hunchback!" or "Sparta, Ahh-OOH!" His last words are "My Queen! My wife! My love!!" Love is literally the last word of a movie fundamentally about stoicism, battle, and war.

Same with *Gladiator*. As Maximus lies dying in the arena, having saved Rome from the depraved clutches of the Emperor Commodus, he hallucinates images of his home, and of his dead wife and child. His deepest desire was never for glory, fame, or "the win." All he ever wanted was to be reunited with his beloved family.

From tiny monkeys to the blockbuster world of Hollywood, love and connection reign supreme and remain fundamental to our thriving. However, the way we do love is increasingly more complex, no longer as simple as monkeys choosing snuggles and heroes dying (pun intended) to be with their wives. We must therefore rethink the way we interact and relate, because if we continue to do so based on old norms, we set ourselves up for a fall when one or the other partner fails to meet those expectations. Traditional wedding vows, for example, include statements like "I promise to forsake all others," and "till death do us part." *I promise to forsake all others.* As much as my poor romantic heart would love to believe this is a natural desire when one finds their true love, a world replete with dating apps, and prolific "cows" and the bulls that chase them, makes this a rare occurrence.

Till death do us part. Or, till I find a better job in a new location. It's a truly global arena now, and we're no longer beholden to our legs to determine how many miles we can traverse. With planes, trains, and automobiles of all kinds, we can travel far and wide with ease. And even when it's not voluntary, we may involuntarily be relocated to a new country for a job—a whole new set of customs, cultures, and dating pools to go along with it. We have so much more freedom to roam than we ever did, and staying sedentary is not in our genetic code anyway. We like to move, to be stimulated by new sights and sounds, to explore and grow. I never met a person who said they didn't want or like to travel, unless they had never been outside of their comfort zone and didn't know the difference. Given the chance, we'd rather be free than chained, and "till death do us part" sounds an awful lot like signing up for shackles than liberation.

Let me assure you, I don't say any of this out of cynicism. I am as much a champion for love and monogamous partnership as I ever was. I simply have a responsibility to address the paradigm shift we're living into and hopefully help you navigate it with more ease. I've been married and understand firsthand how much we can suffer when we're not in the right partnership. I also realize a world in which many of my "happily married" friends doing it the "till death do us part" way aren't all that happy. Perhaps this is because they entered the arrangement for less than true love; perhaps they are coming up against technology and the global arena like exotic animals whose habitat is slowly shrinking around them. The point is, having to confront changing times can lead to a serious questioning of one's ideals. And that's giving way to some really unique, revolutionary, and downright radical new scenarios. I encounter such variegated forms of partnership and coupling these days, I'm rarely shocked. In fact, I have come to understand and really appreciate alternative styles. The landscape of my life—I'm a woman in my late thirties who has been loathe to entertain relationships that put my spirit at risk—compels me to do so.

The hetero-homo coupling scenario is an example. This generally looks like a gay man and a straight woman deciding to have children together, coexisting not as much in passion as true partnership. I've got some absolutely fabulous gay friends who I adore and spend a good chunk of my time with. If I wake up feeling an innate and strong desire to have children, more than one of them would make fine fathers and partners in child-rearing.

It still makes me laugh when I remember how some years ago my brother-in-law was convinced I'd find someone to settle down with in grad school, erasing the memories of my painful divorce and the star-crossed love that followed. He was somewhat on target... I did emerge with two new partnerships, but it wasn't some polyandrous double marriage; I scored two gay besties.

As an aside, it begs pointing out that what you truly desire at a soul level, the Universe provides. I always longed for a gay best friend, someone with whom I could be open and unabashedly honest, without the complication of being desired sexually, or the constant fear that I'd offend the sensitivity of one of the females in my inner circle. I got not one, but two. Don't be careful what you wish for, just be deliberate about it, so you magnetize only what you truly want at the soul level, as I pointed out before. And when you finally get it, remember to appreciate it and feel grateful for it because you have a tangible manifestation of your soul's longing. And that, whenever it is realized, is magic.

The magic of finding my own gay besties has helped me to understand why a heterosexual single woman would choose to couple with a homosexual man. In fact, just the other day, one of my closest friends, a handsome uber-talented gay man, proposed. Well, the idea of us having a baby together anyway. In the next few years, if it was something we both wanted and neither of us had yet, would I consider it? Without missing a beat, I said that I would. Romantic or not, I was refreshingly open to the possibility.

Such is the changing world we live in. In partnership, especially where children are involved, the ideal environment is one infused with harmony, not fraught with conflict. During my training in clinical psychology, in a practice specializing in couples and families, my mentor would often say, "The greatest gift a couple can give to their offspring is a happy marriage." Coming from an expert adept at helping families discover joy and harmony, I took that observation very much to heart.

That said, passion and fire are often inversely correlated with stability and security. I've had my share of such relationship scenarios, arguments and melodramas feeding the intrigue while simultaneously creating untenable anxiety. It's like riding a huge swell of a wave versus floating in a boat on a placid lake. One's risky and thrilling and brings on a rush of adrenaline as you navigate waters that threaten to take you under; the other is predictable and guarantees safe passage.

There are merits in both, and as human beings, we certainly crave both, but which is more responsible parenting as far as your progeny's safety and survival? Having them strapped to your back as you commandeer a tumultuous wave, or nestled inside a boat as you row along unperturbed waters? Perhaps for exactly this reason, there are increasingly more examples of scenarios that allow people to raise children in the boat, and seek the big waves outside the comfort of the home. Partnerships where both individuals are free to explore romantic relationships that satisfy them, in which they mutually decide parameters around how to navigate in the best interest of the family unit they're creating, are gaining in popularity. Talk about evolved.

That includes heterosexual couples who allow each other to entertain intimate or romantic scenarios outside the marriage to keep it stable and flourishing. Though it sounds counterintuitive, it seems the liberty to be completely oneself, without judgment, consequence, or the need to deceive, acts as a kind of glue that keeps some partners together. "Open marriage" is one label for it, though that tends to make people desperately uncomfortable and squirmy. I rather prefer "explorative partnership." I recently saw a movie that addresses this subject matter quite poignantly and elegantly. It's called 5 to 7, and in case you haven't seen it, don't worry, I won't do the spoiler thing again just to make my point. I'll simply assign this movie to you as important research and leave you to it.

In the meantime, an example from my own life: I was recently introduced to a married couple, a young Asian woman and her Nordic-looking mate, both strikingly attractive. Immediately upon being introduced to me, the wife shoved our mutual friend and her husband aside to edge in closer to me. A yellowjacket bee-lining to golden brown honey, she enfolded me in an embrace that was intimate and lingering. I laughed at the overt nature of her attraction; she made no attempt to conceal it nor was she in the least bit apologetic. Her husband stood by plain-faced. As soon as she had completed her dynamic overture, she stepped to my side and I introduced myself to her mate. I wondered if he was upset or embarrassed by what had just transpired. If so, he didn't show it. After I had shaken his hand, I whispered an inquiry to my friend, *"What just happened there?"* He replied that her husband knew of her interest in women, and was supportive of her exploration. He was allowing her the freedom to be her real self, and at the end of the day, that's fundamental to our thriving in partnership.

Choose the adventure that feels right for *you* on this journey of life, not someone else's version or projection. After all, you've only got one (in this physical form anyway), so make it the most truthful and authentic it can be. Just make sure that no matter which way you choose to live, you do so with integrity and grace. Your relationships are among your greatest blessings, and how you handle them is of utmost importance. Whether an entrance into, an exit from, or navigation through, every relationship dynamic can be conducted gracefully.

The key is communication. A strong way to begin any relationship is to be honest about your expectations. For example, if you want your partner to share equally in all of the finances and chores, express that up front instead of silently hoping they'll live up to the standard you set. Entering into relationships with agreements formed early on will minimize confusion and upset later (and it's a short hop from confusion and upset to anger and resentment).

My best friend and I recently took a road trip together, and before we left, we laid out some ground rules around finances so we wouldn't have to have awkward conversations along the way, wondering who would pay for what. That sort of forthright communication is the foundation for all aspects of our relationship. When one or the other of us feels hurt or upset, for example, we bring that truth to each other even if our inclination is to retreat. Most people avoid difficult conversations because they are uncomfortable or disruptive. We've all lost friends in our lives, oftentimes because we've spoken truths that can't be retracted. That makes us scared to speak up. We'd rather swallow down our hurt and hope it will eventually dissipate than risk losing a connection in which we're so heavily invested. Here's another good opportunity to choose faith, not fear; have the courage to communicate honestly. If the relationship is based on love and mutual respect, it will be able to withstand such candor and flourish through it. If not, let it go, knowing your growth depends on your ability to be open and free and you play small when airs or facades restrain you. These communications are mirrors for self-reflection that we tend not to want to acknowledge. Don't diminish your growth potential by avoiding your mirrors. Face them. All connections exist to help us evolve, and not all are meant to be in our lives for the long haul. Trust the higher purpose in the design of your life, accept the impermanence of all things, and you can live your real truth, with conviction instead of needless suffering.

Given a landscape where most communication is happening online, or via text, it is becoming easier to avoid difficult conversations, especially when it comes to a parting of ways. Have you heard of "ghosting"? It alludes to the act of disappearing on someone after a date, a hook-up, or maybe even a short relationship, without any communication to indicate an end. It's probably so common because of how many apps and hearts we seem to be juggling at once. We want the thrill and satisfaction of all those cows and bulls, but don't seem to have the wherewithal to retain our humanity and integrity around keeping that many exchanges active. It's fantastically disrespectful to engage someone in a relationship of any kind and then just pull a disappearing act. At best, a person is left hanging until they themselves realize they've been ghosted and move on. At worst, their self-esteem takes a major hit. Denying someone closure keeps them guessing around what went wrong, and ultimately, leads to self-doubt and low self-esteem. It's unnecessary suffering that can have ripple effects through future relationships and communications, leaving cynicism and jaded mistrust in its wake. Don't be the jerk that pays *that* forward. After all, wouldn't you rather contribute to the total tonnage of happiness in the world than add to the suffering?

Have the maturity to acknowledge an end if there must be one, and rise above your own fear or hesitation and communicate your position honestly and delicately. Wish the recipient well and send them off in light and love. Even if not in the moment of their most acute pain, the receiver of your words will ultimately value your honesty. They'll look back on the time you shared with appreciation, instead of through a lens colored with negative emotions.

It's a tragedy to see hearts closing down or scarring over because someone didn't respect themselves enough to give another closure. Yes, I said "themselves," because not having the courage to speak formidable truths aloud ultimately boils down to weakness in ourselves, a fundamental lack of self-respect because we can't own our truth, be who we truly are. That is to say, we play, and stay, small. Make the strong effort to close out every relationship you begin with integrity, so that all hearts involved stay open and receptive.

21
Growing Pains

You desire to know the art of living, my friend?
It is contained in one phrase: Make use of suffering.
—Henri Frédéric Amiel

Some life experiences trigger intense negative emotions to come bubbling to the surface of our conscious experience. These emotions don't feel good, and they're not meant to, because the more agitated or upset we are, the more likely we are to pay attention. If we are committed to growth, we'll use that attention to see the pain for what it really is: a reflection of the very space within ourselves that we can use as leverage to evolve.

Patience is one of those areas for me. I haven't been a historically tolerant person, quick to dissolve into irritation or imbalance when my limits are tested. As such, I've gotten potent help in learning how to cultivate more obliging of my life, in the form of mindfulness training, and scenarios that require me to bring this virtue to my interactions, like when spending time with my niece and nephew.

It isn't easy to change these sticky areas of our personalities. Growing pains hurt, and we suffer if we aren't patient with the expansion and space being created for our newer, bigger selves. If we doubt or resist, we end up in turmoil. The key is to stay calm and in equanimity no matter what life serves you, trusting that eventually, all will unfold in perfect balance and harmony. A daily mindfulness practice is central to helping you cultivate this ability.

I've got an acquaintance who seems to emulate every professional move I make, finding success from my original ideas, no apparent compunctions about taking them as her own. I've been through my share of upset about it, feeling a spectrum of emotions ranging from irritation to anger. I did a good amount of work reflecting on why she triggers me so, and realized it's a strong pattern in my life that keeps manifesting. I get a rush from devising original thought, from making new connections or putting things together in unique ways to create experiences that reflect the road "less traveled." It feels hard to have another claim my ideas without credit, to feel like my edge is being tenderized toward the generic when all I want is to project a unique persona that contributes something fresh to the world. It means a great deal to me that my voice might change the world for the better in a way that only I could do. I suppose I feel like this gives me singular purpose, and validates my existence.

If I step outside of myself, I realize this reaction is my ego flaring up. It's the "me" part of me that wants to remain separate and individuated. #playingsmall. That anyone would follow my lead should be the ultimate complement, an indication that my unique identity is being recognized and appreciated (caveat: plagiarism is still wrong!). On a larger level, playing big means using that "competition" as momentum to drive me further and higher, flexing my creative muscles constantly to stay fresh—just as Olympians use each others' progress to hit new peaks and *break records*.

Here's another opportunity to be an Olympian of your thriving. Use negative emotions to spurn you on rather than to shut down or become a lesser version of yourself. Smile when your creativity sparks another flame, because the combination of the two is much brighter than either alone, if you choose to see it that way.

And when you've grown out of your container to the maximum capacity that your mind and body can handle in any given moment, ask for help from the Universe. If you acknowledge that it all exists in the interest of your highest evolution, and you ask from that place of reverence and purity, the help *always* comes.

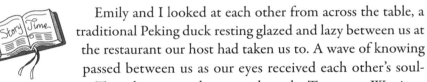 Emily and I looked at each other from across the table, a traditional Peking duck resting glazed and lazy between us at the restaurant our host had taken us to. A wave of knowing passed between us as our eyes received each other's soul-awareness. The others wanted to go and see the Terracotta Warriors, a desire they expressed with gusto. Our hesitation made obvious that we didn't feel called to that experience. Almost in unison, we vocalized that we wanted to "see monasteries!" her voice just a fraction behind mine, like an overlapping echo. Our eyes went wide with amusement and magic, lighting up at the convergence and consequent "rightness" of what we were being drawn to.

Back at the hotel a short while later, we made some inquiries. We were in Beijing to present at China's first conference on positive psychology, and we had just one day free. The concierge opened a guidebook to a section on "monasteries," and as we perused our options, we were both immediately on the same page (#pagepun) about a placed called Wu Tai Shan. It's description read, "a spiritual center of the world." Wu Tai Shan was nestled in the mountains, several hours away from Beijing, and he explained that he could book us tickets on the train for the outbound journey, but we would need to procure tickets for the way home when we arrived. My slight apprehension around not having a return secured given our conference commitments the next day was quite overshadowed by the pull to experience the journey, and we found ourselves on an overnight train that evening, heading deep into the mountains toward enlightenment.

We rested peacefully in our sleeper car, awaking to the mousy screeching of the train slowing to a halt at its depot. We disembarked in the pre-dawn indigo, filing out of the compartment to find not one, but several buses lined up in angular rows. Having no idea which one was ours, Emily and I locked together at the forearms and moved forward, swept up in the tide swelling toward the humming vehicles. I was so grateful for the sheet on which the hotel concierge had written various phonetic pronunciations of keywords and phrases in Mandarin: "Train station," "Please," "Wu Tai Shan," "Hello," and "Beijing," among them.

We began at the first bus, making our way down the line and pointing at the phrase "Wu Tai Shan" to each driver. We were repeatedly met with shakes of the head "no," and I was beginning to wonder if something hadn't gotten lost in translation at the concierge desk. My nervousness at last gave way to relief when the inquiry was met with a nod "yes." It's like that in such situations, persistent excitement and anxiety around the unabating stream of unknowns, rotund moments of relief when a variable becomes a constant.

We boarded the bus, and secured the only two empty seats amongst the rows packed with locals. Our seats happened to be just in front of the only other foreign faces on the bus, a mousy-haired bloke in his twenties seated alongside his flaxen-tressed girlfriend. While Mandarin phrases saturated the air, adding vertigo to our baseline discombobulation, I extracted a thin strand of comprehension from the din. The couple behind us seemed to be speaking . . . *French*? I had studied the language for several years in school, wondering often if I shouldn't have studied Spanish instead for how rarely French was of practical use to me. Validation from the Universe, because it was about to save our a**es.

I asked first if they spoke English, to which they shook their heads "no." *Seulement Francais*. "Bien," I continued, and then in my slightly grammatically challenged French, inquired about how to secure passage back to Beijing. Our new friends obligingly conveyed that they would show us to the bus depot once we got to Wu Tai Shan.

The depot office was closed when we arrived, but the young Frenchman assured us it would open later to meet the afternoon traffic heading out of the mountains. Placated, Emily and I went in search of breakfast.

As we made our pilgrimage through Wu Tai Shan, it was like being enveloped by an energetic potential that seeped further into my cells with each passing hour—like plugging into a power outlet with higher voltage. My cells were buzzing and I felt alive with life force. A testament to the magic surrounding us, we stumbled upon a chanting meditation at a monastery that rested on the tallest of the scattered mountain peaks. We were welcomed right in, and discovered we had just hooked into a very special moment, a celebration that happened but once every hundred years. We joined the other pilgrims as they walked slowly in a large clockwise circle, holding tiny tea lights and singing chants. We were welcomed in with gentle smiles and nods, as if they were expecting us, these two foreign bodies from a faraway land.

Over the next few hours, we saturated ourselves in the magic of that holy place, receiving the gifts of its frequency.

Around mid-afternoon, we returned to the bus depot to arrange our departure. We were satiated but spent, and ready to make our way back. We approached the counter and began to explain that we needed return tickets to Beijing. Despite the cue cards, we were met with blank stares and apathetic shoulder shrugs. My frustration and anxiety mounted as I contemplated how blind Emily and I were flying, quickly running out of cash in a place with no ATMs and zero sense of the bus schedule or whether there would even be one that day to return us to the train station. I envisioned doomsday outcomes like being no-show's for our presentations, or worse, ending up stranded in these remote lands with no place to stay.

Feeling helpless and desperate, I told Emily I needed some air. As we exited the office, there was a tug from deep inside me to "plug in." I closed my eyes, dove into my depths, and asked for assistance. The journey so far had been enlightening and powerful, tears shed at the top of that highest monastery as I resolved to move through a broken heart to healing. The ceremony we had converged with, conducted once a century, that we happened upon at the very instant it was taking place? That was a magical blessing we were meant to receive. I prayed for guidance lest this fear and worry flooding my body erode the beauty that had been our experience so far. I was exhausted, teary, and hitting my limit of self-regulation. I was also growing impatient and short, and had already snapped at Emily. In this place of magic and love, those emotions would sully the purity of the experience, and that was unacceptable to me. I willed a path to clear and save me from that darkness.

When I opened my eyes, I had a renewed faith, from which sprouted fortitude, and marched right back into the ticket office, ready to make our needs understood.

As I opened my mouth to express the desire for two tickets, pulling out the translation card to supplement our foreign tongue, a young woman, who had not been there before, responded. *In English.* I could barely comprehend the grace in this blessing, floored by the miracle of prayers answered. I explained that we needed two tickets on the next bus back to town, so we could catch the train to Beijing. She confirmed that the bus would leave at 4:00 p.m., and once we arrived, we'd need to purchase the train tickets for Beijing at the station there. As we made our way out of the small office, my relief was palpable, a coating of tears slicking my eyes. With what little change we had left, we went in search of supper.

Later that night, we found ourselves back at the town where we had depot'd not twenty-four hours earlier. Closed when we had arrived, the train station office was finally open for business. We made our way to the front of the long line, and I inquired about two tickets in the sleeper car back to Beijing. The attendant understood very little English, but got enough of the gist from my gestures—hands folded together and tucked under my cocked right ear like a pillow—that I was asking for sleeping accommodations. He laughed and shook his head, there were no such tickets left. His laughter implied they were sold long ago, our lack of understanding of the protocol evident in our late request.

With a resigned sigh, I said we'd like two seats, sitting back into an imaginary chair to illustrate. He shook his head. "Only standing," he conveyed in heavily accented English. My shock and dismay must have been evident on my face, for he looked almost apologetic before his annoyance at the growing line behind me took over and he pressed me for a decision. I looked at Emily in alarm. *A whole night awake on the train . . . standing?* It felt like some kind of torture sentence. Given our tremendous fatigue, I was loathe to even consider it. Yet, it was our only option if we were going to make it back in time to give our presentations the next afternoon. I nodded my head in slow motion, begrudgingly accepting our fate to stand on the overnight train back to Beijing.

As we waited in line to board, I felt another surge of negative feelings, their presence once again threatening the purity of the experience. Enervated and on the verge of tears, I stepped back from the line, telling Emily I needed a moment. She was by now familiar with "the process," and in her buoyant faith, smiled happily at what magic might unfold. I leaned against a column in the station, and closed my eyes. I reconnected to my underbelly, the spacious place of pure potential residing deep within, and willed for the journey to be comfortable. In whatever way this might unfold, I simply wanted us to be able to power down and find respite after such an ardent pilgrimage.

I emerged from my meditation just as the line was surging forward, Emily and I again hooking arms as we were swept along to the train doors. Climbing aboard, we were met with the inevitable: a sea of full seats and a mass of people. We wove our way to the center of the train car, not quite sure where to stand or how to place ourselves. That's when I noticed him. The hazy glow that surrounded his body was a beacon that drew my focus and held my gaze fixed to it. This gently smiling monk dressed in a staid brown toga was gesturing for us to take his seat, as he moved across the aisle to find space in an already crowded berth. Somehow, the other passengers simply made room for him, seamlessly shifting their bodies to accommodate the holy man. The whole operation seemed to take place in one graceful maneuver, as if scripted. As I stared at the empty space designated for Emily and me, I felt God.

*****

That story is powerful evidence of the virtue of following your heart, having faith in the unfolding of your life, learning to tap into higher energetic potential, and asking for help from the Universe when you really need it. The last one is key, given that all of our moments of deep discomfort signify opportunities for growth. We'll grow as much as we can take the pain. When we max out, we can scale back and find relief, but also a staving off of that growth. Don't cheat yourself of growth opportunities before you're truly maxed out. Be mindful of the difference (only you know where your personal line is), and learn to embrace the pain and discomfort as your evolutionary levers.

Life unfolds perfectly when you act from a pure and righteous place because, law-of-attraction-style, you magnetize exactly that back. *Trust* this. It can be tempting to go to a negative or dark place when adversity strikes, sliding us out of faith in the divine unfolding of our lives. This is how we create our own "bad" situations, though we may work consistently at being good and doing good. Challenging situations befall the best of us, and there is always learning to be gleaned and purpose to be revealed, if we can be objective enough with our pain to see it.

Think about the mother who lost her thirteen-year-old daughter to a drunk driver, and then started the campaign Mothers Against Drunk Driving. One life, and a mother's commitment to its memorial, saved countless others. Or Amy Purdy, an avid snowboarder who, at just nineteen years old, lost both legs to a life-threatening bout of meningitis. She went on to develop a prosthesis that would allow her not just to snowboard again, but become a world champion in the sport. The planet is full of such examples: human beings who overcome immense tragedy, incredible odds, and tests of survival to contribute something powerful to humanity and find deep meaning and purpose in the process.

Take a look in the mirrors of your own life—particularly at past adversities and traumas. When you confront your pain-points, you can begin the work of recognizing the many ways in which the Universe provides you these vehicles as opportunities for growth. They are your greatest teachers, the ultimate rocket boosters to becoming a more divine being. We often resist these vehicles, for we do not immediately recognize them. They feel injurious, affronts that we question with *Why me? What have I done to deserve this? How is this fair?!* Instead, we should be asking for grace, in recognizing the blessings through our pain, as necessary routes to a more spiritual whole. This takes awareness, and practice. Through a mindful lens, you can receive your world in this way and find absolute grace as you elevate.

My best friend and I had been talking of late about how we wanted to get out more and meet new people (er, men). We set a goal, and were accountable to each other for meeting it: Sign up for one new event each week that we could sweeten with our energy and hopefully magnetize some candy back.

It was my first outing of the initiative—an evening at Fork, a restaurant of great repute in downtown Philly owned by a fellow Whartonite—and I was already running late, stuck at our family business office. It wasn't until after five on most days that the hectic pace of the day calmed down some and we—myself, my mother, and my father—had some space to discuss more meta level matters pertaining to our operations and future directions. At this point in time, we had decided to close down the business and were in the process of selling the properties we owned and managed to free up resources to do our humanitarian work of mindfulness advocacy. The decisions were complex and layered, as well as intense and emotional. We had to proceed cautiously so as not to sell for too low a price and risk my parents' retirement pension while simultaneously working as quickly as possible to make sure that my father, already in his eighties, would still have some energy left to do his real passion work with our non-profit. We couldn't be conscientious enough with these deliberations, and conscientiousness takes time. That was, therefore, the resource I was short on.

Standing at the office door, I was ready for departure. My father was still talking as I held one hand on the doorknob, not wanting to leave in the midst of his thought stream, also not wanting to be harried and rushing. When I finally emerged from the vortex and got into my car, it was 6:40 p.m. The dinner was to start at 7:00 p.m. and was all the way across town, a thirty-minute drive on a good day.

At just after seven, I rolled up to the restaurant. My heart sank as I scanned the block to my right and left looking for an open space and found not a one. I felt the stress creep in. My muscles began to tense and warmth prickled my arm pits as my frustration mounted. I felt resentful and angry, ruing everything and nothing in particular. Raging hormones from my impending menstrual cycle surely had something to do with it, but still, I was exhausted from a long day and not keen to add stress to it. I dared not blame my parents, often the easiest targets and the least culpable, or the traffic, over which any attempt to exercise control or express dismay never seemed to move the cars any faster. I took some deep slow breaths and began to feel my nervous system calm and my body cool off, *I am always protected* whispered from somewhere deep within. Whenever I was late, whatever the scenario, things seemed to work out okay. In fact, I had frequently noticed that whether I was early (rarely), or late, I would walk in just at the right time to connect with a VIP, make an entrance, or avoid a precarious situation. This night was no exception; I just didn't know it yet.

As I looped around block after block looking for parking, faith in the divine unfolding of my life once again gave way to doubt and aggravation. Parking in Philadelphia was free on Wednesday evenings after 6:00 p.m., and I wanted to snag a spot on the street. It would represent a small triumph in the constant battle with the Parking Authority, and I craved that victory. I got more and more incensed as the minutes ticked by, still no parking and now it was ten-past-seven.

The event was a sit-down dinner hosted by the restaurant owner who was also giving a talk on her journey to becoming a successful restaurateur. I was excited about the chance to learn from an insider and fellow alum what Hollywood often depicted in films as fraught with tension and scandal. Cutthroat competition and backstabbing during quests for Michelin stars came to mind, Bradley Cooper's smoking hot visage in *Burnt* top of that mind. Somehow these images were doping me up with anticipation and a simultaneous fury. My frenzied mind, distracted by its parking quest, was perhaps not clear enough to parse out my Bradley Cooper associations with the dinner I was running late for, so it was basically as if I was running late to a dinner with Bradley Cooper.

I was reaching my limit of patience and finally gave up the search and pulled into a nearby lot already crowded with cars. I inquired about space and the attendant lifted up his pointer finger, "one," and then slowly lowered it to aim in the direction of a gentleman in an ancient Mercedes, taking his sweet time lighting a cigar while cajoling his reluctant ride into action. My agitation mounted as I inquired of the lot attendant whether I could leave and he wait on Father Time to dole out another ten years. He demurred, saying it wasn't "that kind of lot," that I had to wait until he parked and gave me the key back. I was jumping out of my skin when the attendant finally sauntered over to me. It was almost amusing how very slowly everything was going, as if too coincidental to be coincidence, but I was too riled up to see that meta truth. I lurched forward to grab the key from him, my body flaring up with fight or flight mechanics. I sped-walked the two blocks to the restaurant, my cheeks growing hot as I imagined bursting disruptively into the intimate and ceremonious gathering, a rebel alone without a cause beyond the desire for free parking.

At 7:18 p.m., I scurried into the restaurant and told the waitress I was there for the Wharton Club dinner. I could have sworn her eyes held reproach as she led me to the private dining room in the back. I steadied myself for my entrance, holding my breath so as to make as little noise as possible, and pushed the door open . . .

What greeted me was typical of virtually every scenario in which we formulate an outcome in our minds that is a product of anxiety and anticipation—it's spot off. As I crept gingerly into the dining room, what enveloped me was not silence but the din of chatter as folks stood conversing in small groups of two and three. A few glanced my way, but for the most part, my entrance went largely unnoticed. I placed my name badge on my dress and looked around the room, wondering who might be interesting to talk to—or who might be interested in talking with me. It was clear any attempt to jump into the conversations already in motion would be awkward and energetically expensive. I could scarcely muster the will. I made my way to the long table in the center and placed my bag down on a chair. I glanced up once again, promising myself I'd override my tiredness and interact if I got a smile or some eye contact to draw me in. Finding none, I pulled out my phone and proceeded to busy myself with a displeased rant to my best friend about why it was I didn't open myself up to these things more. I was moody, stressed, and exhausted, and in this context I now had to make an effort to be sociable and make small talk and hope my dream guy showed up? That didn't seem likely anyway, as the predominant demographic in the room was silver-haired retirees.

Several minutes and a seat change later (I was ousted from my chair by a middle-aged woman who claimed she had saved the one I was in with a dirty napkin), and dinner was only just getting underway. I immediately realized that had I stayed in flow and had faith in the fact that the Universe and its divine design always protect me, I would have arrived right on time. Those precious extra minutes that I could've spent wrapping up with my parents, scoring coveted street parking, or even taking a moment to interact with the lot attendant to inquire about his day or share a laugh were squandered rushing to a dinner that hadn't started yet. In the words of U2, running to stand still. In retrospect, it would've been far more pleasant to stay in the moment and let it unfold as it was trying to, without me pushing or resisting.

Of course, as with so many truths we instinctively know to be real, we still find ways to doubt. And on this day, running late and harried, I couldn't tell my mind to quiet down long enough to heed the whisper of this truth. Had I, I would have walked in at the perfect time, plopped down into the empty seat next to an extremely handsome Wharton professor (who, minor detail, also happened to be seated alongside his beautiful wife) and had a perfectly lovely evening, all without the precursors of agitation, stress, and paying for premium parking.

22
Seeing the Light

What is to give light must endure burning.
—Victor Frankl

You may recall from Section II the armed robbery in which my mother was terrorized. The negative consequences of the incident are clear and overt: not just that it happened, but also the reverberations of PTSD that have plagued her since, including chronic insomnia, up-swells of panic when contractors come into the office without warning, and waves of distrust and paranoia.

The more subtle and potent question is whether there is any light to be revealed from this darkness, if there is a way we can derive meaning from this ostensible tragedy. Did my mother *need* this experience to further her soul's journey? To evolve into a higher self?

At face value, it's like victimizing the victim. And it's my own mother, so it stings hard to even say it out loud. But bear with me for a moment, as we try to leave emotion at the door, and get to a place of higher understanding. If we can process our lives in a way that makes sense of a seemingly disorderly and chaotic world, we can begin to truly understand—and take ownership of—our place in it. In this way, we can work toward our purpose without suffering. As Einstein said, "Yet, only one thing must be remembered: There is no effect without a cause, and there is no lawlessness in creation."[63]

If there is no effect without a cause, whence did this awful crime that befell my mother come? In a literal sense, the cause was Marcus Johnson, the contractor's son who would come to the office with his father, watching as business was conducted and cash changed hands. Through the quick work of a fastidious and adept detective, the thread of guilt was traced back to him. He had orchestrated the whole thing, sending in two men whom he knew my mother would neither recognize nor overtly fear. No doubt he was playing to the same stereotypes we as a society are plagued by every time a young black man is wrongfully shot and killed by a police officer: assumed criminality based on skin color. We might say the inception point was the moment he hatched the scheme in his mind, and called upon help to put it into motion. But what if it were so much bigger than that? What if our own judgments about who is "safe" and who is "threatening" put us exactly in a position to be shown otherwise? Johnson played a hand based on that assumption. Had mom played right into that hand? In that moment at the door, when her instinct told her these men were not to be trusted, her rational mind belied that truth. Among others, this experience presents some salient growth opportunities around the veracity of our inner knowledge versus the temptations of our outer judgments.

A quote by neurologist-psychiatrist Viktor Frankl opened this section because his writings and teachings on meaning are among the most powerful I've come across. Indeed, he has had a profound impact on millions, including some of the greatest thought leaders I know. I've heard his work, particularly ideas from *Man's Search for Meaning*, quoted prolifically at psychology conferences among peers who are asking some of life's toughest and most salient questions.

Man's Search for Meaning describes the inhumane and hellish nature of Frankl's internment at a Nazi concentration camp, and is a powerful manifesto around finding meaning in all facets of existence, even the most brutal ones, so we have the motivation to keep living. Frankl says, "Suffering ceases to be suffering at the moment it finds a meaning."[64]

So, how can we derive meaning from our most severe experiences? To what degree can we think about traumatic events through a lawful (as in, the opposite of Einstein's "lawless") lens?

Here is some of the potent learning I've gleaned from the armed robbery:

- Learning to trust and properly interpret the guidance of the enteric nervous system could amplify our collective intelligence and the scope of the human experience by unimaginable amounts.
- To become aware of stereotypes and biases against those who look like they might cause you harm versus favoring those who often get exempt is fundamental to how our planet will heal itself of racism.
- To forgive those who have hurt and harmed you—and recognize that we all falter—is grace epitomized. It is the ultimate spiritual evolution.
- To leverage our own challenges to help ease the suffering of others allows us to turn our pain into purpose and service.

The moral is this: If you are a righteous energy, with pure and good intentions, the Universe supports you fully in your evolution as a spiritual being on a human journey. If all energy in the Universe is based on one overarching pattern, around which we define algorithms and formulas, as Einstein, Newton, and many other brilliant and beautiful minds have posited, then as constituents of this Universe, our energy undoubtedly follows the same blueprint. We're part of one big rhythm of up and down, in and out, ebb and flow. You, therefore, need never doubt any of your experiences, and can trust the unfolding of your life without suffering, even when painful or aggravating events occur. Think back to Jill Bolte Taylor and her story—as a neuroscientist, who better to have a "stroke of insight"? Taylor endured a terrifying and precarious physical ordeal, but through her voice, many in the science world can give credence to the intense spiritual journey she experienced because her assessment "speaks their language." It feels divine in its design, like Einstein theorized.

In this infinite and orderly algorithm, we're meant to learn, grow, and evolve to become our highest selves. What your highest self represents you will find deep within you, as a fundamental truth you can access through meditation. You will be met with challenges commensurate with the growth you are able to handle, and the leaps you are capable of making. And if this all leads you to your end, you can trust that, too, because you're part of a divine order of balance. *There is no lawlessness in creation.*

If we transcend ourselves enough to allow for this truth to hold, we live each day in joy, not fear. We are given those experiences that will support our unique and personal spiritual evolution. Everyone alive—until their last breath—is learning and growing. It is our choice whether we come to receive those growth opportunities as our friends, or whether we resist them as foes. Post-traumatic stress occurs when we are unable to handle the outcomes of a traumatic event productively. Without the right support, we can spiral into darkness. But with help to find perspective and renewed purpose, we can turn our greatest upsets into assets. We can flourish.

Important and impactful change on the planet—a net gain for humanity—is often inextricable from loss, perhaps in holding the very balance the laws of science dictate. Abraham Lincoln, Mahatma Gandhi, John F. Kennedy, and Martin Luther King Jr. are iconic examples. Even in death, they continue to inspire a better world, their influence perhaps amplified because they were assassinated—a testament to the high-risk–high-reward nature of freedom-fighting, and a constant reminder that we must not allow their deaths to have been in vain. Freedom is the most valuable and essential privilege of humanity, and these champions lost their lives for it. Those lives, and the bravery inherent in them, perpetuate in every movement, memory, and inspired protest in the name of freedom. On a meta level then, even when we meet our end, we can continue to inspire positive momentum and change based on our actions in this life. There can always be a larger purpose to why bad things happen to good people, and in fact, if we change our labels to suit this larger purpose, all things that happen to all people have the potential to be beautiful. Fight to find the meaning in your life, for it will nurture your existence into a thriving one.

In the space below, list five things in your life that have been challenging or painful. This could be a difficult relationship, a loss of some kind, a health issue, etc.

1. _____

_____

_____

2. _____

_____

_____

3. _____

_____

_____

4. _____

_____

_____

5. _____

_____

_____

Use the space below to reflect on how each of these situations has brought you new learning and growth. How are you a more evolved self as a product of these experiences? Also think about how each experience may have contributed to someone else's enlightenment.

_____

_____

_____

_____

_____

_____

_____

_____

_____

_____

_____

_____

_____

_____

_____

_____

_____

_____

_____

_____

_____

_____

_____

23
Getting Served

The best way to find yourself is to lose yourself in the service of others.
—**Mahatma Gandhi**

If you take nothing else away from this book, remember this: Service is the ultimate medicine. It is a potent remedy for negative emotions, and gives you quick and easy access to joy. Aside from the research I quoted earlier on why service has such immense positive impact on well-being, it's also the glue the world needs to survive. We are one energy, and must, therefore, take care of each other. Aggression or anger toward another is like polluting the soup of the Universe in which we are all swimming. But sending more love out there, in the form of any act of service toward another being, is returning that love to the pot and creating more of the same.

When life hands you raindrops, make it rain opportunity.

Over the course of writing this book, I was often confronted with the dilemma of staying home and crafting pages or honoring social commitments. One such weekend, there were two birthday parties and a late-break invite for a picnic. All engagements warranted my attention. The birthday parties were for close friends, and we know well by this point how important connection is to a healthy mental state. As such, there was no question I would make an appearance to celebrate with them on their special days. As for the picnic, I had reservations and some mild debates with myself. It was in the middle of the day on a Saturday, and realistically, by the time I woke up, worked out, and sat down to write, it would be time to go. But this was a crew of mindfulness folks, a new group I hadn't yet connected with, and I felt compelled to attend.

One of my main objectives is widespread and quick dissemination of mindfulness, a vital antidote for so much of what ails us as a species. I've held many mindfulness meet-ups in Philadelphia, my native city, and the gatherings have been a robust and elegant way for me to introduce and teach the concept and practice to a city that desperately needs it. This group seemed keen to start its own mindfulness meet-up initiative, so it was an opportunity I felt averse to refuse.

By the time Saturday afternoon rolled around, my decision to go had been made, and I found myself en route to the picnic. I scooped up a friend on the way, and we drove the several blocks downtown to the designated parking area. From there, we were supposed to walk to a street that I had never heard of (a foreboding sign given that I'm a native Philadelphian) and enter through a hole in the fence. #forebodingsign2. We were then to walk about twenty to thirty minutes along a newly built hi-line to find the gathering location. It all sounded very adventurous and mysterious to me, and I was keen on the exploration. But after many minutes of searching, no closer to the elusive hole, it began to pour rain. My friend and I looked at each other, and without saying a word, made the executive decision to cut and run. We doubled back to my apartment building, deciding to take in the rain for a while on the veranda outside. Heck, since I was already out, I figured I might glean some inspiration for my book. And boy did I.

Two young African men appeared quite out of the blue. Or rather gray, given the rainy sky. Dressed in colorful batik print shirts, black dress pants, and sandals, they were not the usual sight in that neighborhood. They were also clearly lost, staring at their phones and struggling to decipher their whereabouts. I overheard them speaking French to one another, and asked *en francais* (it comes in handy, again! Take that, Spanish!) if they needed help. They explained that they were on their way to a dinner, and weren't sure of the location. As I looked closer at the address, I realized they had gotten completely turned around, getting off the subway entirely too soon and ending up on the opposite end of the city from where they were meant to be. Walking back to the subway and heading downtown again would land them at the dinner very late, that is if they made it at all.

Even as my hyper linear left brain was shouting the time, analyzing and computing how many pages I'd fall behind in writing if I lingered any longer, my right brain was recognizing the universality of the experience, as if I myself was lost. The ensuing empathy I felt sealed the decision, my brain and its computations powerless against my spirit-level desire. I jumped up, simultaneously asking my friend if he was down for an excursion (he was), and told the young men to "follow me." Out to my car we went, through the pouring rain, and piled in. I took them downtown, right to the doorstep of their destination. While leaving the car, one of the young men, Muhammad, said *"Vous etes des anges."* You are angels. *"Vous comprenez?"* I did understand; I replied, *"Oui, j'ai compris. Mais c'etait un honneur—mon plaisir—de vous aider."* The rough translation in my unpracticed and somewhat broken French (though beautifully accented thanks to my Parisian teacher): "but it was my honor—my pleasure—to help you."

*****

If all the research on service as a strong predictor of happiness doesn't convince you, just try it. It feels *so damn good* to help another being. A light and warmth infuse you, more powerful than any sunrays you absorb or beautiful objects you obtain, connecting you to your essential humanity: the ability to give love not because you have to, but because you want to. And that is what I felt, all the way home and up to my apartment, my soul shining so brightly on that rainiest of days. I promptly opened my laptop and let the story gush from my heart, through my fingers, and onto this page.

A Final Thought
We Found Love in a Hopeful Place

It seems that every intellectual or spiritual point I endeavored to make in this book had a counterpart in my personal experience. In fact, it was not uncommon for these events to occur in tandem with the writing. I'd think of a topic, and an example would pop up in my life to support it. This convergence of concepts and ideas having real-life analogues made the words come alive with authenticity and truth, humanizing them, solidifying them, and validating me in feeling they were important to write. The experiences are the reason I wrote the book, and the book is the reason I lived them, just as with many of the figures I've cited, Weiss and Taylor among them.

The process I wrote is the process I've lived, bringing it from the realm of the possible to the realm of the truth. I'm a lover and abider of the real, so this was the motivational magic I needed to continue the acquittal of the words onto the page, knowing I was supported by a higher energy because I was living and writing to help and to serve. This process has been my humble attempt to follow the flow of that service. Divine intervention, in the form of magical convergences, manifests when we're onto something good and pure and worth pursuing. It's the Universe telling us to keep going, because we're on the right track. From that hopeful place, we'll all find more love.

I hope these words have helped you get on, stay on, or lean toward your own right track.

May you always be steeped in light, exuding that into the world and magnetizing it right back.

All for love,

Pax

Appendix
Pax's Stalwart Smoothie Recipe

Serves 1

Ingredients:
Kale
Walnuts
Blueberries (feel free to substitute/mix with strawberries, raspberries, blackberries, etc.)
Banana (Substitute avocado for an equally creamy, but less sugary, option)
Ground flax
Unsweetened almond milk, soy milk, or coconut water
Cubes of ice

Directions:

Place the leaves of one stalk of kale into a powerful blender (I use a Vitamix; they didn't pay me to say that). Toss in a handful of walnuts, a handful of blueberries, and one small banana or half of an avocado. Add 1–2 tablespoons of ground flax.

Pour in the liquid of your choice (almond milk, soy milk, or coconut water) until contents of blender are half-immersed. Add 4–5 small cubes of ice.

Blend on low/slow for 2–3 minutes, then increase speed to medium/high until berry skins are completely blended.

Place your hand on the side of the blender to make sure temperature is cool. Stop blending before mixture becomes temperate to the touch—you want a green smoothie, not green soup!

Endnotes

1. *US News & World Report,* "Mindfulness in Schools: When Meditation Replaces Detention," www.health.usnews.com.

2. Dictionary.com.

3. Danielle LaPorte, *The Desire Map* (Boulder, CO: Sounds True, 2014), 61.

4. *Huffington Post,* "These Educators Reveal the Ways Teaching Kindness Gives Kids a Leg Up in Life." www.huffingtonpost.com.

5. Mandy Oaklander, "The Mindful Classroom," *Time Magazine*, October 3, 2016.

5a. "Compassionate Schools Project Offers New Take on P.E./Health Curriculum," https://news.virginia.edu.

6. M. D. Mrazek, M. S. Franklin, D. T. Phillips, and J. W. Schooler, "Mindfulness Training Improves Working Memory Capacity and GRE Performance While Reducing Mind Wandering," *Psychological Science* 5, no 24 (2013): 776–81.

7. Kashmira Gander, "The World's Happiest Man Reveals What Makes Him Happy," *Independent*, October 18, 2016.

8. "Annual Sleep in America Poll Exploring Connections with Communications Technology Use and Sleep," https://sleepfoundation.org.

9. Harvard Health Blog, "Mindfulness Meditation Helps Fight Insomnia, Improves Sleep," www.health.harvard.edu.

10. "Is There a Difference between Mindfulness and Meditation?", www.oprah.com.

11. "Meditation," www.dictionary.com.

12. "Meditation," www.dictionary.com.

13. Nancy Gibbs, ed. *Mindfulness: The New Science of Health and Happiness* (Time Inc. Books, 2016), 49.

14. Dictionary.com.

15. "Why Does Breathing Calm You Down?", www.livestrong.com.

15a. Michael C. Dillbeck, Carole Bandy Banus, Craig Polanzi, and Garland S. Landrith III, "Test of a Field Model of Consciousness and Social Change: The Transcendental Meditation and TM-Sidhi Program and Decreased Urban Crime," *Journal of Mind and Behavior 9*, no. 4 (Autumn 1988), 457–85.

16. "Water," www.whatthebleep.com.

17. "The Fascinating Scientific Reason Why Money Doesn't Buy Happiness," www.alternet.org.

18. Christopher Peterson, *A Primer in Positive Psychology* (New York: Oxford University Press, 2006), 4.

19. Sheldon Cohen, Cuneyt Alper, William Dole, et al., "Positive Emotional Style Predicts Resistance to Illness after Experimental Exposure to Rhinovirus or Influenza A Virus," *Psychosomatic Medicine* 68, no. 6 (2006): 809–815.

20. ThePositivePsychologyProgram.com.

21. *Huffington Post*, "Top 5 Regrets of the Dying," www.huffingtonpost.com.

22. "Being Kind Is Good for Your Health,"www.cbc.ca.

23. Nancy Gibbs, ed. *Mindfulness: The New Science of Health and Happiness* (Time Inc. Books, 2016), 5.

24. "The ABC Model," http://www.davidbonham-carter.com.

25. "The Relationship Blog," www.gottman.com.

26. "Kindness Health Facts," www.dartmouth.edu.

27. "Find Your Strengths and Focus on Them," www.actionforhappiness.org.

28. "Signature Strengths," www.viacharacter.org.

29. Daniel Coyle, *The Talent Code* (New York: Bantam Books, 2009), 20–22.

30. "Humans Are Genetically Hard-Wired to Prefer Fat and Sugar," www.cleveland.com.

31. "Hunter-Gatherers to Farmers," www.historyworld.net.

32. "An Evolutionary Explanation for Why We Crave Sugar," www.businessinsider.com.

33. "Evolution of Diet," www.nationalgeographic.com.

34. "Inflammation: Causes, Symptoms and Treatment," www.medicalnewstoday.com.

35. "How Stress Influences Disease: Study Reveals Inflammation as the Culprit," http://sciencedaily.com.

36. "Chronic Stress Puts Your Health at Risk,"www.mayoclinic.org.

37. E. S. Ford, "Does Exercise Reduce Inflammation? Physical Activity and C-reactive Protein among U.S. Adults," *Epidemiology* 13, no. 5 (2002) 561–568.

38. "What Are the Benefits of Eating Banana Peels?", www.livestrong.com.

39. "Brain Basics: Understanding Sleep," www.ninds.nih.gov.

40. "Lack of Sleep: Can It Make You Sick?", www.mayoclinic.org.

41. "Alcohol and a Good Night's Sleep Don't Mix," www.webmd.com.

42. "The Importance of REM Sleep," www.azumio.com.

43. "4 Habits That Weaken the Immune System," www.askdrsears.com.

44. "Here's What Lack of Sleep Can Do to You in Just One Day," www.huffingtonpost.com.

45. "How to Fall Asleep Faster," www.nymag.com.

46. "Decaf Coffee Isn't Caffeine-Free," www.webmd.com.

47. "Think Twice: How the Gut's 'Second Brain' Influences Mood and Well-Being," www.scientificamerican.com.

48. "Men Overtake Women as Cause of Infertility," www.independent.co.uk.

49. "5 Facts about Smoking and Infertility," http://attainfertility.com.

50. "How Exercise Keeps Your DNA Young," http://time.com.

51. Elizabeth Blackburn, PhD, and Elissa Epel, PhD, *The Telomere Effect: A Revolutionary Approach to Living Younger, Healthier, Longer* (New York: Grand Central Publishing, 2017), 172–179.

52. "Newton's Apple: The Real Story," www.newscientist.com.

53. "The Three Laws of Thermodynamics," www.boundless.com.

54. "The Spiritual Wisdom of Albert Einstein," http://upliftconnect.com.

55. "Ayahuasca Healing in Peru," www.kirasalak.com.

56. Brian Weiss, *Many Lives, Many Masters* (New York: Fireside, 1998), 24.

57. "What Does It Mean to Be Human?", http://humanorigins.si.edu.

58. "Jada Pinkett-Smith—Take Care of YOU, First," www.youtube.com.

59. Diener, Emmons, Larsen, & Griffin (1985).

60. Harry F. Harlow, "Love in Infant Monkeys," *Scientific American* 200 (June 1959): 68–74.

60a. Cacioppo, John T., and William Patrick, *Loneliness: Human Nature and the Need for Social Connection* (New York: W. W. Norton, 2008).

61. "'There's No Stigma': Why So Many Danish Women Are Opting to Become Single Mothers," www.theguardian.com.

62. "World Happiness Report 2017," http://worldhappiness.report/ed/2017.

63. "The Spiritual Wisdom of Albert Einstein," http://upliftconnect.com.

64. Viktor Frankl, *Man's Search for Meaning* (New York: Pocket Books, 1984).

Bibliography

American Psychological Association. "Why Sleep Is Important and What Happens When You Don't Get Enough." www.apa.org/topics/sleep/why.aspx.

Benson, Herbert, and Miriam Z. Klipper. *The Relaxation Response*. New York: Quill, 2001.

Coyle, Daniel. *The Talent Code*. New York: Bantam Books, 2009.

Csikszentmihalyi, Mihaly. *Flow*. New York: Harper Perennial Modern Classics, 2008.

Diener, E., R. A. Emmons, R. J. Larsen, and S. Griffin. "The Satisfaction With Life Scale." *Journal of Personality Assessment* 49 (1985): 71–75.

Frankl, Viktor E. *Man's Search for Meaning*. New York: Pocket Books, 1984.

Fredrickson, Barbara L. *Positivity*. New York: Crown, 2009.

Gilbert, Elizabeth. *Big Magic*. New York: Riverhead Books, 2015.

Gottlieb, Daniel. *The Wisdom We're Born With*. New York: Sterling Ethos, 2014.

Gunaratana, Bhante. *Mindfulness in Plain English*. Boston: Wisdom Publications, 2011.

Kring, Ann M., and Denise M. Sloan, eds. *Emotion Regulation and Psychopathology: A Transdiagnostic Approach to Etiology and Treatment*. New York: Guilford, 2009.

LaPorte, Danielle. *The Desire Map*. Boulder, CO: Sounds True, 2014.

Peterson, Christopher. *A Primer in Positive Psychology*. New York: Oxford University Press, 2006.

Peterson, Christopher, and Martin E. P. Seligman. *Character Strengths and Virtues: A Handbook and Classification*. New York: Oxford University Press, 2004.

Post, Stephen. *Why Good Things Happen to Good People*. New York: Broadway Books, 2007.

Ratey, John J. *Spark*. New York, NY: Little, Brown, 2008.

Seligman, Martin E. P. *Authentic Happiness*. New York: Free Press, 2002.

Taylor, Jill Bolte. *My Stroke of Insight*. New York: Viking, 2008.

Verni, Kevin A. (Consultant). *Happiness: The Mindful Way*. London: Penguin Random House, 2015.

Weiss, Brian L. *Many Lives, Many Masters*. New York: Fireside, 1988.